Taste the Tradition

The best traditional cooks in Ireland, Scotland, Wales, and Cornwall center their menus around the same simple foods that have fed the Celtic people for generations: fresh meats and fish, nutty grains, wild fruits, rich dairy cream and butter, and home-grown vegetables. And, through the generations, this delicious fare has inspired a rich crop of proverbs, legends, and songs. Now you can feast upon this delectable folklore and the food it honors with *Celtic Folklore Cooking.*

Charming as a whitewashed cottage and cozy as tea and scones by the fire, *Celtic Folklore Cooking* will draw you into the culture, folkways, and character of the Celts, who have traditionally lived close to the land and the changing of the seasons. These pages blend food folklore, recipes, and associated Pagan and Christian holidays so anyone can celebrate feast days, Sabbats, rituals, or just plain good eating in traditional Celtic fashion.

Whether you need an idea for the perfect beverage to serve at a spring gathering (Blas Meala), a special bread for Good Friday (Hot Cross Buns), or a warm, filling meal for a chilly evening (Irish Stew or Poacher's Pie), you can relish the same tasty foods the Celts have enjoyed for generations. *Slainte!*

◆

About the Author

Joanne Asala is the author of over twenty-five books on traditional folktales, customs, and cooking, including *Recipes from Ireland*; *Folktales of the Slav Peasants and Herdsmen*; *Whistling Jigs to the Moon: Tales of Irish and Scottish Pipers*; *Irish Saints and Sinners*; *German Recipes*; *Christmas in the Midwest*; *Words of Wisdom from the Vikings*; and *Irish Tales of the Strange*. She has traveled extensively throughout Europe and the British Isles in order to collect material firsthand. She was taught the proverbs, songs, stories, and plantlore in this book at pubs, farmhouse parlors, and at local festivals. Currently Ms. Asala lives and works in Chicago.

To Write to the Author

If you wish to contact the author or would like more information about this book, please write to the author in care of Llewellyn Worldwide and we will forward your request. Both the author and publisher appreciate hearing from you and learning of your enjoyment of this book and how it has helped you. Llewellyn Worldwide cannot guarantee that every letter written to the author can be answered, but all will be forwarded. Please write to:

Joanne Asala
℅ Llewellyn Worldwide
P.O. Box 64383, Dept. K044-2
St. Paul, MN 55164-0383, U.S.A.

Please enclose a self-addressed, stamped envelope for reply,
or $1.00 to cover costs. If outside U.S.A., enclose
international postal reply coupon.

Celtic

FOLKLORE COOKING

JOANNE ASALA

2001
Llewellyn Publications
St. Paul, MN 55164-0383, U.S.A.

FIRST EDITION
Third Printing, 2001

Book design and editing by Rebecca Zins
Cover art and interior illustrations by Rijalynne
Cover design by Anne Marie Garrison

Library of Congress Cataloging-in-Publication Data
Asala, Joanne.
    Celtic folklore cooking / Joanne Asala.—1st ed.
       p.   cm.
    Includes bibliographical references and index.
    ISBN 1-56718-044-2 (trade paper)
    1. Cookery, Celtic.   I. Title.
  TX717.2.A83 1998
  641.59'2916—dc21
                                          98-3993
                                            CIP

Note: These recipes have not been tested by the publisher. Personal sensitivities to ingredients should be researched before using.

Author's Note: It was an oversight on my part to neglect to acknowledge the kind permission of HarperCollins to adapt several recipes from *Great British Cooking*, ©1981 by Jane Garmey, in the first printing of this book. I would also like to thank University of Toronto Press for permission to adapt recipes from *Pleyn Delit: Medieval Cookery for Modern Cooks*, ©1976 by Constance Hieatt and Sharon Butler, in the first printing.

Important Note: Herbs are very powerful and potent ingredients. Many of these traditional Celtic recipes make use of herbs that, if taken in large quantities, may cause adverse reactions. Before trying any new herb, sample a small quantity to determine if you have any allergic reactions. It is recommended that you consult a doctor or licensed medical herbalist if you are pregnant or nursing.

Llewellyn Worldwide does not participate in, endorse, or have any authority or responsibility concerning private business transactions between our authors and the public.

    All mail addressed to the author is forwarded but the publisher cannot, unless specifically instructed by the author, give out an address or phone number.

Llewellyn Publications
A Division of Llewellyn Worldwide, Inc.
P.O. Box 64383, Dept. K044-2
St. Paul, MN 55164-0383, U.S.A.
www.llewellyn.com

Printed in the United States of America

The Pedigree of Food

In the fanciful Vision of Mac Conglinne, *Mac Conglinne traces the genealogy of the monk Manchin all the way back to Adam. This "pedigree" gives a rare look into the types of food eaten in the early middle ages of Celtic Ireland and Britain.*

Bless us, O cleric, famous pillar of learning,

Son of honey-bag, son of juice, son of lard,

Son of stirabout, son of pottage, son of fair speckled fruit-clusters,

Son of smooth clustering cream, son of buttermilk, son of curds,

Son of beer (glory of liquors!), son of pleasant bragget,

Son of twisted leek, son of bacon, son of butter,

Son of full-fat sausage, son of pure new milk,

Son of nut-fruit, son of tree-fruit, son of gravy, son of drippings,

Son of fat, son of kidney, son of rib, son of shoulder,

Son of well-filled gullet, son of leg, son of loin,

Son of hip, son of flitch, son of striped breast bone,

Son of bit, son of sup, son of back, son of paunch,

Son of slender tripe, son of cheese without decrease,

Son of fish of Inver Indsen, son of sweet whey, son of bastings,

Son of mead, son of wine, son of flesh, son of ale,

Son of hard wheat, son of tripe,

Son of fair white porridge, made of pure sheep's milk,

Son of rich pottage, with its curls of steam,

Son of rough curds, son of fair oatmeal gruel,

Son of sprouty meat-soup, with its purple berries,

Son of the top of effeminate kale, son of soft white midriff,

Son of the bone-nourishing nut-fruit, son of Abel, son of Adam.

Fine is thy kindred of choice food, to the tongue it is sweet,

O thou of staid and steady step, with the help of pointed staff.

◆

To Ceridwen, Mistress of the Cauldron
to Bridgit, Guardian of the Hearth
and to my mother, Donna Jean,
who made the journey home with me.

————◆————

Table of
Contents

I tell of festivals, and fairs, and plays
of merriment, and mirth, and bonfire blaze;
I tell of Christmas mummings, New Year's Day,
Of Twelfth Night Kings and Queens and children's play;
I tell of Valentines and true love's knots
of omens, cunning men, and drawing lots.
I tell of brooks, of blossoms, of birds and bowers.
Of April, May, of June, of July Flowers.
I tell of maypoles, hock carts, wassails, wakes,
Of bridegrooms, brides, and of their bridal cakes.
I tell of groves, of Twilights, and I sing,
The court of Mab, and of the Faerie King.

ROBERT HERRICK (1591-1674)

◆

Introduction

The goal of *Celtic Folklore Cooking* is to help you select foods to serve at your celebrations of the Sabbats and Esbats. It may also be seen as an introduction to Celtic culture. I myself love to take a cookbook to bed as nighttime reading, and I hope that as you thumb through these pages you get a sense of the traditional customs that once made up a way of life in the highlands and islands. Included are recipes that have evolved over the thousands of years that make up Britain and Ireland's history. Some are meals that were eaten by the early Celts and, because of their perishable ingredients, are tied to certain times of the year. The more modern recipes are those that have come to be recognized as national dishes of Wales, Cornwall, Scotland, Ireland, and England.

Celtic civilization cannot be viewed as a stagnant moment of our far-distant past, but as a centuries-long evolution of a people. Today's Celtic nations are an amalgamation of both Pagan and

Christian traditions, a combination of Celtic, Saxon, Roman, and Norse influences. Throughout this book I have chosen to deal freely with these traditions, for all of them make up who the Celts are today.

I gathered the majority of these recipes on four subsequent trips to Ireland and Britain, where many people still cook in the traditional manner of their ancestors, passing down recipes from generation to generation. I stayed with friends on their farms and visited them in the cities. I traveled extensively through small fishing villages and mountain retreats, visiting old libraries and churches. The men and women whose kitchens I visited typically worked from family cookbooks that were well loved—the pages frayed at the corners and stained in places that had come too close to the cooking. The recipes in this book come from meals I was served at hotels, bed and breakfasts, and restaurants; others I enjoyed in the homes of friends. Of great help to me was Maura O'Byrne of Co. Carlow, Ireland. She and her husband own a dairy farm where I spent one terrific summer, and learned a lot about Celtic cooking firsthand. As well as tending the household chores, Maura serves up three meals a day to her husband and six sons.

Celtic cooking is by and large a wholesome cuisine based on the richness and generosity of the Goddess' bounty. It is simple and tasty, reflecting the quality of its ingredients—fresh meat and seafood, rich milk and cream, fruit, vegetables, and wonderful, wholesome breads. Some of the older recipes make use of such exotic ingredients as rose petals and gillyflowers. These dishes were once more common than they are now. I've left a few of these recipes in their original form, so you may see for yourself how the method of cooking has changed.

Any of these meals will lend a Celtic atmosphere to your home when brought into your circle, offered as a libation, or shared with family and friends. All can be found in countless variations throughout the Celtic lands.

When discussing the Sabbats, I have listed the foods sacred to each, and throughout the book I have matched each recipe with its associated festival or holiday. As these days are primarily agricultural and pastoral celebrations, each one has a long-standing tradition of the kinds of foods that would be served.

You may wonder why I have not included very many recipes from Brittany or Gaelicia. I have chosen to deal primarily with the Irish and British Celtic history and traditions, rather than those of mainland Europe, for two reasons.

The first is a personal one. For as long as I can remember, I have been drawn to Ireland. Although I have many family members who are Irish, I myself am not. On my first trip there with my mother in 1993, we decided to travel by boat from Fishguard, Wales to Rosslare Harbor. As the ocean mists parted and I caught my first sight of the green, rolling headlands, I turned to my mother and said, without thinking, "It'll be good to be home again. I've been gone for far too long." She merely smiled and said, "I know how you feel." I had never before felt such a sense of homecoming, and each subsequent journey to Ireland has been the same. I'm convinced that I once lived there, though when I cannot say.

The other reason for focusing on Britain and Ireland is a more practical one. A great many early Celtic traditions of the isles survived well into the Middle Ages—still others up until the present century—relatively unchanged. Mainland Celtic customs were more significantly altered by Germanic and Roman influences, while those of the islands changed little due to their isolation.

Yet we must keep in mind that what we do know about the old Celts and their traditions is still based on supposition, conjecture, and plain guesswork. The Celts did not call themselves Celts, nor did they speak "Celtic." The term is merely a convenient one for discussing the various tribes from which the modern Irish, British, Bretons, Scots, Cornish, Welsh, and Gaels have descended. Aside from a wonderful body of mythology and a precious few works of art, there is little left to tell us of the people themselves. Many of their ways have been cloaked under a blanket of other influences. What we know today is based on scholarship and the traditions said to be passed down in Pagan groups and by hereditary witches.

Finally, what we do know is that the Celts celebrated their Sabbats with music, dance, games, food, and drink. Whether you are a solitary practitioner or part of a larger group, food and drink should always be a part of your festivities, rituals, and ceremonies.

Blessed be!

Midsummer, 1998

Joanne Asala

On the day of the feast at the rise of the sun
And the back of the ear of corn to the east
I will go forth with my sickle under my arm
And I will reap the cut the first act.

I will let my sickle down
While the fruitful ear is in my grasp
I will raise mine eyes upwards
I will turn me on my heel quickly
Rightways as travels the sun
From the airt of the east to the west
From the airt of the north with motion calm
To the very core of the airt of the south.

I will give thanks to the King of the field
For the growing crops of the ground
He will give food to ourselves and to the flocks
According as he disposeth to us.

CARMINA GADELICA

The Celtic Wheel of the Year

Among the most important questions humans have asked are those that deal with our own origins: Who are we? Why are we here? What is the meaning of our existence and what happens to us when we die? In an attempt to understand the world and all it contained, early humans created identities for the powerful forces of nature. It was only natural that, in personifying the earth, humans chose woman as a role model. A woman's ability to bring forth new life and create another human being from her own body was seen as powerful magic—something to be respected and revered. Like a woman, the earth brought forth new life by a miraculous process. And, like a mother who cares for and nurtures her children, the earth also fed and cared for all her creatures.

Ancient images of the great Mother Goddess have been found from as far back as 30,000 B.C.E.—the Stone Age of human civilization. They were fertile images, emphasizing hips, thighs, buttocks, and breasts, and often showing a full, pregnant belly. Shrines to the Goddess appear between 7000 and 8000 B.C.E., and by 3000 B.C.E. her worship was spread throughout the known world.

◆ 5

For thousands of years the Goddess reigned alone. She was the source of all life, present in all forms of life. Her arching body filled the sky—she was the sun, the moon, the stars, and the planets. The earth was her body, the rivers and streams her veins, the oceans her womb. She was Mother Nature, and through the cycle of seasons her body changed from a fresh young maiden, to the bountiful mother, to the old and dying crone. All life was born from her, lived a brief time upon her, and returned to her at death.

And then the Goddess created for herself a companion.

The earliest form of male deity was probably the Horned God, often known as Kernunnos, borne of a time when the harsh cold of the Ice Age prevented an abundance of plant life, and humans depended on animals for survival. Skins provided clothing and shelter. Feathers, bones, teeth, hooves, and horns were transformed into personal jewelry, ritual items and, most importantly, tools. These animals were among the Goddess' most precious and sacred gifts, and early forms of the God were associated with hunting these animals. Oftentimes he is portrayed as a ram, or a goat, an elk or a bison, and sometimes a stag. Cave paintings throughout the world show men wearing the horns of deer, bulls, or goats, fused together in a divine image of hunter and hunted.

As situations change and perceptions alter, humans revise their myths. In the Fertile Crescent (now the modern countries of Israel, Jordan, Iran, Iraq, Turkey, and Lebanon), grain was first planted, harvested, ground into flour, and baked into bread. This new knowledge quickly spread throughout human civilization. The advent of agriculture, combined with a general warming of the earth following the Ice Age, allowed people to settle in one place and cultivate crops for winter storage. A new incarnation of the Goddess and God was born. She became the Grain Mother, and was associated with a great many aspects of creativity—planting, gathering, harvesting, building shelters, making fires, weaving, brewing, cooking, sewing, bread baking, healing, music, and poetry.

The God became both the consort and child of the Goddess. As the Corn King he was a son of the Earth Mother, a Green Man. He was believed to dwell in crops of grain or grapes. He was also her lover, fertilizing her body with his seeds. During the winter he lay in the Earth's womb. When the Goddess gives birth, he is the new plant life. When her growing season ends, he will again fertilize her with seeds for next year's harvest.

These male and female aspects of nature were personified by the early Celts as the White Moon Goddess and her consort, the Horned God. The Goddess and the God were worshipped together and separately in the turning of the seasons, as well as in the annual solar cycle and the monthly lunar cycle. This is the basic idea still held by modern Pagans, although they, like our Celtic ancestors, celebrate various aspects of these deities. The Celts believed that all gods are in truth one God, all goddesses are really aspects of one Goddess, and the two are united in a sacred marriage. They furthermore embraced the idea of polarity—that all aspects of good, evil, and indifference are found in one being.

Like later Christians, the Celts had the concept of a triune deity—three aspects of a single being. The aspects of the Triple Goddess correspond to the three ages of woman, symbolized in the lunar cycle. There is the waxing moon who is the Maiden, the full moon who is the Mother, and the waning moon who is the Crone. The Goddess can therefore appear in many guises and under many different names. She is the Virgin, the Lover, and bringer of Death. She is the Creator, the Continuer, and the Destroyer. She is with us from womb to tomb, from birth to death to rebirth.

The Maiden, or Virgin as she is sometimes called, is representative of the continuation of all life; her color is white, denoting innocence and new beginnings. She is the springtime, the dawn, eternal youth and vigor, enchantment, seduction, the end of the cold cycle, the victor over death, the waxing moon. But she is not a virgin in the modern sense of the word. The term more accurately means "unmarried woman," and the Goddess here retains her independence and her separateness, awaiting the arrival of her consort.

Likewise, the Goddess as Mother is a misleading term. Rather unlike the traditional Mother's Day image of a devoted figure whose very existence is for the service of her children, the Mother Goddess is life, a figure who revels in the full power of her womanhood and sexuality. She is a wonderfully fertile figure. The Mother is the ripeness of womanhood, the richness of life. Her color is red, the color of menstrual blood and the life source; the most ancient Goddess figures are painted with ochre to depict this. The Mother is summer, long days, vibrant health, abundance of food, the full moon.

The Crone, or Dark Mother, is personified by winter, night, and the waning moon. She is wisdom and good counsel, she is the gateway to death, and she is the keeper of secrets. Her color is most often black, the darkness of the womb where all life rests to await rebirth.

Many of the faerie tales that have been handed down to us have kept alive the memory of the Goddess. The colors white, red, and black are deeply rooted in legends and songs of the faerie realms. The most famous is probably Snow White, who had skin as white as snow, lips as red as cherries, and hair as black as night.

While the Goddess is eternal, the God is not. He lives and dies and is reborn throughout the year. The Goddess gives birth to the God at Yule, grows with him, takes him as her lover, watches him die at Samhain, and gives birth to him again at Yule. Unfortunately, his Celtic names have been lost in a distant past, and he is usually referred to as Kernunnos, his Greek name. He is the God of the Woods and the forests and the green, growing places. He is a patron of music and dance, of fertility and sex, and of play. He is usually depicted with horns but sometimes appears as the Green Man. His third face is that of a Sun God. The sun is the daytime counterpart of the White Moon Goddess.

There are a number of feasts celebrating the various aspects of these deities. The Celtic year is divided into a dark and light half, and a series of solar and lunar festivals, called Sabbats, round out the year. The four Great Sabbats, based on the change of seasons, are Imbolg, Beltaine, Lughnasadh, and Samhain. They are frequently called "fire festivals," for they are often celebrated with bonfires. They marked important agricultural/pastoral events in the Celtic calendar. The four Lesser Sabbats were adopted later and are marked by the passage of the sun: the solstices and the equinoxes.

Most celebrations were held at night, as the Celtic day began at midnight. The Celtic year begins on November 1 and is based on the thirteen lunar months. Monthly Esbat celebrations in honor of the White Goddess are held at or near the full moon, the height of people's psychic power. The bright half of each month was made up of fifteen days of the waxing moon, while the dark half was fifteen days of the waning moon. The waxing moon is the time for positive magic, while the waning moon is the time for bindings and dark magic. Although moon and sun provide the basis for the two cycles of festivals, the cycles are by no means mutually exclusive. There is considerable overlap between the two as, over the centuries, different cultures have mixed.

Originally the Celts were a herding people rather than farmers, so it is not surprising that their feasts would coincide with major periods of the pastoral year. When they adopted agriculture, their celebrations began to have associations with plant fertility and the sun.

Samhain and Beltaine were the two major holidays, as they divided the year into two parts—winter and summer. At Samhain livestock was rounded up and brought into stockades for the winter, and excess livestock were slaughtered. That is why meat dishes are so prevalent during the winter festivals. At Beltaine, the animals were brought to summer pastures, and the foods of summer—milk, cheese, vegetables, and later grains—would feature prominently in the feasting.

The eight Sabbats described below represent the turning of the Wheel of the Year. The solar festivals mark the points along the sun's annual journey— usually when the sun has reached an extreme, such as the solstices, or a balance, such as the equinoxes. The others mark the change of seasons. Each Sabbat honors a stage in the eternal life cycle of the God and Goddess.

Today the Wheel of the Year is a very common metaphor to help conceptualize the ever-turning cycle of life, death, and regeneration. The life, death, and rebirth of the Goddess and the God in their various incarnations were cycles of crucial importance, for the survival of the species depended on them. If the earth failed to complete her circular journey through death to renewal, if the sun failed to return and bring back light and warmth, we were doomed. At each of the joints or hinges of the year, people held festivals in which magic, ritual, and ceremony generated sufficient energy to rotate the Wheel into the next phase. In Pagan mythology the Goddess herself turns the Wheel of the Year, bringing everything its season, just like the old song, ". . . there is a season, turn, turn, turn . . ." In artwork the Year is often symbolized as an eight-spoked wagon wheel, a wreath, a ring, or a snake holding its tale—the worm Oruburos. Below is a model of the Wheel of the Year, which begins with Samhain and follows clockwise.

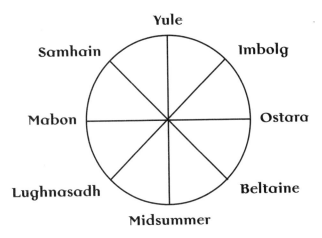

In *Celtic Folklore Cooking* I have chosen to give only a brief look at the holidays the Celts once celebrated, and which modern Pagans still do. Because there are already a number of fine books out there which tackle the subject in far greater depth than I could do here, I would recommend you turn to them for further reading. Try Scott Cunningham's *Wicca: A Guide for the Solitary Practitioner;* Edain McCoy's *The Sabbats: A New Approach to Living the Old Ways;* Pauline Campanelli's *Ancient Ways;* and Diana Ferguson's *The Magickal Year.* You will find a wealth of information on the history and traditions of these feast days, as well as detailed descriptions of appropriate rituals.

Samhain

Samhain is the Celtic Feast of the Dead and the night of the Wild Hunt. From dusk to dawn, the veil between this world and the Otherworld is thinnest, and the spirits of the dead walk the earth, visit friends and family, and join in any celebrations. Food and drink should be left out for any spirit travelers, and candles should be placed in the window to guide your loved ones home. As well as marking the end of the harvest season, Samhain is the Celtic New Year, and the most important festival of the Wheel. On this night the old God dies, returning to the land of the dead to await his rebirth at Yule. The Goddess goes into mourning for her consort/son, and the world turns dark and gray. We are now under the aegis of the *cailleach*, the Goddess as Old Woman.

The rituals of Samhain are concerned with the dead, and because the veil between the worlds is thinnest on this night, it is an excellent time for divinations. Many Celts of Pagan and Christian traditions visit graveyards at this time. Feasts are made in remembrance of those who are gone and as an affirmation of continuing life. It is a time for throwing out old ideas and influences, of visiting elderly relatives, and of self-reflection. At your own feast, in addition to serving the foods of harvest, it is a good time to make those dishes that were special to an honored friend or relative.

Date	October 31
Other Names	Halloween, Hallowmas, Samana, Samonios, Samhuinn, All Saint's Day, Ancestor Night, Feast of the Dead, November Eve, Calangaef
Associated Celtic Deities	Ceridwen, Gwyn ap Nudd, sacrificial/ dying gods, crone goddesses
Customs	Bonfires, apple games, costumes, fire calling, tricks, pumpkin carving, Dumb Supper (meal eaten in silence to which the dead are invited)
Symbols	Jack O'Lanterns, disguises, corn husk bundles, poisonous herbs, skulls, black cats, bale fires
Traditional Incenses	Apple, mint, nutmeg, heliotrope, sage
Sacred Foods	Acorns, apples, red meats, red wine, root and vine vegetables (squash, potatoes, parsnips, carrots, turnips, etc.)
Threshold Time	Midnight

They dance, the nine Korrigans,
with crowns of flowers and robes of white,
they dance about the fountain in the pale moonlight.

TRADITIONAL

Yule

Yule, one of the oldest and most widely observed of the Sabbats, was not a part of the Celtic calendar until the invading Norsemen introduced it. Many of the holiday's traditions are even older and come from the Roman feast of Saturnalia, when the Solar God went into the Underworld.

Traditionally Yule takes place on the winter solstice, the shortest day of the year, and celebrates the subsequent rebirth of the Sun God. From this day until Midsummer, the sun grows ever stronger. Yule is also a time to honor the Goddess in her Virgin aspect, and to observe the battle between the Holly King, God of the waning year, with the Oak King, God of the waxing year.

At the solstice, the sun is at its lowest point. Yule should therefore be a festival of light that encourages the return of the sun/son. Fill your home with candlelight and welcome the divine child.

Date	ca. December 21, Winter Solstice
Other Names	Alban Arthuan, Gehul (Saxon), Häul (Welsh), Midwinter, Christmas, Winter Rite
Associated Celtic Deities	Mabon, Cernunnos, virgin goddesses, the Triple Goddess, newborn gods, Holly and Oak Kings
Customs	Yule logs, kissing under the mistletoe, bell ringing, spinning wheels
Symbols	Yule tree, pine boughs, stag horns (symbolizing the winter lord), mistletoe, evergreens, Christmas trees, holly and ivy
Traditional Incenses	Cedar, bayberry, pine, rosemary
Sacred Foods	White wine, white cakes, bitter herbs, mints
Threshold Time	Dawn

Imbolg

The first day of February is the old Celtic festival marking the reawakening of the earth, and is seen as a celebration of newness. It is a promise of fertility, new life, and new hope. The Goddess is seen as a young bride awaiting her consort, and the *cailleach*, the crone aspect, is in retreat.

Imbolg is a time of cleansing and celebrating new beginnings. Take care of your spring cleaning and air out your home. This is the time of year when new lambs are born and ewes are in milk—in the days when the Celts depended on the cycle of seasons for fresh food, these were important events. Celebrate Imbolg with a feast rich in milk, cheese, and other dairy products.

Date	February Eve, February 1
Other Names	Oimelc, Imbolc, Groundhog Day, Candlemas, Brigantia, St. Brigid's Day, Bride's Day, Lady Day
Associated Celtic Deities	Bridgit, Danu, Epona, virgin goddesses, sun goddesses, child goddesses, young male gods
Customs	Candle burning, relighting the hearth
Symbols	Candles, candle flame, hearth and home, grain dollies, burrowing animals, milk-producing creatures
Traditional Incenses	Basil, myrrh, wisteria
Sacred Foods	Milk, cheese, dairy products
Threshold Time	Midnight

If Candlemas be bright and fair

Winter will have another year

But if it be dark with clouds and rain

Winter is gone, and will not come again.

TRADITIONAL

◆

Ostara

The name "Ostara" is derived from Eostre, the Goddess of Spring, and celebrates the Vernal Equinox. It is believed that Ostara was introduced to the Celtic world by the Saxons around the year 600 c.e. to mark the official beginning of spring. Many people still go bird watching on this day to catch sight of returning flocks. At this time the courtship between the God and Goddess begins, a relationship that will be consecrated on May Day (Beltaine). Ostara is a balance of light and dark, and a time of sowing in the northern countries. Many creatures give birth at this time, so symbols of fertility—such as eggs—are traditionally eaten at this time. The most popular food is probably Hot Cross Buns, originally a cake with the crescent moon symbol of the Goddess.

Date	ca. March 21, Vernal Equinox
Other Names	Alban Eiler, Eostre, Lady Day, Easter, Festival of Trees
Associated Deities	Young gods and goddesses
Customs	Collecting/decorating eggs, bird watching, egg hunts, burying eggs in fields
Symbols	Rabbits, chicks, eggs, equilateral cross
Traditional Incenses	Violet, jasmine, rose, sage, strawberry
Sacred Foods	Fish, sweets, sweet breads, eggs
Threshold Time	Dawn

Beltaine

The first day of May has long been celebrated in song and verse, as it is the official beginning of summer. It is a time to honor life in all its many forms. On this day the God and Goddess are united in sacred marriage. It is primarily a fertility festival with nature enchantments and offerings to wildlings and Elementals. The powers of elves and faeries are growing and will reach their height at the Summer Solstice. A time of great magic, it is good for all divinations and for establishing a woodland shrine. The guardians of your home should be honored on this day.

May is a month of sexual freedom in honor of the Great Mother and Horned God of the Woodlands. Trial marriages of a year and a day could be contracted at this time. If it was unworkable, partners simply went their separate ways. Green, worn at this time to honor the earth mother, was later called unlucky by the Christians in hopes that people would discontinue the practice of trial marriages.

Date	May Eve/May 1
Other Names	Rudemas, Giamonios, Bhealltainn, May Day, Lilac Sunday, Lady's Day, Walpurgisnacht, Cyntefyn, Ruod Day
Associated Celtic Deities	Belinos, Flora, Blodeuwedd, flower goddesses, divine couples, animal spirits, deities of the woodlands and the Hunt
Customs	Sexual license, Maypoles, gathering flowers, wearing green, fire calling, feasting
Symbols	Maypoles, flowers, bright colors, sunshine
Traditional Incenses	Frankincense, rose, lilac, hawthorn
Sacred Foods	Sweets, mead, cakes, cookies, fruit, milk products
Threshold Time	Dawn

*On May Day young men doe use commonly to runne
into woodes at night time, amongst maidens, to set bowls.
So much as I have heard of tenne maidens whiche went
to set May and nine of them came home with childe.*

UNKNOWN SIXTEENTH-CENTURY CHRONICLER

Midsummer

The waxing sun reaches its highest point before beginning its slide into darkness. It is the longest day of the year and the earth is lush and green. In terms of the sacred marriage, the God is at the peak of his power and the Goddess heavily pregnant with new life. As a holiday, it was not celebrated by the Celts until they came into contact with the Norse.

As often happens with ancient festivals, many of the customs of Beltaine are also celebrated at Midsummer—maypole dancing, fertility rites, and divination spells, to name a few. But the most famous tradition is probably the bonfire. Even today in northern countries, Midsummer blazes dot the landscape, encouraging and strengthening the sun.

Midsummer marks the turning of the Wheel from the light half to the dark of the year. The day is symbolized by the Green Man in his guise of Oak King. Just as the Holly and Oak Kings battled at Yule, they again battle for supremacy now; but this time it is the Holly King, God of the waning year, who will win.

Traditionally, herbs gathered on this day are extremely powerful. Decorate your home or altar with fresh flowers, particularly yellow ones that represent the sun. On this night elves and faeries gather in great numbers, so do not forget to honor them in your observances.

Date	ca. June 21
Other Names	Alban Heruin, Aerra Litha, Gathering Day, Feill-Sheathain, Summer Solstice, St. John's Day, Mehefin, Mother Night
Associated Celtic Deities	Ogmios, Huon, Math, pregnant goddesses, sun gods/gods at their zenith

Customs Bonfires (traditionally kindled with friction of fir and oak twigs), faerie hunting, picking sacred sun flora (St. John's Wort, wild rose, oak blossoms), gathering herbs, maypole dancing, handfasting and fertility rites, divination

Symbols Oak, bonfires, mistletoe, feathers, roses

Traditional Incenses Frankincense, myrrh, pine, rose, wisteria

Sacred Foods Mead and wine, first vegetables of summer, bread, new cheese (particularly golden cheeses), edible flowers

Threshold Time Dusk

Saint John's Wort, Saint John's Wort

My envy whosoever has thee

I will pluck thee with my right hand

I will preserve thee with my left hand

Whoso findeth thee in the cattle fold

Shall never be without kine.

TRADITIONAL HIGHLAND CHARM

Lughnasadh

Lughnasadh is a festival to honor the Celtic God Lugh, and represents the first of the harvest festivals. Lugh was a poet, silversmith, healer, warrior, magician, musician, and a blacksmith. He was also a God of harvest, light, fire, and the sun. Samildánach, as he was also known (a name that means "master of every art"), was king of the Tuatha de Dannann and said to be the consort of the Goddess Danu.

Although Lugh is a solar deity, the festival of Lughnasadh is primarily a harvest celebration, with corn, wheat, and barley products prominent at the feasts. (Your own feast should feature breads and August fruits and vegetables.)

It is believed that Lughnasadh replaced an older fertility festival. Also, it was the high summer gathering of Celtic tribes to discuss harvest concerns and plans for the upcoming year. Contests of strength and skill were performed at this time, and marriages arranged. Again, trial marriages could be made at this festival, with couples swearing to stick it out for a year and a day, and to part with no regrets if it did not work.

At this time the Goddess is honored as the Grain Mother who gave birth to this great bounty, and the God is honored as the father of prosperity.

Lughnasadh is the turning point in the life cycle of the divine couple. Here the Goddess begins to age and will soon cease to bring forth new life. Her son, the spirit of the grain, is cut down and his seeds scattered. In nearly every culture and civilization, this cycle of death is portrayed as the seasonal death of a vegetation spirit or fertility figure. It may seem sad, but the death of the God must take place in order for life to go on. He has to be cut down—slain—in order to be reborn.

Date	August 1 or 2
Other Names	Lammas, August Eve, Elembiuos, Halfmass, Feast of the Assumption, Festival of First Fruits
Associated Celtic Deities	Lugh and other solar deities, harvest and grain deities, mother goddesses

Customs	Celebrating life in its fullness and honoring the earth for the richness of her bounty through games, singing, dancing, poetry/storytelling competitions, contests of strength and skill, feasting, and handfasting ceremonies
Symbols	Wheat stalks, loaves of bread, scythe/sickle, sun symbols
Traditional Incenses	Aloe, rose, sandalwood
Sacred Foods	Bread and all foods made with grain, wine (particularly those made with summer harvest fruits), poultry and other domestic fowl, fish and other sea foods, porridge, oatmeal, pancakes, strawberries, blueberries, and other ripe fruits
Threshold Time	High Noon

Prepare yourself, Harvest commeth on
The field is the staff we all rely on.
For kings and people from the field are fed
and poor folk do expect their share of bread.

TRADITIONAL SCOTTISH

———◆———

Mabon

Once again the hours of day and night are in balance. However, at Mabon the sun is weakening, not gaining, in strength. The time has come when the great God must return to the Underworld, whether in the form of the Corn King who has been cut down and who fertilizes the earth with his seed, or as the dying sun who is swallowed in the encroaching darkness.

Traditionally, Mabon is the second of the great harvest festivals. It is a time of rest after labor, and a chance to give thanks for the earth's generosity. Although it is not celebrated in the United States until late November, Thanksgiving Day is the modern equivalent of this great feast. The season is associated with wild game (particularly fowl), the apple harvest, and is a celebration of grapes and viniculture. Your Mabon feast should be filled with these late-season foods.

Above all, Mabon is a time to welcome the Goddess in her crone aspect.

All preparations for the dark of the year and the year's ending should be made at this time. Mabon is a time of meditation. Think about what the past year has brought you, and take an opportunity to reflect on who you are and what you hope to become.

Date	ca. September 21
Other Names	Alban Elved, Wine Harvest, Feast of Avalon, Feast of Ungathering, Autumnal Equinox, Harvest Home, Thanksgiving
Associated Celtic Deities	Mabon, Bran, Branwen, wine gods, harvest/grain deities, gods and goddesses of the Hunt, sun gods, aging gods and goddesses
Customs	Harvest feasting, meditation
Symbols	Grapes, corn bundles, fish, cornucopia, gourds
Traditional Incenses	Myrrh, sage
Sacred Foods	Red wines, wild game (particularly fowl), squash, melons, cakes, stews, pomegranates
Threshold Time	Dusk

The Esbats and the Celtic Tree Calendar

The moon is perhaps humankind's oldest form of reckoning time. The Celts divided their year into thirteen Esbats, or celebrations of the full moon. Esbats are times to honor the Goddess in her Mother aspect, and can be spent in either solitary observance or as a celebration with family. The word "esbat" comes from the French *esbattre*, "to frolic."

The Celts assigned each of their full moons a corresponding tree image, with each tree being sacred to either the God or the Goddess. Although there seems to be a debate as to the polarity of each of these trees, I have assigned them with the aspect of divinity I've most commonly encountered. Some of these trees have a long association with magic and the faerie realms, others belong to an herbal tradition of medicine, healing, and self-improvement. While there is also some disagreement between scholars and the various Pagan groups as to the proper order of these trees, the cycle of the thirteen esbat moons as written below are the ones most commonly accepted.

Birch Moon

Month	November or December
Gender	Feminine
Properties and Associations	Protection, exorcism, purification, new beginnings, creativity, friends and family

Rowan Moon

Month	December
Gender	Masculine
Properties and Associations	Healing, protection, travel, improving psychic powers, divination, astral travel

Ash Moon

Month	January
Gender	Androgynous
Properties and Associations	Prosperity, seas, oceans, and other waterways, health, healing, women's mysteries

Alder Moon

Month	February or March
Gender	Masculine
Properties and Associations	Protection, self-guidance and teaching, self-improvement, self-reliance

Willow Moon

Month	March
Gender	Feminine
Properties and Associations	Love, fertility, divination, healing, balance

Hawthorn Moon

Month	April
Gender	Masculine
Properties and Associations	Fertility, happiness, peace (both inner and external), prosperity

Oak Moon

Month	May or June
Gender	Masculine
Properties and Associations	Potency, fertility, fidelity, wisdom, luck, strength, security, the sun

Holly Moon

Month	July
Gender	Masculine
Properties and Associations	Dreaming, protection, luck, sex, divination, trust

Hazel Moon

Month	August or September
Gender	Feminine
Properties and Associations	Fertility, dreaming, wishes, wisdom, secrets, old age

(Grape) Vine Moon

Month	September
Gender	Feminine
Properties and Associations	Fertility, wisdom, creativity, inspiration, joy

Ivy Moon

Month	October
Gender	Androgynous
Properties and Associations	Healing, resilience, exorcism, personal growth

Reed Moon

Month	October or November
Gender	Feminine
Properties and Associations	Health, happiness, truth, love, family, hearth and home

Elder Moon

Month	November
Gender	Feminine
Properties and Associations	Protection, prosperity, healing, exorcism

The counting of the Celtic tree calendar begins with the full moon nearest Yule, in midwinter. This is probably due to the Norse influence that began the new year at this time. When you have determined which moon that is, count off the thirteen moons of the coming year and mark your calendar with their names. Keep the properties and aspects of that particular moon in mind when honoring the holiday. If you have a problem or issue with love, for example, you might wish to focus your magic during the Willow Moon. If you seek guidance and counseling, work your appropriate spells during the Oak Moon.

Beverages

Thirst is the end of drinking,
and sorrow is the end of love.

MANX PROVERB

Syllabub

A seventeenth-century manuscript reads, "Fill your syllabub-pot with cyder, put in a good quantity of sugar, and a little nutmeg; stir these well together, then put in as much thick cream by two or three spoonfuls at a time, as if you were milking it; then stir it round very gently, and let it stand two hours, then eat it. If it be in the field, only milk the cow into the cyder, and so drink it."

The cream needn't be that *fresh to enjoy the following recipe:*

Juice and grated zest of 3 lemons
¾   cup sherry
5   tablespoons sugar
3   cups heavy cream
½   teaspoon freshly ground nutmeg
Twists of fresh lemon peel

Stir together the lemon juice, grated zest, sherry, and sugar in a ceramic mixing bowl (do not use metal). Cover loosely with a clean cloth and store in a cool place for about an hour.

Strain liquid into another bowl and add the cream. Beat with a wire whisk until the cream becomes thick and forms ribbons. Pour syllabub into individual dessert glasses and refrigerate for at least two hours.

Before serving, sprinkle each portion with a pinch of nutmeg and decorate with a twist of lemon peel. Many people still serve syllabub with triangles of shortbread (page 309) fresh from the oven.

ASSOCIATED HOLIDAYS: IMBOLG, BELTAINE, MIDSUMMER

SERVES 8

Alternate Recipe for Syllabub: *Records from Bordeaux show wine exports to Irish kings as far back as 2,000 years ago. This recipe, from Co. Donegal, Ireland, uses white wine instead of sherry.*

- 1 quart heavy cream
- 3 tablespoons sugar
  Grated rind and juice of 2 lemons or 2 oranges
- 1 bottle of white wine, chilled

In a blender, beat together the cream and sugar. Add grated rind, fruit juice, and wine. Beat ingredients just until blended, pour into tall glasses, and serve.

SERVES 8

A Third Syllabub Recipe: *This one comes from* The Country House-wife and Lady's Director, *1732:*

"Put a pint of white wine, a pint of mulberry, or black cherry juice into a wooden bowl; add also a pint of cream, sweeten it with sugar, and put in a large perfumed comfit, put a branch or two of rosemary stript from the leaves, among some willow twigs, etc. together very well, and melt the butter in a little thick cream. Then stir your syllabub well together, and whip it up till it froths, take off the froth with a spoon, and put it into your glasses, and squeeze some spirit of lemon peel between every layer of froth, and let it stand till the next day."

A Fourth and Final Syllabub Recipe:

- ¼ cup whipped cream
- 1 tablespoon brandy
- 5 tablespoons rose preserves (page 322)

Beat all ingredients together and serve.

SERVES 1

Blas Meala

Choose your company before you drink (Welsh proverb).

  1½ cups fresh-squeezed orange juice
   1 tablespoon clover honey, or to taste
   2 jiggers Irish Whiskey
     Heavy cream, lightly whipped
     Toasted oatmeal, optional

If desired, sprinkle oatmeal on a cookie sheet and heat in a slow oven until golden brown. Heat the orange juice until near-boiling in a small saucepan. Add the honey and stir. Pour the juice into 2 separate glasses, add a jigger of whiskey to each, and top with a generous dollop of whipped cream. Sprinkle with hot toasted oatmeal and serve with a hearty *slainte!*

ASSOCIATED HOLIDAYS: IMBOLG, BELTAINE, MIDSUMMER

SERVES 2

Scottish Spiced Ale

Drunkenness and anger speak the truth (Scottish proverb).

        4 eggs
4½ plus ½ cups Scottish ale
        ¼ cup clover honey
        2 tablespoons butter, melted
        ¼ teaspoon nutmeg
        ¼ teaspoon cinnamon
        ¼ teaspoon cloves, or to taste

With a wire whisk, beat the eggs with ½ cup of the ale until frothy. Heat the remaining ale in a small pot until hot, being careful not to let it boil. While continuing to beat the eggs, pour the hot ale over the mixture. Return the mixture to the pot and add the honey, butter, and spices. Heat again but do not boil, or you will end up with scrambled eggs in your drink. Pour into large mugs and drink hot, preferably in front of a cozy fire.

ASSOCIATED HOLIDAYS: LUGHNASADH, SAMHAIN, YULE

SERVES 2

Herbs to Spice Usquabath (Whiskey)

Yarrow is a native English plant, and has long been used in witches' spells. It promotes love and a happy marriage, and aids in the pains of rheumatism. Placing leaves in the nose will ease migraines, but plucking yarrow will sometimes cause a nosebleed. Hang a bunch of dried yarrow in the home to promote a good marriage.

Wormwood has a long tradition of use, and is said to have sprung up in the tracks of the serpent as he left paradise. As the herbalist Culpepper tells us, "This herb being laid among clothes will make a moth scorn to meddle as much as a lion scorns to meddle with a mouse." Ancient cookbooks recommend soaking it in red wine or brandy and drinking it as a general tonic. Wormwood is used in divination spells and if sprinkled in a cauldron aids in scrying. It is sacred to the moon, and if carried will protect you from enchantment, as well as any snakes or sea serpents you might encounter. It will keep you safe on the road. Burned at Samhain in a graveyard, wormwood will cause the dead to rise.

Fumitory, if rubbed on your shoes, will bring you wealth—either material or spiritual. Hang your clothes in the smoke of fumitory incense to achieve the same.

Tormentil tea should be taken by mediums, spiritualists, and channelers prior to undergoing a trance. This will prevent a spirit from taking permanent possession.

Anise is one of the most powerful herbs of protection, and can be utilized in a variety of ways. It is good to scatter anise seeds and fresh leaves around the perimeter of your magic circle to protect yourself and others from dangerous spirits. Place them in your pillowcase if you've been having nightmares; this will keep them from troubling you and provide you with a deeper night's sleep. Anise seed cookies, which my mother bakes every Christmas, have always been a comfort to me.

From The Queen's Closet Opened, *1655:*

"Take agrimony, fumitory, bugloss, wormwod, hart's tongue, cardus benedictus, rosemary, angelica, tormentil, each of these for every gallon of ale one handful, anniseeds, and liquorice well bruised half a pound. Still all these together and when it is still you must infuse cinnamon, nutmeg, mace, liquorice, dates, and raysins of the sun, and sugar what quantity you please. The infusion must be till the color please you."

Whiskey You're the Devil

Shane O'Neil lived in the Rushy Mountains of Munster, just as his father did and his father before him. Shane remembered his grandfather as a belligerent sort, often drunk and singing to the cows at milking time. But he was smart, too. He taught his children that it made more sense to convert their grain into alcohol. "Twenty bushels of corn will only bring you six pounds sterling," he'd say. "Make it into *poitín* and you can earn twenty-six." He passed on his love of moonshine to his grandson, along with his set of pipes.

Shane was a fine player, despite his reputation for being a wild fellow who, like his father and grandfather, was a wee bit too fond of his own drink. His pipes were his prize possession and many was the starlit night that he could be found on the oak stump by his back porch, playing jigs to the moon.

One night Shane was playing to himself, long after his wife and daughters had gone to bed, and every now and then he would take a swig from his jug and gaze up at the heavens. Was he ever startled when one of the stars fell from the sky and landed right in his yard! There was a flash of black light, and a man with an oak-wood case stood facing him. He brushed some stardust from his shoulders.

"And who might you be?" Shane asked.

"The devil," the man replied.

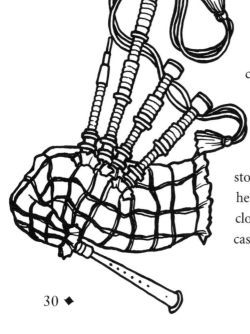

"Go on, now, quit your kidding. I'm serious. Who are you?"

"It's the truth I'm telling you, Shane Murphey O'Neil!"

"But you don't *look* anything like the devil," Shane challenged. "Where are your horns? Your cloven feet? Your spiked tail?"

"Oh, *really*," the man said in a rather bored way. "You people are too much. I was, after all, once an angel. But if you *insist*." There was another black flash, and before Shane stood the devil himself, just as he always imagined he would look like. He was a red, hairy fellow with cloven hooves, tail, and horns. He still held the oak case in his clawed hand.

"Can I offer you a drink?" Shane held out his jug.

"When was it made?" the devil asked suspiciously.

"Last night. It was the last thing I did before going to bed. Well," he paused, "before my prayers, that is."

The devil grimaced. "But doesn't age improve *poitín*?"

"I don't know who told you that," Shane chuckled. "I once kept a batch around for a *whole week* one time, and I couldn't say that it was a bit fresher or better tasting than when it was first made. So take it and drink, and if you don't mind my asking, what brings you to my mountainy home?"

The devil took a long swig and nearly choked. He handed it back to Shane and in a wheezing voice said, "Ah, a fine batch, indeed." Then he looked the moonshiner in the eye. "You aren't afraid of me, are you, Shane O'Neil?"

Shane sniffed at the jug. It smelled like brimstone and graveyard dirt and sulphur. He carefully wiped the neck with his coat sleeve before taking another drink. "I can't say as I have any reason to be. Afraid, that is. I've been to Mass and I've made my confession and I've said my prayers. Besides, I wouldn't want it known that I'd turned a thirsty soul away from my home. Not even yours."

"Fair enough," said the devil. "The priest of the parish has taught you well."

They passed the jug around a few more times and both were soon well into their cups. "Shane," said the devil, "have I mentioned yet that I'm a piper, too?"

"Go on!"

"It's the truth I'm telling you! How about the two of us having a piping contest?"

"All right," agreed Shane, intrigued by the challenge.

The devil opened up his case. "I'll start us off then."

"Funny how you just happened to bring your pipes," Shane remarked. "You never know when they'll come in handy." The devil strapped his pipes around his waist, placed the bellows under his arm, and let rip with a few fiery scales.

"Ready?" asked Shane.

"Ready!" said the devil. He played a slow air first, and it was so eerie that shivers ran up and down Shane's spine. "I call it *Fall from Grace*," said the devil. Then he launched into a jig, and with a band of goblins that had appeared from nowhere, finished off with an unearthly reel.

"Well," said Shane as he looked at the devil's smug face. "You're pretty good. But say, we never did set a wager."

"Oh," sniffed the devil nonchalantly, "how about we battle for your soul?"

"My soul? You get right to it, don't you? And if I win?"

"Why!" the devil grinned. "You can have my pipes; a finer set you'll never own."

"They *are* mighty sweet." Shane eyed them critically. "Okay, it's a deal." Then he played his own pipes, the ones his grandfather had given him, and the angels must have been smiling on him despite his arrogance, for he played hornpipes, jigs, and reels better than the Prince of Darkness.

The devil could hardly believe his ears, but he was a gracious loser. He set the pipes on the ground at Shane's feet. "Although it burns me to be beaten by a mortal, I have to admit you're the finest piper I've seen on either side of the ocean." Without another word, he sank into the earth and was gone.

"Wait!" shouted Shane. "Take a jug of the spirits with you! As a token of good will!"

"Keep it!" The devil's head popped up from the earth. "It's warm enough down here as it is, and I'm already sure of getting a nasty hangover from your *poitín*. It's a most devilish brew!"

"Suit yourself." Shane grinned and went inside with both sets of pipes. He tried to get into bed, but his wife had other ideas.

"You reek of *poitín* and smoke! You've had an accident with the still, haven't you? Well! You're not coming in here, stinking up the bed clothes as you are! Off to the shed with you!"

Shane stood alone in the front yard, contemplating the horror of a bath. Then he shrugged, took up his new pipes, and played a sad lament before going to the river to wash himself.

And so that is the tale, as it is told in the Rushy Mountains of Munster, of the time Shane Murphey O'Neil gave the devil his due, and how the devil got his revenge.

◆

Welsh Posset Cup

Posset is a very old drink made of sweetened and spiced milk curdled with ale, stout, or wine. You will rarely find it served in a pub, but try it once at home. Be warned! Mixing milk and stout is not to everyone's taste.

2¾	cups whole milk
2	tablespoons oatmeal
	Pinch of salt, or to taste
1	tablespoon honey
2½	cups Guinness or other stout
½	teaspoon each cinnamon and nutmeg, or to taste

In a small saucepan, heat milk, oatmeal, and salt to just below boiling, stirring continuously. Remove mixture from heat and let stand for 10 minutes. Strain the liquid into a clean pot and add honey, stout, and spices. Heat mixture, stirring to combine ingredients thoroughly, but do not boil. Drink immediately.

Variation: Taken from the cookbook of Robert May, 1671:

Rosemary purifies and wards off negative emotions, so is an excellent additive to a spring tonic. It is also well loved by faeries. The Celts and Saxons used ivy, also known as gill, to season their beer. Places where beer is sold are sometimes still called gill houses.

"For a posset of herbs take a fair scoured skellet, put some milk into it and some rosemary; the rosemary being well boiled in it, take it out and have some ale or beer in a pot, put to it the milk and sugar (or none). Thus of thyme, cardus, camomile, mint, or marigold flowers."

ASSOCIATED HOLIDAYS: OSTARA, MABON

SERVES 2

Take the drink for the thirst

that is to come.

WELSH PROVERB

Cakes and Ale

The ceremony of cakes and ale is probably one of the most ancient of rituals, utilizing the concept that we become what we consume. Celtic warriors, as well as other Indo-European tribes, are reported to have eaten parts of their dead so that they could be reborn within the group. Celtic mythology is full of stories of people who are consumed in some manner, and reborn in another. The Welsh bard Taliesin is one.

According to tradition, the cake (or if you prefer, bread) is symbolic of the Goddess as Mother Earth while ale (or wine) is symbolic of the moon, of spirit, and of water. Eating and drinking these items is an expression of our desire to unite with the Goddess. So widespread was this ceremony that the early Christian church adopted it as their own communion ritual to speed the conversion of the masses.

Today, most observers of the Celtic tradition will use this ritual in their monthly Esbat celebration. Any of the ales, beers, or wines listed in this chapter will serve the purpose. Refer to the bread chapter to pick an appropriate bread. Crescent moon rolls (page 110), reminiscent of the moon, would be a good choice. Several recipes in the dessert chapter could also be utilized, such as the Lammas cookies (page 316). Oftentimes the bread or cake is molded and baked into the shape of a desired goal or petition.

An alcoholic may be cured if he drinks from a cup made of ivy wood.

ENGLISH FOLK BELIEF

Eggnog

A narrow neck keeps the bottle from being emptied in one swig (Irish proverb).

3   eggs, separated
6   tablespoons sugar, divided
1   cup whole milk
½   cup rum or brandy
½   teaspoon vanilla
⅛   teaspoon salt, or to taste
½   cup heavy whipping cream
3   egg whites
    Ground nutmeg or cinnamon

Separate eggs. Set egg whites in a metal bowl and place in the refrigerator. In a small mixing bowl, beat egg yolks until blended. Gradually add 3 tablespoons of sugar, beating at high speed until thick and lemon-colored. Stir in the milk, rum or brandy, vanilla, and salt. Place egg yolk mixture in refrigerator to chill thoroughly, about 2 hours.

Whip the cream. Remove the egg whites from the refrigerator and beat until soft peaks form (if using same beaters, make sure they are thoroughly washed). Add remaining sugar, beating the mixture into stiff peaks. Fold yolk mixture and whipped cream into egg whites. Serve immediately in a silver bowl decorated with hollyberries and ivy leaves, with a dash of nutmeg or cinnamon on each serving.

Variation: If you would like to serve a non-alcoholic eggnog, simply follow the recipe above, but omit the rum or brandy and increase the milk to 1½ cups.

ASSOCIATED HOLIDAYS: OSTARA, YULE, NEW YEAR'S EVE, WINTER CELEBRATIONS

SERVES 8

John Barleycorn

It is believed that barley was the first grain cultivated by the ancient European tribes. In the following traditional song, we see the life cycle of John Barleycorn, the personification of the grain, and his eventual transformation into that much-beloved drink, whiskey.

> There came three men from out of the west,
> Their fortunes for to try,
> As they had sworn a solemn oath,
> John Barleycorn must die.
> They ploughed, they sowed, they harrowed him in,
> Throwed clods upon his head,
> And these three men made a solemn vow,
> John Barleycorn was dead.
>
> Then they let him lie for a very long time
> 'Til the rain from heaven did fall,
> Then little Sir John sprung up his head,
> And soon amazed them all.
> They let him stand 'til midsummer
> Till he looked both pale and wan,
> And little Sir John he growed a long beard
> And so became a man.
>
> They hired men with the scythes so sharp
> To cut him off at the knee.
> They rolled him and tied him by the waist,
> And served him most barbarously.
> They hired men with pitchforks
> Who pricked him in the heart,
> And the loader he served him worse than that,
> For he bound him to the cart.

They wheeled him round and round the field
'Til they came unto a barn,
And there they made a solemn mow
Of poor John Barleycorn.
They hired men with crab tree sticks
To cut him skin from bone,
And the miller he served him worse than that,
For he ground him between two stones.

Here's little Sir John in a nut-brown bowl,
And brandy in a glass;
And little Sir John in the nut-brown bowl
Proved the stronger man at last.
And the huntsman he can't hunt the fox,
Nor so loudly blow his horn,
And the tinker he can't mend kettles or pots
Without a little of Barleycorn.

◆

Celtic Prayer

Every day I pray to Bridgit that
No fire, no flames shall burn me,
No lake, no sea shall drown me,
No sword, no spear shall wound me,
No king, no chief shall insult me.
All the birds shall sing for me,
All the cattle shall low for me,
All the insects buzz for me,
God's angels shall protect me.

◆

Hot Whiskey

A few centuries ago, it was common to flavor whiskey with such items as pepper, fennel seeds, raisins, fruit, cloves, or liquorice. People even laced their spirits with bits of spiced toast. Although the Celts no longer put bread into their whiskey, the term "toast" has survived to refer to any special words expressed before imbibing. It was not until the 1600s, when the great distilleries opened, that whiskey became a standardized product made only from barley, yeast, and water.

When suffering from a cold, I always like to take a glass of hot whiskey to bed along with a good book.

	Boiling water
2	**teaspoons sugar, or to taste**
	Irish Whiskey
	Cloves, slices of lemon to taste (optional)

Heat a stemmed whiskey glass by running it under hot water and pour in fresh boiling water to half full. Dissolve sugar in glass and add the whiskey, cloves, and lemon. Stir with a silver spoon and drink at once.

ASSOCIATED HOLIDAYS: LUGHNASADH, SAMHAIN, MABON, YULE

SERVES 1

Water is a good drink

if taken in the right spirit.

IRISH PROVERB

———◆———

Hot Buttered Rum

What butter and whiskey won't cure there's no cure for (Scottish proverb).

A combination of cinnamon and nutmeg promotes prosperity, protection, success, and general good wishes, which is why buttered rum makes an excellent festival drink.

½   cup butter, softened
½   cup brown sugar
¼   cup powdered sugar
½   teaspoon nutmeg
½   teaspoon ground cinnamon
1   cup vanilla ice cream, softened
6   jiggers of rum, or to taste
   Boiling water

In a small bowl, beat butter together with brown sugar, powdered sugar, nutmeg, and cinnamon. Beat in the softened ice cream. Pour the ice cream into a freezer-proof container, seal, and freeze. When ready to serve, put about ⅓ cup of the ice cream mixture into individual mugs. Add 1 jigger of rum and ½ cup boiling water to each. Stir well and serve. Some people like to add an extra dollop of whipped cream, but this is not necessary.

Variation: Place 2 jiggers dark rum, a twist of lemon peel, and a cinnamon stick in an ale mug. Fill with boiling hard cider, add a pat of butter, and stir with a cinnamon stick.

ASSOCIATED HOLIDAYS: YULE, ESBAT CELEBRATIONS

Three things that foster high spirits:

self-esteem, courting, and drinking.

WELSH TRIAD

Black Velvet

It may seem strange to mix two already perfect ingredients, but this drink is surprisingly good and well worth a try. Black Velvet is a wonderful party drink, and a nice alternative for New Year's Eve celebrations.

2 cans Guinness stout (Do not use bottled variety)
1 bottle of champagne

In tall glasses, mix the champagne with equal measures of stout. Serve immediately, while drink is still bubbly.

ASSOCIATED HOLIDAYS: YULE, NEW YEAR'S EVE, NAME DAYS/BIRTHDAYS

SERVES 8

Wassail

A fine way of serving wassail is to put an apple in each mug and ladle the hot brew over it. Provide each of your guests with a spoon so they can eat the apple afterwards.

12 small tart apples
6 pints ale
2 cups brown sugar
2 teaspoons each ginger, cinnamon, nutmeg
4 whole cloves
Zest of 2 lemons
2 pints red wine

Peel and core apples and dry roast them (no sugar) in a slow oven until they almost burst. Combine ⅓ of the ale with sugar, spices, and lemon zest. Simmer over low heat for 20 minutes. Add remaining ale and wine and heat but do not boil. Serve.

ASSOCIATED HOLIDAYS: YULE, MIDWINTER

SERVES 12

Mulled Cider

In ancient Ireland, apple trees were one of three things (the other being a hazel bush or an oak grove) that could only be paid for with other living objects—money could not exchange hands. In Tir-na-nÓg, the Celtic land of the ever-young, apple trees bore both fruit and flowers at the same time. It is interesting to note that in the Christian myth of paradise, no specific fruit is ever mentioned for the Tree of Life, but everyone interprets it to mean an apple. When picking apples, respect their sacred origins. Three of the finest apple specimens should be left as an offering to the Goddess and to the faeries who tend the grove.

This is a good harvest drink, and perfect for a Samhain feast, as it aids in divination spells.

    8   cups apple cider
    ½   cup brown sugar
        Pinch of ground nutmeg
    6   inches of stick cinnamon
    1   teaspoon whole allspice
    1   teaspoon plus 8 whole cloves
    8   orange wedges, rind attached
        Cheesecloth

In a large saucepan, combine cider, brown sugar, and nutmeg. Place cinnamon, allspice, and 1 teaspoon of whole cloves in cheesecloth and tie with string. Add spice bag to cider mixture; bring to boiling. Reduce heat, cover, and simmer for another five to ten minutes. Remove spice bag and discard. Serve cider in mugs with a clove-studded orange wedge in each. You may also reserve the cinnamon sticks for a decorative touch.

ASSOCIATED HOLIDAYS: LUGHNASADH, SAMHAIN, MABON,
HARVEST SUPPERS, ESBAT CELEBRATIONS,
NAME DAYS/BIRTHDAYS, YULE

Never lean against a public house

except when you are drinking.

WELSH PROVERB

Here We Go A' Wassailing

Wassail, wassail, all over the town

Our bread is white and our ale is brown

Our bowl is made from good maple tree

We be good fellow all

I drink to thee!

The warm, spiced punch served at Christmastime is a descendant of the old English wassail, a drink of hot spiced ale and apples. The name "wassail" comes from the Saxon *wes hæl,* or "be whole," and to wassail meant to drink to someone's health. While drinking the punch could be a family affair, it was more often a communal event. At the winter solstice people would carry a large bowl of spiced cider from house to house, where everyone drank the blood-red brew. (Perhaps, long ago, wassail was the warm blood drunk from sacrifices, ensuring the health and qualities of the sacrificial animal.) Many of the songs wassailers sang along the way have come down to us as familiar Christmas carols. You may remember "Here we come a-wassailing among the leaves so green, here we come a-wassailing so fair to be seen." The reference to greenery is probably of holly, a favorite midwinter decoration.

Stand fast root, bear well top,

give us a young crop

every twig, apples big,

every bough, apples enough.

For centuries Somerset, England, has been known as Cider Country. Right to this day the residents of many a village wassail their orchards. Wassailing the apple trees is an ancient custom. It was done on Christmas Eve, New Year, or Twelfth Night, depending on the locale. The men and boys of the farm, sometimes

accompanied by the woman, servants, and even the local vicar, went to the orchard carrying cider, pots, pans, kettle, and guns. Anything to create a ruckus! Around the turn of the century the custom was nearly lost, but due to recent revivals it can still be enjoyed.

In Carhampton, Somerset, the Twelfth Night tradition has never been broken. The citizens will mull some cider and take it out to a selected tree and drink to its health. The tree need not be the oldest, or the largest; whatever tree is selected represents all the trees in the orchard. The cider is poured over the roots of the tree, and the host will bow three times. Pieces of bread, soaked in cider, are placed in forks in the branches. The following song, or some such variation, is then sung:

> Old apple tree, we wassail thee
> and hope that thou wilt bear
> For the Lord knows where we shall be
> till apples come another year.
>
> For to bear well, and to bear well,
> so let us merry be.
> Let every man take off his hat,
> and shoot to the old apple tree!
>
> Old apple tree, we wassail thee,
> and hoping thou wilt bear
> Hatfuls, capfuls, three-bushel bagfuls,
> and a little heap under the stair!

Noise is mandatory. Shotguns are fired to rouse the sleeping tree spirits and to frighten away evil spirits and bad luck. Because of this ceremony, an abundant apple crop is assured for the coming year.

◆

Milk Punch

There's no cure for spilled milk but to lick the pitcher (Irish proverb).

Milk punch, also known as *scáiltín*, can be made in several ways. The most common method is to mix equal measures of hot whiskey and warm milk. Melted butter, sugar, cinnamon, nutmeg, or cloves can be added, according to taste.

ASSOCIATED HOLIDAYS: IMBOLG, BELTAINE, YULE

Atholl Brose

Though honey is sweet, do not lick it off a briar (Breton proverb).

3 cups uncooked oatmeal
8 ounces honey
1 cup cold water
2 pints whiskey

Stir together the oatmeal, honey, and cold water. When they are thoroughly mixed, slowly add the whiskey. Stir briskly until the mixture foams. Bottle and cork tightly in sterilized containers. After a day or two remove the cork, strain the mixture, and toast your friends with a hearty *sláinte agus saol agat!* Health and long life to you!

ASSOCIATED HOLIDAYS: IMBOLG, YULE

Bread when you're hungry
drink when you're dry
rest when you're weary
and heaven when you die.

BRITISH PROVERB

◆

The Moonshiner (Traditional)

I've been a moonshiner for many a year,
I'll spend all my money on whiskey and beer,
I'll go to some hollow and set up my still,
I'll make you a gallon for a two-dollar bill.

Chorus:
Moonshine, dear moonshine, oh how I love thee,
You kill'd my poor father but dare you try me.
Bless all moonshiners and bless all moonshine,
Its breath is as sweet as the dew on the vine.

I'll go to some hollow in this coun-ter-y,
Ten gallons of wash I can go on the spree.
No woman to follow and the world is all mine,
I love none so well as I love the moonshine.

Chorus

I'll have moonshine for Liza, and moonshine for May,
Moonshine for Lu and she'll sing all the day,
Moonshine for me breakfast, moonshine for me tea,
Moonshine, me hearties, it's moonshine for me.

Chorus

Irish Coffee

In the 1940s, Irish Mist liqueur inspired Joe Sheridan, chef at Foynes, a boat house located on the Shannon Estuary in Co. Clare, to concoct this now-classic beverage as a pick-me-up for transatlantic travelers arriving by seaplane. He later took the recipe to the States, where variations can be found in every Irish pub from New York to San Francisco. Legend holds that the recipe for Irish Mist, thought to be the heather ale of Celtic folklore, is 1,200 years old.

1	cup hot black coffee
1½	ounces Irish Mist liqueur
2	tablespoons whipped cream

Heat a stemmed whiskey glass by running it under hot water. Pour in coffee, add Irish Mist. Do not stir. Top with freshly whipped cream. The hot spirit-laced coffee is then drunk through the cold cream—a delightful sensation!

Variation:

1	heaping teaspoon soft brown sugar
1	cup strong black coffee, hot
1	jigger Irish Whiskey
1	tablespoon cream

Place sugar in a heated whiskey glass and add coffee to dissolve sugar; stir well. Add the whiskey to fill within an inch of the brim. Hold a spoon, curved side up, across the glass and pour the cream slowly over the spoon. Do not stir; the cream should float on top of the coffee.

ASSOCIATED HOLIDAYS: NAME DAYS/BIRTHDAYS, SAMHAIN, MABON, YULE, ESBAT CELEBRATIONS

SERVES 1

To Your Health!

It is still common to lift a glass and wish health and good will to a friend. From the *Laws of Drinking*, 1617, we find the following passage:

"It seems to have been formerly usual for a man in company, not contented with taking what he chooses, to bid another to drink the same quantity that he does. In the following passage one proposes a health which another pledges to honor by drinking to it an equal quantity with him that proposed it."

> Oh, how they'll wind men in, do what they can,
> By drinking healths, first unto such a man,
> Then unto such a woman. They they'll send
> A health to each man's mistress or his friend;
> Then to their kindrels or their parents dear,
> They needs must have the other jug of beer.
> Then to their captains and commanders stout,
> Who for to pledge they think none shall stand out,
> Last to the king and queen, they'll have a cruse,
> Whom for to pledge they think none dare refuse.

◆

There is more friendship in a jigger of whiskey
than in a churn of buttermilk.

MANX PROVERB

———◆———

Saffron Cordial

As for rosemary I lette it runne all over my garden walls, not onlie because my bees love it, but because it is the herb sacred to remembrance and to friendship (Sir Thomas Moore).
From The Good Housewife, *1736:*

"Fill a large still with marigold flowers, adding to them of nutmegs, mace, and English saffron, of each an ounce. Then take three pints of red wine, and with a sprig of rosemary dash it on the flowers. Distil it off with a slow fire, and let it drop on white sugar candy, draw it off till it begins to be sour. Save a pint of first running to mix with the other waters of an extraordinary occasion. Mix the rest together to drink it by itself."

ASSOCIATED HOLIDAYS: MIDSUMMER, LUGHNASADH, SUN FESTIVALS

Homemade Irish Cream

Irish cream can be used in a variety of ways, from drinking straight to spicing up coffee.

- 3 eggs
- 1 can condensed milk
- 1 cup whiskey
- 1 tablespoon chocolate syrup
- 1 tablespoon vanilla

Blend all ingredients together and keep refrigerated. Discard unused mixture after 1 week.

ASSOCIATED HOLIDAYS: NAME DAYS/BIRTHDAYS, NEW YEAR'S EVE

You can't expect a big egg

from a little hen.

MANX PROVERB

◆

Sowans

Sowans is a particularly bitter drink that was made from the "sids," the husk and chaffe residue of milled oatmeal. It was steeped in water for up to three weeks while it fermented, then strained to create a milky liquid known as Bull's Semen or White Bull's Milk. Although the connection with bulls is unclear, it is perhaps a reference to the great God. While the Goddess sometimes takes on the form of a white cow, it is natural that her consort take on the form of a white bull. White cattle are also said to originally come from faerie herds.

While it was usually drunk during haymaking season, Sowans was also made at Samhain for the dead who were believed to visit their former homes on this night. It was once the custom to prepare a bed near the hearth and to lay out tobacco, whiskey, and sowans for the departed relatives.

While it tastes nothing like the drink described above, this is another harvest drink with the name sowans. It is a large recipe, making approximately 6 gallons.

- 3 quarts buttermilk
- 6 cups yogurt
- 2 cups sour cream
- 2 cups sugar
- 1 tablespoon vanilla
  Crushed ice

Mix together buttermilk, yogurt, sour cream, sugar, vanilla, and enough crushed ice to chill the lot.

ASSOCIATED HOLIDAYS: SAMHAIN, MABON,
HARVEST SUPPERS

Home Brewing

In years gone by the Celts enjoyed many a home-brewed beverage made from the land's bounties. They drank whiskey, heather ale, and wine; *nenad-min*, a cider made from wild apples; *fraochán*, brewed from blueberries; and *graggert*, made by fermenting ale and honey together. The most famous of drinks, however, is mead, a potent honey brew. Bards sang of its praises, and it was the choice drink of any celebration. At one such feast in Ulster, 100 barrels were served, and the drunken sound of singing was said to have disturbed the residents of Munster (the next province). According to Celtic tradition, brews will be tastiest if made during the last two quarters of the moon. Also, the first libation should be poured out in honor of Bridgit, patron goddess of brewing.

An Olde Mead Recipe

Don't argue with drunken warriors, mead steals the minds of many (Celtic proverb).

An infusion of eyebright, as its name implies, makes a soothing eyewash. I've used it after spending too many hours staring at my computer screen. It also aids in clairvoyance and psychic powers.

A British folk belief: Betony is one of the sacred herbs to be burned in the mid-summer fire. Jumping through the smoke will rid the body of illness. If added to food or drink, it will end lovers' quarrels.

From a seventeenth-century cookbook:

"Put a handful of thyme, rosemary, sweet briar, eyebright, wood betony, scabious, wormwood, agrimony (of each a like quantity), and steep for twenty-four hours in a wooden bowl, uncovered, then boil them in another water till it be very high coloured; then change the water and boil them till it is coloured green, and as long as any green mess remains, then set it by for twenty-four hours more. Then strain the liquor from the herbs and put a pound of honey to every two quarts of the liquor and when it will bear an egg to three pence breadth above the water work it together till the honey is dissolved; then let it settle for a night; the next day boil it with the shells and whites of half a dozen eggs; then strain it, set it by to cool; then put it up into the cask, then bruise cinnamon, nutmeg, cloves, mace, and put them in a bag and hang them in the cask and stop it up. If you would have it fit to drink in a little time, beat together the whites of three eggs; add to them a spoonful of yeast, two spoonfuls of honey, and put them into the cask and then temper some Clay with Bay salt and stop it up close."

Mead

A popular spring drink was a mixture of cow or sheep blood that was mingled with their milk (the animal was not killed). This was thought to ward off evil faeries.

In ancient Ireland and Britain, mead made the year before was often drunk in celebration of spring. It was thought to be an aphrodisiac, a gift from the goddess Bridgit. When making mead, be sure to dedicate the first libation to the goddess, and leave out a small quantity as a gift to your house spirits.

½	gallon water
1½	cups honey
¼	cup lemon juice
⅛	teaspoon nutmeg
⅛	teaspoon allspice
1	package brewer's yeast

Heat water, honey, lemon juice, nutmeg, and allspice together in a large stock pot. Blend well and remove from the heat. Stir in brewer's yeast and pour the mead into a wooden cask. Allow to ferment for 6 months. During this time the cask should be aired daily to allow gasses to escape. At least once a month it should be poured into a fresh cask.

Variation: Many older cookbooks recommend a variety of herbs to add flavor to mead. Try brewing with lemon balm, thyme, sweet marjoram, rosemary, burnet, cloves, ginger, mint, elderflowers, cloves, angelica, borage, or bugloss.

ASSOCIATED HOLIDAYS: IMBOLG, OSTARA, BELTAINE

Raisins-of-the-Sun Wine

When worn in your hair, cowslips will help to preserve your youth. William Turner, a sixteenth-century botanist, wrote, "Some women sprinkle ye floures of cowslip wt whyte wine and after distill it and wash their faces wt that water to drive wrinkles away and to make them fayre in the eyes of the world."

- 4 pounds pitted raisins
- 2 pounds sugar
  Juice of 4 lemons, peels of 2
- 4 gallons water
  Cowslips and gillyflowers (optional)

Place raisins, sugar, lemon juice and peel in a large pot and cover with water. Add cowslips and gillyflowers if in season. Let boil for half an hour. Remove from heat and let stand covered for 3 or 4 days, stirring twice a day. Strain into sterilized bottles and cork tightly. Do not fill the bottles all the way, or else they may shatter. Store in a cool place for a fortnight's time before drinking.

ASSOCIATED HOLIDAYS: MIDSUMMER, LUGHNASADH

From the bonny bells of heather,
They brewed a drink langsyne,
'Twas sweeter far than honey,
Was stronger far than wine.

ROBERT LOUIS STEVENSON

Heather Ale

Scottish Highlanders built their summer shielings of heather stems bound with grass and held together with a mortar made of peat. Roofs were also thatched with heather. Heather is not a native American plant, but was probably brought here by the Scots in heather-filled mattresses. At one time young heather shoots were used to flavor beer instead of hops.

In Ireland I was once approached by a gypsy tinker woman selling magical white heather that would bring luck and protect me from violence. She told me I could burn it with fern to bring needed rain.

I first sampled this recipe from a farmer in the Welsh mountains who swore his ancestors brought it from Scotland. But is this the celebrated recipe once used by the ancient Celts? We may never know for sure.

Heather bells
Hops
Ground ginger
Treacle
Yeast

Take the heather bells when the heather is in full bloom and wash in cold water. Fill an enamel pot with the heather, cover with water, and boil for an hour. Strain the liquid into a clean wooden tub, and for every dozen pints of liquid add a half-ounce of hops, an ounce of ground ginger, and a pound of treacle. Boil again for another 20 minutes. Strain off once more, and when almost cold, add five tablespoons of barm (yeast). Cover with a cloth and allow the mixture to ferment, undisturbed, for at least 24 hours. After that, carefully skim the surface and gently pour into a tub, leaving the barmy sediment behind. Pour into sterilized bottles and cork tightly. Put the bottles in a dark place for about a week, and then drink.

ASSOCIATED HOLIDAYS: IMBOLG, LUGHNASADH

Heather Wine

While Ireland and Britain are not known for their grape industry, heather wine and ale were highly prized, and the manner of their brewing was a well-kept secret. Heather is a sacred flower, and placing it on your Samhain altar encourages the presence of faeries. White heather is used in generating a protection spell, red for promoting an affair.

1–2	pounds fresh heather (upper stalks and flowering heads)
1	gallon water
4	cups sugar
¼	teaspoon nutmeg
½	teaspoon allspice
¼	cup lemon juice (optional)

In a large soup pot, boil the heather in a gallon of water until you have a heavily colored tea. You may need to add more plant material if the color is weak; you should not be able to see through the liquid if poured into a clear glass. Remove the mixture from the heat and strain. Discard plant material. When mixture has cooled slightly, add sugar, nutmeg, allspice, and lemon juice. Pour the mixture into casks and allow to ferment about 6 months.

ASSOCIATED HOLIDAYS: IMBOLG, LUGHNASADH, ESBAT CELEBRATIONS

Wine is sweet but

the results are often bitter.

SCOTTISH PROVERB

Lemon Wine

This recipe comes from the cookbook of my Grandmother O'Kelly. It was a popular summertime drink when she was young.

24 large lemons, divided
2 quarts brandy
1 gallon spring water
  Sugar to taste
1 quart white wine

Take a dozen large lemons and pare off the rind. Cut the lemons in half and squeeze out the juice. Put the rinds and juice in a bowl and pour brandy over. Let it stand in a tightly closed earthen vessel for 3 days. Squeeze another dozen lemons into a pot, add a gallon of fresh spring water, and as much sugar as will sweeten the whole of your palate. Boil it together to dissolve sugar and let stand till cool. Add a quart of white wine and the lemon brandy mixture. Run it through a cheesecloth and into a sterilized cask. Let stand 3 months and bottle it off for use. Keep the bottles well corked and store in a cool, dark place. It will be fit to drink in a month or so.

ASSOCIATED HOLIDAYS: MIDSUMMER, LUGHNASADH, SUN FESTIVALS

Wine makes old women wenches.

SCOTTISH PROVERB

White Metheglin

In my research of British literature, I have come across several references to an herbal drink called metheglin. The recipe I found will make a rather large quantity, and I have yet to come across an occasion to serve it.
  From Sir Kenelm Digby, 1699:

"Take of sweet-bryar a great handful; of violet-flowers, sweet marjoram, strawberry leaves, violet leaves, and one handful, agrimony, bugloss, borage, and half a handful of rosemary; four branches, Gillyflowers (the yellow wallflowers with great tops), anniseeds, fennel, and caraway, of each a spoonful, two large Mace. Boil all these in twelve gallons of water for the space of an hour; then strain it, and let it stand until it be milk-warm.

"Put in as much honey as will carry an egge to the breadth of sixpence at least; then boil it again, and scum it clean. Let it stand until it be cold. Then put a pint of ale-barm (yeast) into it, and ripen it as you do beer, and tun it. Then hang in the midst of the vessel a little bag with a nutmeg quartered, a race of ginger sliced, a little cinnamon, and mace whole, and three grains of musk in a cloth put into the bag amonst the rest of the spices. Put a stone in the bag, to keep it in the midst of the liquor. This quantity took up three gallons of honey; therefore be sure to have four in readiness."

ASSOCIATED HOLIDAY: MIDSUMMER

Mead isn't the blessing to men

that many say it is.

The more you drink

the less you stay the master of your wits.

NORMAN-IRISH SAYING

———◆———

Sloe Gin

I never considered making sloe gin from scratch until I met Remmy Jones, a vintner from North Wales. I have not purchased the store-bought variety since then.

- 1 gallon sloes (see note)
- 1 pound sugar
- 1 gallon gin

Crush the fruit in a large bowl, remove the stones. Add the sugar, mix well, and pour into a sealable sterile jar. Pour over the gin. Seal the jar and let stand in cool dark place. In 6 weeks it is ready to be strained and bottled in sterilized containers.

Note: Sloes can be purchased at specialty stores or grown yourself—they're a plumb-like fruit of the blackthorn tree.

Associated Holidays: Lughnasadh, Mabon

A Slower Gin

Whuppity Scoorie, celebrated on March 1, is a Celtic custom in which people would go out and tap the earth three times with a staff, calling out for the goddess to "wake up." It is a rowdy holiday, with much noisemaking and drinking. Celebrate with your own brew.

- 4 cups sloes
- 1 quart gin
- 2½ cups brown sugar
- ¼ cup white sugar

Prick each sloe several times with a fork and place in a large, sealable jar. Pour in gin and add sugars. Stir with a wooden spoon to dissolve as much sugar as possible. Seal and leave in a cool dark room for 3 months. Each day turn the jar upside down and give it a good shake. Strain several times through a linen cloth until the mixture comes out perfectly clear. Do not squeeze the fruit. Bottle in sterile bottles and store for 1 year before using.

Blackberry Wine

Blackberries, which were sacred to the goddess Bridgit, ripen in late summer and early fall, and blackberry wines were made and dedicated to her. In Ireland there was, and still is, a folk taboo against eating blackberries after the autumnal equinox, but all berries made into wines for the goddess were permissible to use. Blackberries are traditionally baked into pies at Lughnasadh.

> 2½ pounds fresh blackberries (handpicked if possible)
>   Enough hot water to make 1 gallon of liquid when
>   mixed with the berries
> 3–6 cups sugar

Let the berries sit out in a large bowl for about 4 weeks, stirring them occasionally. The berries will get a rank smell and may even begin to mold. With mortar and pestle, crush the berries into as smooth a pulp as possible. Add the hot water and stir in the sugar. Pour the wine into casks to ferment for 8 to 10 months. The longer it is kept, the better it will be. The wine will have to be aired every few days to allow building gases to escape.

ASSOCIATED HOLIDAYS: IMBOLG, LUGHNASADH, NAME DAYS/BIRTHDAYS

Egg Punch

Seldom are hunger and thirst together (Manx proverb).

> 1½ quarts wine
> 1 quart water
> 1¼ cups sugar
>   Juice of 1 lemon
>   Nutmeg and whole cloves
> 8 eggs, beaten

Combine all ingredients except eggs, and heat. Add eggs and beat until mixture is frothy. Do not boil or you will end up with scrambled eggs. Serve at once.

ASSOCIATED HOLIDAY: OSTARA

SERVES 8 TO 10

Spring Wine

Undoubtedly the best known of all herbal wines is the traditional May Wine, flavored with sweet woodruff and drunk in celebration of Beltaine. Many other herbs can be used to flavor wine, but you should do so sparingly and with consideration to the flavor of the wine itself, as well as the magical properties of each herb. Dry white wines work the best, but feel free to experiment. Adding herbs to a young wine has the practical purpose of improving the harsh taste.

    1   bottle dry white wine
  3–4   sprigs of herb

In a non-metallic container, steep the herbs in the wine and set in a cool, dark place overnight. Some herbs, such as rose petals, may need to steep for several weeks to take on the characteristic flavor, so you should place the wine in sterilized jars and seal. Filter before serving.

Variation: Sometimes strawberries are steeped along with sweet woodruff for Beltaine Wine, or else they are floated on top. If you do not have time to make it yourself, it is possible to purchase several good German varieties at your local wine shop.

Associated Holiday: Beltaine

Serves 6

A drink is shorter than a story.

Scottish Proverb

Chamomile Wine

Chamomile has the benefit of calming one and promoting relaxation. It is good to drink in wine (if in moderation) and tea to clear the mind before spell work.

   4   cups red or white wine
½–1   cup dried chamomile flowers
   1   tablespoon lemon zest
   1   tablespoon orange zest
2–3   tablespoons brown sugar

Place all the ingredients in a glass jar with a tight-fitting top and steep in a cool, dark place for about a week. Filter and bottle.

Associated Holidays: Midsummer, Yule

Yields 1 quart

Hypocras

Last time I went to London, I brought back with me packets of hypocras to spice my midwinter wine cups. The mixture was based on a seventeenth-century recipe:

"To make hypocras take four gallons of claret wine, eight ounces of cinamon, and Oranges, of Ginger, Cloves, and Nutmegs a small quantity, Sugar six pounds, three sprigs of Rosemary, bruise all the spices somewhat small, and so put them into the Wine, and keep them close stopped, and often shaked together a day or two, then let it run through a jelly bagge twice or thrice with a quart of new milk."

On the day Dechtine sat at her wedding feast, a mayfly flew into her cup of wine, and she swallowed it without noticing its presence. When she slept that night she dreamed that the sun god Lugh approached her and said, 'It was no mayfly you swallowed, beautiful one, but my own essence.' Not long afterwards the maiden gave birth to a son, Sétanta, who would one day grow up to be the great hero Cúchulainn.

Tain bo Cúchulainn

Strawberry Summer Liqueur

Strawberries tend to attract faeries and friendly spirits, and when combined with rose petals produce a love potion.

> 4 pints strawberries
> 1 cup rose petals
> 4 cups vodka or other grain alcohol
> ½ cup white wine, dry
> ½ cup water
> 1 cup sugar

Combine the strawberries, rose petals, vodka, and wine in a sterilized jar with a tight-fitting cover. Place in a cool, dark place to steep for at least 1 month. Crush the berries slightly against the sides of the jar with a fork and steep for another week. Press as much of the juice from the berries as possible, then strain and filter the liquid through a cheesecloth. In a small saucepan over medium heat, dissolve the sugar in the water. Cool and gradually stir sugar water into the liqueur, tasting as you do so. When it has reached its desired sweetness, bottle and age for another 2 to 3 weeks in a cool, dark place. You may wish to try using clay bottles or jars and make your own labels.

ASSOCIATED HOLIDAYS: MIDSUMMER, LUGHNASADH

Bring us in good ale!

Bring us in good ale!

For our blessed Lady's sake

Bring us in good ale!

TRADITIONAL SCOTTISH SONG

Orange Brandywine

Orange peels are used in spellcraft to bring love and good fortune. Share this drink with one you would like to get to know better.

4 cups dry white wine
½ cup sugar
½ cup brandy, preferably orange brandy
Zest of 2 oranges, absolutely no pith should be attached
1 tablespoon orange juice
¼ cup mint
Mint leaves to garnish

Combine wine and sugar in an enamel pot and bring to a boil. Remove from heat and stir to completely dissolve sugar. Cool to lukewarm and add the brandy. In a sterilized jar, place orange zest, orange juice, and mint. Pour in wine mixture, seal, and store in a cool, dark place for at least 1 week. Filter before drinking. Garnish each glass with mint leaves.

ASSOCIATED HOLIDAYS: LUGHNASADH, SUN FESTIVALS

From *The Fionn Cycle:*

Fionn called together the seven battalions of the Fianna, and the place where they gathered was on the hill that was called Fionntulach, the White Hill. They often stopped on that hill for a while, and spear-shafts with spells on them were brought to them there, and they had every sort of thing for food, beautiful blackberries, haws of the hawthorn, nuts of the hazel, tender twigs of the bramble bush, sprigs of wholesome gentian, mint, and watercress at the beginning of summer. And there would be brought to them birds out of the oakwoods, and squirrels, and speckled eggs from the cliffs, and salmon out of the river, and eels, and woodcocks, and otters from the hidden places, and fish from the coasts, and dulse from the bay. But above all there was drink.

◆

Wine Cup

I serve this punch at my annual Samhain gathering, as the combination of fruit and spices is a particularly potent spell for love and success. Therefore, it is best shared with friends.

5	cups rhubarb or apple wine
3	cups orange juice
2½	cups cold water
1¼	cups apple juice
½	cup sugar
¼	cup grated lemon peel
2	tablespoons honey
6	whole cloves
½	teaspoon cinnamon
½	teaspoon nutmeg
2	quarts ginger ale
	Crushed ice

Combine all ingredients except ginger ale and ice. Refrigerate overnight. At serving time, strain, add ginger ale, and pour over ice.

ASSOCIATED HOLIDAYS: LUGHNASADH, SAMHAIN, MABON, HARVEST SUPPERS, ESBAT CELEBRATIONS, NAME DAYS/BIRTHDAYS

The sweetest wine makes

the sharpest vinegar.

WELSH PROVERB

Witchwood (Elderberry) Wine

There is a great deal of folklore surrounding witchwood. If you burn it while green, you promote bad luck and invite the devil into your home. You should apologize three times to the Elder spirit before cutting the wood, and never use it to make furniture. Drinking elderberry wine promotes faithfulness in your lover, encourages prophetic dreams, and will enable you to see faeries.

½	bushel elderberries
6	gallons water
6	pounds Demerara sugar
2	pounds valencia raisins
1	tablespoon ginger
8	cloves
4	tablespoons fresh brewer's yeast
	Cognac

Pick the elderberries at midday on a hot, sunny day. Add water, Demerara sugar, valencia raisins, ginger, and cloves. Clean the berries and pour on them the boiling water. Leave set for 24 hours. Strain through a muslin bag, breaking the berries to extract all the juice. Add the other ingredients and boil, removing the scum. Remove from the fire and leave the pot to stand until the contents are blood-heat. Strain through muslin into a cask and allow 4 tablespoons fresh brewer's yeast to each 9 gallons of wine. Leave to ferment a fortnight. Then to every gallon of wine allow a quarter pint of old Cognac. Seal tightly and allow to ferment for 4 months before bottling.

ASSOCIATED HOLIDAY: MIDSUMMER

"*I will give them a gift,*" *said a young man of the Tuatha de Danaan.* "*A horn I will give them, and a vat. And there is nothing wanting but to fill the vat with pure water, and it will turn into mead, fit to drink, and strong enough to make drunken. And into the horn you have but to put salt of the sea, and it will turn into wine on the morrow.*"

LADY AUGUSTA GREGORY, GODS AND FIGHTING MEN

Dandelion Wine

Where wine goes in, wit goes out (Breton proverb).

1	quart dandelion blooms
4	pounds of Demerara sugar
3	lemons
1	gallon of water
½	package yeast
1	slice bread, toasted

Boil blooms in water for 20 minutes. Strain boiling liquor onto the sugar. Halve the lemons, peel, and remove the seeds. Put remainder into liquor. Place yeast on a small piece of toast and lay it on the liquor when it has cooled to blood warm. When it has fermented about two days, skim off the yeast and toast and discard. Bottle the wine, adding the lemon peel.

Variation:

9	quarts water
9	quarts dandelion heads
1	(1-inch) piece ginger
10	whole cloves
8	cups sugar
1	lemon
1	package yeast
1	slice toast

Place the flower heads in a saucepan with the water, crushed ginger, and cloves. Boil for 30 minutes. Add sugar and rind of lemon. Boil 30 minutes more. Strain into an earthenware vessel. When cool, spread yeast on both sides of a piece of toast and float in liquid. Cover container with thick, clean cloth and let ferment 2 weeks. Strain into clean bottles, cork securely, and store 6 months.

Suggestions: Try adding orange and lemon zest.

Associated Holidays: Midsummer, Lughnasadh

A Perfect Pot of Herbal Tea

There is nothing better than a cup of herbal tea if you are feeling out of sorts. Just the ritual of brewing tea can be comforting: heating the water, holding the warm mug in your hands, and feeling the steam rise to your face are all soothing after a long day's work. Drinking a cup of tea prior to any magical working can clear your mind and aid in divination work.

While herbal teas help you relax, many herbs contain properties that can be used in connection with certain spell work. It is a good idea to pick up a guide to magical herbs and keep a variety of herbs in your cupboard for helping you create perfect tea combinations.

Please note: *Although all of these herbs have traditionally been brewed and served as a tea, many have adverse side effects if taken in large doses. Pregnant women and nursing mothers in particular should consult a reputable herb book or visit an herbalist before experimenting with herbal blends.*

Let the cold water run from your faucet for several seconds. Do not use hot water from the tap, as it contains too many impurities. Fill a teakettle with water and bring to a brisk boil. Rinse a china, pottery, or other non-metal teapot by swishing around some of the hot water. Toss in 2 tablespoons of fresh or 1 tablespoon of dried herbs (roots, seeds, pods, leaves, or whatever you are using) for every cup of water you'll be using, plus an extra 2 tablespoons of fresh or 1 tablespoon of dried "for the pot." It is best to use a ritual spoon of wood; oak is a good choice, as it symbolizes the Green Man. One you carved yourself is even better. Pour in the boiling water and let the tea steep for about five minutes. Draw on the powers of the herbs, envisioning a problem that might be troubling you. Keep the pot or teapot covered to retain heat. Steeping time will vary, depending on what herbs you're using, so periodically check the flavor until you are satisfied. Strain the herbs out as soon as the tea has reached the desired strength. Do not use cream, as it will tend to curdle. Serve herb tea with honey, sugar, lemon, orange slices, or fresh herb sprigs. The following combinations work well; experiment to make your own tea blends.

> **lemon and peppermint**
> **mint and strawberry leaves**
> **yarrow roots, leaves and flowers**
> **bergamot**
> **sweet woodruff and strawberry leaves**
> **elderflower, nettle, burdock, mullein, rosehips**

lemon verbena and borage
roseleaf and petals
fresh or dried violet leaves
elder blossom and peppermint
chamomile flowers and honey
rosemary, thyme, and cloves
horehound and mint
sage and lemon
ground ivy, hyssop, and apricot
agrimony
southernwood and nutmeg
tansy leaves and flowers (a spring tonic)
rosemary and honey
chamomile, rosehips, elder
rose petals and gillyflowers
angelica, clove, orange peel, and nutmeg
spearmint, elderberry, and lemon balm
anise, chamomile, and costmary
nettle tops (a spring tonic)
borage and heather
chamomile and honey
hawthorn leaf
meadowsweet leaves and flowers
pennyroyal, peppermint, and ginger
blueberry leaf, beebalm, and ginger
woodruff and strawberry
nettle, ginger, and hyssop
thyme, sassafras, and strawberry leaf
lemongrass, rosemary, and thyme
jasmine, orange peel, and sage
rose petals, rosehips, and raspberry leaf
horehound and chamomile
elderberry, rosehips, and bay
chamomile and apple mint
fennel and goldenrod
chamomile and valerian
chicory, ginseng, and cinnamon

A Perfect Pot of Tea

*There is a great deal of folklore related to serving tea. If the lid of the pot is acci-
dentally left off the teapot, this foretells the coming of a stranger or, in some places,
simple bad luck. It is unlucky to stir the tea in the pot, as to do so will cause quarrels. This is where the phrase, "A tempest in a pot of tea," rises from. If two women
pour from the same pot, one of them will have a baby before the year is through.*

Tea should always be made with freshly drawn, boiled water. Too often I've
seen people float a tea bag in milk, pour in some microwaved water, and
mash the tea bag against the side of the cup with a spoon. Dreadful! To be
honest, I was long guilty of "brewing" tea in this manner, a holdover from
my university days when I seldom had time for the soothing ritual of tea
preparation. I quickly discovered what I'd been missing after moving to
Chicago. My neighbors in the flat below were from central Ireland, and tea
and conversation soon became an after-work ritual. Tea brewed the proper
way, and shared with others, makes a huge difference to the day.

Let the cold water run from your faucet for several seconds. Do not use
hot water from the tap, as it contains too many impurities. Fill a teakettle
with water and bring to a brisk boil. A whistling tea kettle, besides providing you with perfectly boiled water, adds a homey touch. Rinse a china,
pottery, or other nonmetal four-cup teapot with some of the water, then
empty the water out. (Nonmetal pots keep the tea pure in flavor and hot
while it brews.) Using good-quality tea, put 3 to 5 teaspoons, depending
on taste, into the warmed pot. Bring the water back to a boil and immediately pour into the teapot. Cover the pot with a tea cozy and allow to steep
for five minutes—any shorter and the flavor will not have developed, and
any longer and the bitter tannin will leech out. Tea should never be
reheated. Black tea wards off negative influences and adds strength. It is a
good base for many herbal blends as well as love potions.

Tea seldom spoils if water boils.

Scottish Proverb

Floral Punch

According to Arthurian legend, Guinevere rode out early on Beltaine morning to gather wildflowers and greenery. She is an aspect of the flower maiden, the virgin goddess, and embodies the sovereignty of Britain. No king could reign without her. Honor her by serving this punch in a pretty bowl decorated with flowers.

1	quart red grape juice
4	tablespoons sugar
40	mint leaves
1	quart red wine
1	quart strong tea, cooled
	Juice of 3 lemons
	Array of edible flowers, such as nasturtiums, marigolds, primroses, pansies, borage, orange and apple blossoms

Heat grape juice with sugar until sugar has dissolved. Add mint leaves and steep overnight. Strain liquid, discarding leaves, and add wine, tea, and lemon juice. Chill for at least 2 hours.

ASSOCIATED HOLIDAYS: MIDSUMMER, BELTAINE, ESBAT DINNERS

I liken love nowadays into summer and winter; for like as one

is hot and the other cold, so fareth love nowadays; therefore all

ye that be lovers call unto your remembrance the month of

May, like as did Queen Guinevere, that while she lived she was

a true lover, and therefore she had a good end.

SIR THOMAS MALLORY, *LE MORTE D' ARTHUR*

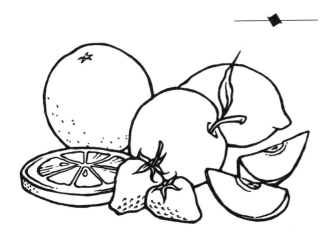

Breads, Porridges, and Breakfast Foods

*Never scald your lips on
another man's porridge.*

SCOTTISH PROVERB

Porridge

On my first trip to Ireland, my mother and I arrived in Rosslare Harbor on a passenger ship from Wales. It was late at night, cold, and rainy. By the time we found a bed and breakfast with room available we were tired and very, very hungry. Our hostess, Kathleen, made us change into dry clothes, sat us down before a blazing peat fire, and brought us each a bowl of steaming porridge. It was the best meal I've ever had.

In ancient times, porridge was made from barley and wheat, as well as oatmeal, and could be cooked in buttermilk or plain water and seasoned with salt, honey, or butter. The seventh-century Celtic Brehon Laws clearly spelled out what types of porridge could be eaten by which classes of people:

> The children of inferior classes are to be fed porridge made of oatmeal and buttermilk or water taken with old butter, and are to be given a bare sufficiency; the sons of chieftains are to eat their fill of porridge made of barley meal with fresh milk and butter; and the sons of kings and princes are to be fed on porridge made of wheaten meal and new milk, and taken with honey.

Many of today's Irish cooks suggest adding raisins and fruit to porridge, while the Scots insist that for a traditional porridge it must be made with fresh spring water, served in a wooden bowl, and eaten with a horn spoon. The majority of Welsh, however, prefer to serve it with liberal amounts of cream and sugar. If you are starting out with fresh ingredients, any of the methods will provide you with a wholesome and satisfying meal.

1 cup water (or half-and-half mixture of milk and water)
3 tablespoons oatmeal
Large pinch of salt

Bring the oatmeal to a boil in the water. Add the salt and stir continuously. When oatmeal begins to thicken and bubble, turn down the heat and let it sputter away for five minutes. Stir occasionally, and add more liquid if desired.

ASSOCIATED HOLIDAYS: ANYTIME, ESPECIALLY ON A COLD WINTER'S EVE

SERVES 1

Let broth boil slowly but let

porridge make a noise.

IRISH PROVERB

No Butter!

One Christmas Eve in the Orkneys, so far back that no one can quite say when, a servant girl wanted to tease the spirit of the farm and play a little trick on him. She hid the butter at the bottom of the Christmas porridge, instead of placing it on top, and set the porridge bowl out in the barn. She knew how much the little sprite loved his butter, and she couldn't wait to hear what he would do when he discovered there was none.

But she got more than she expected! When the faerie lad saw that there was no butter on his Christmas Porridge, he flew into a rage. He immediately went to the cow shed and killed the best cow, even though he had cared for it tenderly all the year. "No butter, eh?" he muttered spitefully. "That will make them sit up and take notice. How dare they be so stingy as to deny me a little butter!"

However, he ate the porridge anyway, and there, at the bottom of the bowl, he discovered the butter. How terrible he felt about killing the cow! How he cried and wailed!

That same Christmas Eve, the little faerie crept over to a farm in the next village, and took the best cow he could find, although it did not look half so fine as the one he had tended. But give him time.

◆

Faerie Porridge

This recipe is for the traditional Christmas porridge given to the faeries in Scotland, Norway, and the Faero Islands.

In medieval Ireland and Britain, it was thought that the Devil could be raised by running widdershins and backwards around stone circles. It could only be done at midnight on Midsummer Eve, and the devil would soon arrive with a bowl of porridge in exchange for the runner's soul. (I have yet to discover what the advantage to that was!)

> 1   quart cream (not too fresh)
> 1   cup flour (more if needed)
> ¾   quart milk
>   Sugar and salt to taste

Stirring continuously, bring cream to a full boil until foam is gone. Gradually add flour to make a thick mush. Stir until butter appears. Remove butter; reserve. In a separate pot, bring milk to a boil. Gradually add hot milk to the mush, stirring all the while. Simmer 10 to 20 minutes, stirring frequently, until mixture thickens. Add sugar and salt to taste. If serving to your house spirits, don't forget to top with the reserved butter.

ASSOCIATED HOLIDAYS: YULE, CHRISTMAS

SERVES 2 HUMANS (AND AN UNKNOWN NUMBER OF FAERIES)

Burstin, Flummery, and Furmenty

References to these recipes stretch all the way back to the early days of the Celts. A seventeenth-century description of furmenty reads: "Furmenty is made of what is called in some areas 'kneed wheat,' or whole grains first boiled plump and soft, and then put into and boiled in milk sweetened and spiced. I cannot avoid reminding you upon the present occasion that furmenty makes the principle entertainment of all our country wakes; our common people call it firmity. It is an agreeable composition of boiled wheat, milk, spice, and sugar. In some locales it is also eaten for the Christmas breakfast."

Burstin: Burstin is made from hulled six-row barley grains. Place grains in a pot by the fire and let them roast. Hand grind grains in a quern. Place the meal in a bowl, heat some milk, and pour over. Serve hot. Burstin can also be made with cold milk or with buttermilk.

Flummery: Place a cup of uncooked oats in a broad deep pan and cover with water. Stir and let stand for 12 hours. Pour off the liquid. Cover with fresh water and let stand for another 12 hours, and so on for 12 more hours. Remove water. Pour oatmeal into a saucepan; heat and stir continuously until it bubbles and thickens, adding more water if necessary. Pour into dishes. When cool, turn out onto plates and serve with milk, wine, and sugar, or beer and sugar.

Furmenty: Fill a jar halfway with wheat grains, cover with milk and set in a warm spot for 12 hours. The grains will swell and burst, and are known as creed wheat. Furmenty may be heated and served with cream and honey.

ASSOCIATED HOLIDAYS: YULE; SAMHAIN; WAKE SERVICES
AND OTHER FEASTS OF THE DEAD

Pratie Oaten

Pratie oaten are very good as a breakfast side dish with bacon, eggs, and sausage.

   2   **cups warm mashed potatoes**
   1   **cup uncooked oatmeal**
       Salt to taste
  ½ **cup melted butter or lard**

Work enough of the oatmeal into the mashed potatoes to form a soft dough. Add salt to taste and enough melted butter or bacon drippings to bind it together. Scatter oatmeal on board and roll out dough. Cut into triangular wedges and cook on both sides on a hot greased griddle in the oven, or fry in bacon fat on the stove. Serve hot or cold.

ASSOCIATED HOLIDAYS:
LUGHNASADH,
SAMHAIN, MABON

SERVES 4

Apple Fritters

The three most nourishing foods: beef marrow, the meat of a chicken, and Guinness Stout (Irish saying).

4 large tart apples, peeled, cored and sliced into ¼-inch rings
1 tablespoon apple brandy
2 teaspoons lemon juice

For batter:

2 eggs
2 tablespoons sugar
1 tablespoon grated lemon zest
½ cup apple brandy or stout
½ cup buttermilk
1 tablespoon butter, melted
1 cup flour
½ teaspoon baking soda
½ teaspoon salt
Butter for frying
Powdered sugar for sprinkling

Toss the apples with apple brandy and lemon juice. Set aside for 30 minutes. For batter, combine eggs, sugar, and lemon zest. Add brandy, buttermilk, and melted butter; beat after each addition. Sift together flour, baking soda, and salt. Add to batter mixture. Heat butter in frying pan. Dip the apple slices in the batter and fry them on both sides until they are golden brown. Drain them on paper towels and serve sprinkled with powdered sugar.

ASSOCIATED HOLIDAYS: LUGHNASADH, SAMHAIN, MABON,
YULE, ESBAT CELEBRATIONS

SERVES 4

Carrot Fritters

Carrots are commonly said to improve the eyesight and enable some to see in the dark. Modern herbalists recommend carrots for nightblindness and cataracts. The seeds of carrots, if eaten, will help in conceiving a child.

¼	cup lukewarm water
1	package dry yeast
⅔	cup lukewarm ale
1	cup flour
2	eggs, beaten
¼	teaspoon salt, or to taste
3	carrots, sliced
	Fat for frying
4	tablespoons ground almonds
2	tablespoons orange water
	Pinch saffron

Dissolve the yeast in the water and let it rest for a few minutes. Add the ale, flour, eggs, and salt; blend well. Let batter rise in a warm spot for about an hour. Parboil carrots for about 5 minutes; drain and reserve cooking water. Stir the carrot slices into the batter to coat each piece. Fry in deep fat, turning them over so they are brown on all sides. Drain on paper towel. Beat the orange water with the ground almonds until a sauce consistency is reached. Add a pinch of saffron for a more pleasing color and serve alongside the fritters.

ASSOCIATED HOLIDAYS: MIDSUMMER, LUGHNASADH, MABON, ESBAT CELEBRATIONS, SUN FESTIVALS

SERVES 2

Matrimonial Divination

When you go to bed, place under your pillow a prayer book, open at the part of the matrimonial service. Place on the book a key, a ring, a flower, a sprig of willow, a small heartcake, a crust of bread, and the following cards: the ten of clubs, nine of hearts, ace of spades, and the ace of diamonds. Wrap all these in a thin handkerchief of gauze and muslin and, on getting into bed, cross your hands and say:

> Luna, every woman's friend,
>
> To me thy goodness condescend;
>
> Let me this night in visions see
>
> Emblems of my destiny.

If you dream of storms, trouble will betide you; if the storm ends in a fine calm, so will your fate; if of a ring, or the ace of diamonds, marriage; bread, an industrious life; cake, a prosperous life; flowers, joy; willow, treachery in love or friendship; spades, death or a transition; diamonds, money; clubs, a foreign land; hearts, many children; keys, that you will rise to great trust and power, and never know want; birds, that you will have only one child; and geese, that you will marry more than once.

Elder Flower Fritters

Elder is a plant of many uses, and was once called "the medicine chest of the people." An infusion of the flowers can be used to treat colds, and elder flower water is good for both the complexion and eyes. The flowers and leaves are also used in ointments to treat burns, bruises, and sprains. According to seventeenth-century herbalist William Coles, "People gathered the leaves of the elder upon the last day of April (May Eve), which to disappoint the charms of witches they had affixed to their doors and windows." An elder tree should always be planted near your herb garden, for all herbs are said to be in the protection of the Elder Mother. Her permission should also be asked before elder is picked or cut. One should be careful with elder wood, for it is bad luck to burn it and the smoke draws evil intentions. Be sure to stand under an elder tree at midnight on Midsummer Eve, and then you will see the King of Faeries and all his attendants pass by.

Christian folklore states that both the cross of Christ and the hanging tree of Judas were made of elder wood.

"Gather your bunches of elder flowers just as they are beginning to open, for that is the time of their perfection. They have just then a very fine smell and spirited taste, but afterwards grow decayed and faint" (John Nutt).

2 eggs, beaten
1 teaspoon rosewater (see note)
½ cup honey
¼ cup brandy
1 tablespoon port
1½ cups flour
¼ teaspoon cinnamon
   Pinch of nutmeg
2 cups fresh elder flowers
   Oil or lard for frying
   Orange water, lemon juice, or sweet cream (optional)

Combine eggs, rosewater, honey, brandy, and port in a bowl. Sift together flour, cinnamon, and nutmeg, and stir into mixture. Fold in elder flowers (elder flowers should be picked just as they are beginning to open, for that is when they are at their peak flavor). Drop by tablespoon measurements on a hot greased griddle and fry for 3 to 4 minutes on each side. Serve with a sprinkling of orange water or fresh lemon juice, or dip fritters in fresh sweet cream.

Note: To make rosewater: While it is possible to purchase bottled rosewater, it is more satisfying to make your own. Take the petals from 2 red roses and place them in ¼ inch of water in a frying pan. Warm slowly, but remove from heat before it boils. Strain the liquid and store in the refrigerator until needed.

ASSOCIATED HOLIDAYS: OSTARA, BELTAINE, MIDSUMMER, ESBAT CELEBRATIONS

SERVES 3 TO 4

When the elder is white, brew and bake a peck,

when the elder is black, brew and bake a sack.

WELSH SAYING

Beestings Pancakes

I once attended a wedding in Ireland, and later stayed on a farm belonging to the groom's family. Every morning I would get up to milk the cows with Liam, one of seven brothers. Or rather, he would milk the cows and I would watch from a safe distance. I was lucky enough while there to witness (again, from a safe distance!) the birth of one of the calves. I was also introduced to beestings. Colostrum, as it is also called, is the first milk, rich in protein and other nutrients, that a cow produces for several days after the birth of a calf. In some Celtic regions, this milk was highly valued, and it was made into cheese curds and pancakes. It is speculated that these foods were originally used as offerings to the Goddess, but nowadays are a treat to share with family and friends.

Recent medical studies support the positive health benefits of colostrum. As a result, many small businesses are springing up to serve the growing market for this product. If you cannot find it locally, check the Internet. This recipe also works using whole milk.

    5   cups flour
    1   teaspoon baking soda
        Large pinch of salt, or to taste
    1   egg yolk
 2–3   teaspoons sugar
 4–5   cups beestings
        Butter or lard for frying

Mix the flour, baking soda, salt, egg yolk, and sugar in a large bowl. Beat in enough of the beestings to create a batter of the desired thickness. Drop tablespoons of the batter on a hot greased griddle and cook for 4 to 6 minutes on each side. Serve with rich butter, cream, or syrup.

ASSOCIATED HOLIDAYS: BELTAINE, MIDSUMMER, OR WHENEVER YOUR COW CALVES

SERVES 4

These things I warmly wish for you:

Someone to love

some work to do,

a bit o' sun

a bit o' cheer

And a guardian spirit

always near.

CELTIC BLESSING

Welsh Shrovetide Pancakes

Welsh pancakes are a little different from their North American counterparts. They are very thin and are served either rolled up with lemon and sugar sprinkled on top, or flat and piled on top of each other in a method known as a "quire of paper." Pancakes are traditional fare for Shrove Tuesday, a custom that dates back to the Middle Ages when every household had to use up all its eggs and milk before the beginning of Lent. It is customary to present the first pancake to the greatest trollop or lie-a-bed in the party, which commonly falls to the dog's share since no one will own to their due.

2	cups flour
	Salt to taste
2	teaspoons sugar
3	eggs
1	cup milk
1	cup water
	Grated rind and juice of 1 lemon
3	teaspoons melted butter
	Oil for frying
	Powdered sugar, hot treacle or syrup, chocolate spread, jam, or peanut butter for topping

Sift together the flour, salt and sugar. Beat the eggs with a wire whisk and add them slowly to the flour mixture. Add the milk and water and beat until the batter is covered with bubbles. You may also use a blender to combine the ingredients. Add the lemon rind and let the batter stand in a cool place for at least 1 hour. Stir the melted butter into the pancake batter. Heat a little of the oil or lard in a frying pan. When it is very hot, begin to cook the pancakes, using a small amount of batter for each pancake so that it is very thin. Only flip the pancake once. The process tends to be a bit smokey, so be sure to have a well-ventilated cooking space. As soon as a pancake is cooked and you have removed it from the pan, sprinkle it with lemon juice and sugar and serve. If your home is anything like my own, a crowd of people will be standing around the stove, plates in hand, ready to take the pancakes as they come off the griddle!

Variation: For a spicy treat, add brandy, ginger, cinnamon, and nutmeg.

ASSOCIATED HOLIDAYS: SPRING FESTIVALS, SHROVE TUESDAY

SERVES 2

Shrovetide Mumming and Other Customs

Shrove Tuesday comes from the custom of people applying to the priest to "shrive" them, or hear their confessions, before entering the great fast of Lent the following day. After the people have made their confession, they are permitted to indulge in festive amusements, though restricted from partaking of any food beyond the usual substitutions for meat. Mardi Gras ("Fat Tuesday") and Carnival ("Farewell to the Flesh") are other names for this festival. Pancakes are a common shrovetide food, made with the remainder of the milk, butter, and eggs that must be used up before Lent.

In some villages, boys would go around in small parties visiting the houses, headed by a leader who knocks at the door and says:

> Pit a pat, the pan is hot,
>
> we are come a-shroving
>
> for a piece of pancake,
>
> or a piece of bacon,
>
> or a little truckle cheese
>
> of your own making.
>
> Open the door and let us in,
>
> for we are come a-pancaking!
>
> Pit a pat, the pan is hot,
>
> we are come a-shroving;
>
> even with a bit of bread and cheese
>
> we'll be better off than with nothing.
>
> The pan is hot, the pan is cold,
>
> the fat in the pan is nine days old!
>
> Lard's scarce, and flour's dear,
>
> That's what makes us come shroving here!
>
> Eggs in the trencher,
>
> Bacon in the pan,
>
> ale in the cellar
>
> and I can carry the can.

As black as a rook,

As speckled as a pie,

I cannot sing no longer,

My throat is too dry!

Shrove Tuesday is also the official opening day for many of the traditional Celtic sports, such as Gaelic football, rugby, or hurling. While I've witnessed some particularly rough contests in Ireland and Wales, the Cornish, I'm told, have a unique and particularly boisterous game.

In the village of St. Columb, a ball about the size of a cricket ball and covered in silver is tossed up in the market square. The two teams, the Townies and the Countrymen, can score in either of two ways: the Town goal is a stone trough a mile southwest of the square. The Country goal is a trough a mile to the north. If either of these goals cannot be reached, a goal can be scored by taking the ball out of the parish! It is a violent contest, only played by adult men, and reminds one of the various feats of strength and skill Celtic warriors once participated in. Whoever can catch the silver ball will run, struggle, and fight to keep a hold of it. The winner—that is, the one who can score a single point—carries the ball back to town in triumph, where it is carried from pub to pub with the following song:

For we roll, we roll, the country (or town) ball along,

And we roll, we roll the country ball along,

And we roll, we roll, the country ball along,

And we all come marching home.

The ball, which is inscribed with the words *guare wheag yn guare teag* (fair play is good play), is dipped in jugs of beer, and everyone drinks to the toasts of "silver beer!" and dines on shrovetide pancakes.

A similar ball game is played in Jedburgh, Scotland. According to local legend, the game used to be played with the severed heads of English invaders!

◆

Apple Tansy Pancakes

In our house, the first pancake made is given to "the pancake gods," and left outside to share with the earth's creatures. This ensures that all the pancakes to follow will turn out perfect.

1¾	cups flour
	Salt to taste
1	teaspoon sugar
2	eggs
1	egg yolk
1	cup cream
1	cup milk
2	tablespoons tansy tea (see note)
1	small apple, pealed and grated
1	tablespoon melted butter
	Oil for frying
	Cream for dipping
	Powdered sugar for sprinkling

Sift together the flour, salt, and sugar. Beat the eggs and egg yolk with a wire whisk and add them slowly to the flour mixture. Add the cream and milk; beat until the batter is covered with bubbles. You may also use a blender to combine the ingredients. Add the tansy tea and grated apple and let the batter stand in a cool place for at least one hour. Stir the melted butter into the pancake batter. Heat a little of the oil or lard in a frying pan. When it is very hot, begin to cook the pancakes, using a small amount of batter for each pancake so that it is very thin. Only flip the pancake once. The process tends to be a bit smokey, so be sure to have a well-ventilated cooking space. As soon as a pancake is cooked and you have removed it from the pan, sprinkle it with sugar and serve with cream.

Note: For tansy tea, place dry bunches of tansy (both leaves and flowers) in a pint of boiling water. Let set until cool, strain and bottle. Keep refrigerated a few days until used.

ASSOCIATED HOLIDAYS: SPRING FESTIVALS

SERVES 2

A Tale of Harvest Time

One brilliant spring morning, a farmer was sowing barley seed in the rich limestone soils of Trevalen Downs, in south Wales. As he cast his seed to right and left he noticed a fair young woman, dressed as a milkmaid, watching him.

"What are you doing?" asked the maiden as she made her way toward him, and behind each of her footsteps sprang tiny white flowers and shamrocks.

"Sowing barley," replied the farmer.

"Ah," said the strange woman, smiling sadly. "But you must know that this seed which you are sowing will decay in the ground."

"Yes, it will," nodded the farmer. "But it will burst into life again, and grow, and at harvest time I will gather it."

The mysterious woman looked the farmer in the eye and challenged him. "Do you believe," she asked, "that that which is dead can come to life?"

"Of course I do," said the farmer.

"Then go home," said the stranger quietly, "and get your sickle and cut your corn. For I am life reborn."

The farmer thought this very strange, but nonetheless he obeyed the instruction and set off for home in order to fetch his sickle. But as he hurried away the beautiful maiden called to him, "If any should come to this place seeking after me, and should ask if I have passed this way, you shall say to them that you have indeed seen me, but in sowing time."

Later, when the farmer came back to his barley field, the young maiden was gone. But, to his amazement, the barley field was ripe for harvesting—on the very same day it had been sown.

The farmer set to work with his sickle, and suddenly noticed an approaching band of men. They were a rough and desperate-looking lot, each with his head shaved in the classic tonsure worn by the monks. They accosted him rudely, and their leader asked, "Have you seen a young milkmaid pass this way? You cannot miss her, for her hair is of darkest ebony, her lips like fresh strawberries, and her skin like new cream."

"I have seen such a maiden, if memory serves correctly. It was when I was sowing my field." The farmer had answered truthfully, and the men, looking at the ripe barley growing all around them, gave up the chase in despair. They turned and rode back the way they had come. The farmer knew, then, that he had been visited by the Goddess, and when he had finished harvesting his field, he made an offering to her of the last sheaves of his grain.

Hot Cross Buns

Although they are rarely homemade anymore, it is still the custom in Celtic countries to eat these round cinnamon and fruit buns on Good Friday. Each bun is decorated with a cross on top, and while it is said to represent the crucifix of Christ, its arms are of equal length. This combination of cross and round bun is reminiscent of the Celtic Cross, itself a representation of the union of male and female energies, and not at all a Latin Cross.

Many Scottish housewives make an equilateral cross on dough when it is set to rise. Several experienced bakers I know say that this is to prevent the bread from falling, but I have no doubt it was originally made to ask the Goddess' blessing.

1½ plus 2–3 cups flour
  2 packages dry yeast
  1 teaspoon cinnamon
¾ cup milk
½ cup vegetable oil
⅓ cup sugar
  1 teaspoon salt
  3 eggs
⅔ cup currants
  1 egg white, slightly beaten
1½ cups powdered sugar
¼ teaspoon vanilla
     Dash salt

In a large mixing bowl, combine 1½ cups flour with the yeast and cinnamon. Heat milk, vegetable oil, sugar, and salt in a saucepan until warm; stir constantly. Remove from heat and beat for 3 minutes at high speed with an electric mixer. Add all at once to the flour mixture along with the eggs. Beat at low speed with an electric mixer for 1 minute, scraping sides of bowl constantly. Beat 3 more minutes at high speed. Stir in currants and as much of the remaining flour as possible. Turn dough out onto a lightly floured surface and knead in enough of the remaining flour to make a moderately soft dough that is smooth and elastic. Shape into a ball. Place in a lightly greased bowl, turning once to coat surface. Cover and place in a warm spot. Let rise until double, about 1½ hours. Punch dough down and turn out onto lightly floured surface. Cover and let rest for 10 minutes. Divide dough into 18 pieces and form each into a smooth ball. Place on a greased baking sheet 1½ inches apart. Cover; let rise until nearly double (30 to 45 minutes). With a sharp knife, cut a cross in each; brush tops of each bun with some of the slightly beaten egg white (reserve remaining white). Bake at 375 degrees for 12 to 15 minutes or until golden. Cool slightly. Meanwhile, combine powdered sugar, vanilla, dash of salt and the reserved egg white. Add more milk if necessary to give it piping consistency. Pipe crosses on top of buns with a pastry decorator.

ASSOCIATED HOLIDAYS: OSTARA, SPRING FESTIVALS, GOOD FRIDAY

MAKES 18

The Widow's Son

Once a year, on Good Friday, a sailor is invited to the Widow's Son pub in London where he is to add a fresh hot cross bun to a collection that hangs in a net from the ceiling. This is done in memory of a son who never returned from the sea. Afterwards the sailor is given free beer, and hot cross buns are passed out to all customers.

Long ago, a woman who owned a beer hall on the spot of the present pub had a son who promised he would return from the sea in time for Easter. She baked hot cross buns for him, a particular favorite of his, but he never made it home. She set one aside and throughout all the next year she kept it. When it was again Good Friday she set it in a basket and baked another batch. Until she died, she continued to set one bun aside for her long lost son, refusing to give up hope. Afterwards the tradition was kept up by the pub's new owners. Nowadays, it is actually written into the lease that the tradition be upheld. As if to substantiate the belief that the buns will not grow moldy, they only appear to shrivel up and turn black, although many of them are well over 100 years old. So important is it to maintain the tradition that, during World War II, the buns were taken to a place of safety to escape the Blitz. Today there are over 200 buns.

◆

The Origin of Hot Cross Buns

The hot cross buns served on "God's Friday" may actually be descendants of the spicy cakes offered to the Saxon Goddess Eostre, which were decorated with horns that formed a cross shape and represented the four quarters of the lunar cycle. Although little is known of Eostre, it seems that she was worshipped, in various forms, by the Greeks, Romans, Germans, Franks, and Anglo-Saxons, as well as the Celts.

Eostre long remained associated with the lunar cycle, as well as the woodlands and wild places, and her priestesses were called *wudu-maer*, Wood Mothers. The Venerable Bede tells us that the entire month of April was once called Eosturmonath. It was customary to offer these wood mothers gifts of bread, dumplings, and buns. Eostre gave her name to Easter, which in the Christian faith commemorates the resurrection of Jesus—a moveable feast determined by the patterns of the Moon, falling on the first Sunday following the first Full Moon after the Spring Equinox. (If the first Full Moon falls on a Sunday, Easter Day is held on the Sunday following.) Churches throughout Christendom are decorated with flowers for the festival, again harkening to the fact that Easter was once a Pagan spring festival.

Some people will still admit to the belief that the buns baked on Good Friday will never get moldy, and can be used in various charms to combat illness. It used to be the custom that at least one was kept from each year's baking for medicinal use. It was hung in the kitchen and allowed to dry out thoroughly, and then powdered and mixed in a glass of water, milk, or ale to be given to an ill person. Unfortunately, the hot cross buns people purchase at bakeries today are usually baked the day before, and this powerful magic is lost.

Hot Cross Buns!

Hot Cross Buns!

One a penny, two a penny,

Hot Cross Buns!

If you have no daughters,

Give them to your sons!

One a penny, two a penny,

Hot Cross Buns!

British Folksong

Marigold Buns

Marigolds are known as the Sun's Flowers or Summer's Bride because they open at dawn and follow the sun's course across the sky, spreading their petals to receive the light and closing again at sunset. They are therefore appropriate to add to recipes served at sun festivals. Marigolds are also symbols of constancy and enduring love, and can be used in love potions, wedding garlands, and floral wreaths. Marigold buns, full of sunny orange and yellow fruit, are a welcome addition to a Midsummer breakfast.

1	cup plus 1 tablespoon marigold petals
1	cup milk
1	egg
3–5	cups flour
5	tablespoons sugar
1	teaspoon baking powder
¼	teaspoon salt
6	tablespoons butter
½	cup candied orange peel
1	cup sultanas

Place 1 cup petals in a small cloth bag; tie and place in pot along with the milk. Heat over a low flame, careful not to let it boil. Remove petals and discard; beat in egg. In a separate bowl mix flour, sugar, baking powder, salt and 1 tablespoon marigold petals; cut in butter and add the orange peel and sultanas. Add the milk mixture to the flour mixture all at once; beat for 10 minutes. Pour into a well-greased 12-cup muffin tin. Bake 10 to 15 minutes at 375 degrees.

ASSOCIATED HOLIDAYS: MIDSUMMER, LUGHNASADH, SAMHAIN, SUN FESTIVALS

SERVES 12

Good humor comes

from the kitchen.

MANX PROVERB

A Song of Harvest Home, ca. 1580

In harvest time, harvest folke, servants and all,

should make, alltogither, good cheere in the hall,

And fill out the black bol of bleith to their song,

And let them be merie al harvest time long.

Once ended thy harvest, let none be begilde,

Please such as did please thee, man, woman and child.

Thus doing, with always suche helpe as they can,

Thou winnist the praise of the labouring man.

◆

Purgatory Fields

Like Midsummer, Samhain was a time to dance around bonfires and strengthen the sun. Up until the turn of the century bonfires blazed outside of every village. On the following day burning brands were carried to the fields, and sometimes a farmer would toss a bundle of burning straw up into the air. While it was falling, everyone present would pray for their departed relatives and friends. The name "Purgatory Field" often designates the spot where this custom took place. The ashes from the Samhain fires were spread on the fields to both bless and fertilize them. In Pagan and Christian traditions alike, November is a time to reflect on our mortality and remember the dead. In the Christian calendar, the first two days following Halloween honor the saints in heaven (All Saints Day) and the souls in purgatory (All Souls Day).

◆

Boxty

Boxty on the griddle, Boxty in the pan, If you don't eat Boxty, you'll never get a man (Irish saying).

Boxty has probably inspired more rhymes than any other dish. There are several ways of making Boxty, two of which follow:

Boxty in the Pan (Boxty Bread)

1	pound potatoes
2	cups cooked mashed potatoes
4	cups flour
	Salt and pepper to taste
¼	cup butter or bacon fat

Peel the raw potatoes and grate onto a cheese cloth; wring over a bowl, capturing liquid. Place the grated potatoes in a separate bowl and spread with mashed potatoes. When the starch has sunk to the bottom of the potato liquid (about 30 minutes), drain off the water and spread the starch onto the potato mixture. Mix well. Sieve the flour, salt, and pepper over the mixture. Add melted butter or bacon fat. Knead; roll out onto a floured surface and shape into fat cakes. Mark with a cross so that when they cook they will divide into farls (triangles). Bake on a greased baking sheet at 300 degrees for 40 minutes.

ASSOCIATED HOLIDAYS: SAMHAIN, MABON, YULE

SERVES 6

Boxty on the Griddle (Boxty Pancakes)

Use the same ingredients as for Boxty Bread, except add 1 teaspoon baking soda and enough milk to make a batter. Spoon batter onto lightly greased pan or griddle and cook both sides over medium heat. Boxty Pancakes can be served with butter or sprinkled with sugar.

A man who has a loaf

will get a knife to cut it.

IRISH PROVERB

Hallowe'en Barm Brack

Hallowe'en comes from the Celtic celebration of Samhain, known as the "split between the worlds" where time ceases to exist and mortals may get a glimpse of the Otherworld. As Samhain is a time of fortunetelling and divination, various objects may be wrapped up in waxed paper and baked into the barm brack. Traditionally these items include a thimble, representing spinsterhood; a pea, for poverty; a wedding ring; a coin, for wealth; and a stick, representing a walking stick for one who is to travel far. "Barm" comes from the Anglo-Saxon word beorma, *which was a fermented liquor that was used to raise a cake. "Brack" comes from the Irish word* brac, *meaning "speckled." I once attended a feast where the bread was thrown against a wall, and the children then scrambled to collect the trinkets.*

4	cups flour
½	teaspoon cinnamon
¼	teaspoon nutmeg
½	teaspoon salt
2	heaping tablespoons butter
1	package yeast
1	cup sugar, divided
1	cup warm milk, divided
1	egg
1¼	cups golden raisins
1	cup currants
½	cup mixed, candied peel
	Ring, coin, stick, pea, thimble, each individually wrapped in waxed paper

Sift together the flour, spices, and salt; pinch or rub in butter with fingers. Cream the yeast with 1 teaspoon of the sugar and 1 teaspoon warm milk; mixture should froth up. If it doesn't it means the yeast is old. Add the remaining sugar to the flour mixture and blend well. Pour the remaining milk and the egg into the yeast mixture and combine with the flour mixture. Beat well with a wooden spoon. The batter should be stiff, but elastic. Fold in fruit, chopped peel, and wrapped divination pieces. Cover with a cloth and leave in a warm place until the dough doubles in size. Turn out and divide into 2 loaves. Place each loaf in a greased 7-inch cake tin. Cover again and let rise for about 30 minutes. Bake at 400 degrees for 1 hour. Test with a skewer before removing from oven. Glaze with 1 tablespoon of sugar dissolved in 2 teaspoons boiling water and return to oven for 3 minutes. Turn out onto rack to cool. Slice and serve with butter. Barm brack keeps very well, but if it does get a little stale, you may try toasting it.

ASSOCIATED HOLIDAY: SAMHAIN

MAKES 2 LOAVES

Cinnamon Toast

The millstone is a symbol for the universal goddess of grain, harvest, milling, and baking. Many breads were baked with a hole in the middle to represent the stone.

    4   slices whole grain bread
    1   tablespoon cinnamon
    1   tablespoon sugar
    1   tablespoon claret

Toast the bread in the toaster or on a gridiron. Lay them in a baking dish. Combine the cinnamon, sugar, and claret and drizzle over each slice of bread. Warm them in slow oven for several minutes, until hot enough to eat.

Variation: A less elaborate variation would be to butter the bread when it comes out of the toaster and sprinkle the cinnamon and sugar over it.

ASSOCIATED HOLIDAYS: HARVEST FEASTS, BREAKFASTS ON THE RUN

SERVES 2

Onion Bread

This recipe comes from Galicia, a remote region in the northwest corner of Spain. The Galicians speak a language that is their own, closer to Portuguese than Spanish, and their culture, music, and food traditions have more in common with Brittany, Ireland, Wales, and Scotland than they do Castille or Andalusia. Galicia is considered the "world's undiscovered Celtic Country," and a book of Celtic recipes would be incomplete without adding at least one Galician recipe.

Lovage was brought to the Celtic lands by advancing Romans. The leaves of the lovage plant were placed in shoes to revive a tired traveler, and at inns the plant was served in a cordial. If pepper was unavailable, ground roots and seeds of the lovage plant could spice meats and soups. You may still make an herbal tonic that will settle an upset stomach by steeping lovage seeds in brandy sweetened with sugar.

1	package dry yeast
1	teaspoon sugar
1¼	cups warm (not hot!) water
2	teaspoons salt
2½	cups wheat flour
2½	cups flour
1	tablespoon brandy
1	tablespoon vegetable oil
1	onion, peeled and grated
1	tablespoon lovage seeds

Mix the yeast, sugar, and warm water together. Set aside in a warm spot until the mixture grows frothy. Sift together the flours and salt in a separate bowl. Add the oil, yeast mixture, onion, and brandy, kneading to make a soft dough. Turn dough onto a floured board and gently knead for 10 minutes. The dough should be smooth and elastic. Return the dough to the bowl, cover with a damp cloth, and leave to rise for 1½ hours or until doubled in size.

Punch down dough, turn onto the floured surface, and knead for five minutes. Form dough into a loaf shape and place in a well-greased 9 by 5 by 2½-inch loaf pan, turning once to coat all sides. Sprinkle with lovage seeds and let rise for 15 minutes while you preheat oven to 450 degrees.

Bake for 10 minutes, reduce heat to 400 degrees and bake for an additional 20 minutes or until golden. Turn out onto wire racks to cool.

ASSOCIATED HOLIDAYS: SAMHAIN, MABON, WINTER ESBAT CELEBRATIONS

MAKES 1 LOAF

Evaline Carney Shea's Soda Bread Recipe

A friend of mine, Linda Arnold, makes this bread each St. Patrick's Day for her family, just as her grandmother used to. The way to make a perfect loaf, she says, is to keep from over-kneading the dough and to wrap each loaf in a damp cloth as it cools.

- 6 cups flour
- 1½ teaspoons baking soda
- 3 teaspoons salt
- 2½ cups buttermilk
- 1½ cups regular or golden raisins

Preheat oven to 375 degrees. In a large bowl, combine the flour, baking soda, and salt. Slowly stir in half of the buttermilk. Add the raisins and stir in the rest of the buttermilk. Gather dough in a ball and turn onto a floured surface; knead for 2 minutes. Divide the dough into two loaves and quickly shape each loaf into a round. Place loaves on a greased baking sheet and cut a cross on the top of each loaf about 1 inch deep. Bake for 45 to 50 minutes until golden brown. Wrap each loaf in a damp cloth (a cheesecloth or tea towel will do) and put on a rack to cool for at least six hours. It's then ready to slice and eat.

ASSOCIATED HOLIDAYS: NAME DAYS/BIRTHDAYS, ESBAT CELEBRATIONS, ST. PATRICK'S DAY

MAKES 2 LOAVES

If you go into the forest for a day,

take bread for a week.

IRISH PROVERB

Rhubarb Bread

Rhubarb has been cultivated for at least 5,000 years. It is one of those rare food plants that is also extremely poisonous. The leaves—whether raw or cooked—are deadly. The stems, however, are safe for use and are quite delicious.

A Cornish belief states that a piece of rhubarb worn as a necklace will prevent stomach cramps.

2½　cups plus 2 tablespoons flour
1½　cups dark brown sugar
1　teaspoon baking soda
½　teaspoon salt, or to taste
1　egg, beaten
1　cup buttermilk
½　cup vegetable oil
1　teaspoon vanilla
1　cup chopped fresh rhubarb
　　Butter, cinnamon, and sugar for topping

Combine 2½ cups flour, brown sugar, baking soda, and salt in a large mixing bowl. In a separate bowl beat together egg, buttermilk, vegetable oil, and vanilla; add to dry ingredients and mix well. Fold the rhubarb pieces and remaining flour into the batter and pour into four greased 7 by 3 by 2-inch loaf pans. Dot with butter and sprinkle with sugar and cinnamon. Bake at 350 degrees for 45 minutes. Cool in pan for 15 minutes before turning out onto a wire rack.

ASSOCIATED HOLIDAYS: MIDSUMMER, LUGHNASADH, ESBAT CELEBRATIONS

MAKES 4 LOAVES

The Miller's Wife

One day, as a young mother was rocking her baby to sleep, she was surprised, on looking up, to see a strange and beautiful lady standing in the middle of the room. The woman was dressed in a gown of costly green velvet, embroidered round with thread of gold and handsewn pearls. On her head was a crown of pearls and emeralds, and around her neck a strand of the same. As surprised as the young woman was to see such a visitor in her home, she did not forget the rules of hospitality her grandmother had taught her. "Although I'm not sure how you came in without my hearing, sit down by the fire, and warm your bones. It's cold out this day."

"Thank you, no, fair Jennet," the woman said. "But could I trouble you for a bowl of oatmeal if you have some to spare?"

"Oatmeal? Aye, I have that and more, if you need it," replied Jennet. "My husband is the miller, you must know, and I'd be honored to share with you what we have." The woman in green was handed a bowl overflowing with freshly cooked oatmeal. "You have my thanks," she said. "I'll see that your bowl is returned on the morrow." And as silently as she had entered the cottage, the woman left.

The very next day the bowl was returned, and filled to the brim with grain it was. The woman who carried it was a wee sprite of a thing, dressed in the same green as her mistress, but with a screeching, yelping voice. "Braw meal," she squeaked, handing the bowl to Jennet. "It's the top pickle of the sin corn."

And excellent it was, too. All the family sampled the gift, all but one servant boy, who refused to taste even a mouthful. "I'll not eat faerie food," he said. "And if you were wise, Mistress Jennet, you would not either. Such gifts always come at a price." But the stubborn child soon found himself ill, and Jennet and the miller believed it was because he refused to take his share of the meal.

They also firmly believed that their first visitor was the Queen of the Faeries herself, and such a person was of course due great respect. Each evening, before going to bed, the miller's wife would place on the doorstep a bowl of her finest porridge, and each morning would find in its place such delicacies the likes she had never before seen—strange and exotic fruits, honey wine, and sweetmeats aplenty. Her family drank and ate of these fine gifts and thrived. Such is the prosperity of one who befriends the faeries!

Caraway Rye Bread

Caraway was once used to flavor cheese and soup, but nowadays seems to be found only in rye bread. Place the seeds under a child's bed to keep away evil spirits. Place in or around an object to render it invisible to thieves.

3	packages dry yeast
1½	cups warm water
¼	cup molasses
⅓	cup sugar
4	teaspoons salt, or to taste
3	tablespoons caraway seed
2¾	cups rye flour
2	tablespoons shortening
3½–4	cups white flour
1	egg white
2	tablespoons water

Dissolve the yeast in the warm water. Stir in molasses, sugar, salt, and caraway seed. Stir in enough of the rye flour to make a smooth dough. Work in shortening. Using your hands, work in enough of the white flour to make a dough that is easy to handle. Turn onto a floured board and knead until smooth, about 10 minutes. Place dough in a clean, greased bowl, cover and let rise until doubled in bulk. Punch down. Shape dough into two rounds, slightly flattened on top. Place on a large, greased baking sheet with plenty of room to rise. Cover with a damp cloth and let double in bulk. Preheat oven to 375 degrees. Combine egg white and water and brush on the loaves. Bake for 30 to 40 minutes until done.

Associated Holiday: Lughnasadh

Makes 2 loaves

A grain often came whole

from the grinding.

Welsh Proverb

Brown Soda Bread

This is the soda bread version I usually serve. Do not be tempted to knead the bread in the same manner you would yeast bread; too much handling causes the bread to toughen. The process should not take more than a few minutes from the time you add the buttermilk to the time you put it in the oven—any longer and the action of the baking soda is lost. A half-and-half mixture of wholemeal flour and white flour works best.

8 cups wholemeal flour mixed with white flour
   (proportions may vary according to taste)
2 teaspoons salt
2 teaspoons baking soda
3–6 cups buttermilk

Mix all dry ingredients together. Make a well in the center and pour in half the buttermilk. Carefully mix in the dry ingredients, adding enough buttermilk to make a soft dough. Gently and quickly combine the bread. Turn dough out onto a floured surface. Divide into two loaves and quickly shape each loaf into a circle. Place each loaf into a 7-inch greased pie plate, and cut a deep cross on the top with a knife. Bake at 450 degrees for 15 minutes. Reduce heat to 400 and bake for an additional 25 minutes, or until the bread is done. The bread should be lightly browned and sound hollow when tapped on the bottom. Turn out onto a rack when cool.

Variation: For white soda bread the directions are the same, but use white flour only. Spotted Dick uses the same ingredients, but adds sultanas and currants. For Soda Bread with Bacon you may place several slices of bacon in a criss-cross pattern on top of the bread before putting it in the oven.

ASSOCIATED HOLIDAYS: NAME DAYS/BIRTHDAYS,
ESBAT CELEBRATIONS, ST. PATRICK'S DAY

MAKES 2 LOAVES

Scones

The first time I had scones was in college, when I helped my friend Dave make them for our Pipe Band banquet. The ingredients are few, and making scones is about as simple as bread baking gets.

2 cups flour
3 tablespoons butter
   Pinch of salt
½ cup whole milk

Sift flour into a bowl and pinch or rub in the butter with your fingertips. Add the salt and mix in the milk a little at a time. Knead lightly to form a soft dough, adding more liquid if necessary. Roll out ½ inch thick. Cut into scones with a round cutter, but do not twist or they will distort while baking. Or you can cut into 2-inch squares. Place on a greased cookie sheet near the top of a 425 degree oven; bake for 12 to 15 minutes.

Variation: For sweeter version add 2 tablespoons sugar and 1 tablespoon caraway seeds.

ASSOCIATED HOLIDAYS:
EVERYDAY BREAD,
NAME DAY/BIRTHDAY
BREAKFASTS

MAKES 8

Sweet Scones

Split each scone in half and serve with butter, jam, and whipped cream. Sweet scones are commonly taken at tea.

8 cups flour
Pinch of salt, or to taste
⅓ cup sugar
4 teaspoons baking powder
1½ sticks butter
3 eggs
1½ cups milk
Glaze:
1 egg, beaten with a pinch of salt
Sugar for dipping
Butter, jam, whipped cream

In a large bowl, combine flour, salt, sugar and baking powder. Make a well in the center and pinch in the butter. Beat the eggs with the milk and add all at once to the flour mixture. Mix to form a soft dough and turn out onto a floured board. Knead lightly, just until you can shape the dough into a ball. Roll out to about 1 inch thick and cut into rounds. Brush the tops with the egg glaze mixture and dip in sugar. Bake at 475 degrees for 10 minutes, or until golden brown.

ASSOCIATED HOLIDAYS: OSTARA, NAME DAY/BIRTHDAY
BREAKFASTS, ESBAT DINNERS

Many mouths make

an empty dish.

GALICIAN PROVERB

Treacle Bread

Bread baked on Yule contains magical powers. If kept in the house, it will protect the home from fire. If put in a stable or granary or thrust in a heap of corn, it will protect your harvest from rats and weevils. Feed it to your livestock to keep them healthy. If such bread is allowed to dry out it can be crumbled into powder and given to a sick person in a cup of hot broth. Like Hot Cross Buns, the bread will only have these wonderful abilities if baked on the holiday itself.

I received this recipe from Maura O'Byrne of Co. Carlow. During my stay in her home, she took me to a castle south of Dublin. While it seemed like your average Irish castle, with its sprawling gardens, pleasant view, and resident ghosts, the basement housed a temple dedicated to the goddess Isis. The ceiling was Nile blue with suns and stars painted across it, and reminded me of the nobles' tombs I saw in the Valley of the Kings in Egypt. What a delightful surprise!

1½	cups flour
1	teaspoon baking soda
½	teaspoon cream of tartar
½	teaspoon salt
3	tablespoons butter
1	tablespoon sugar
1	egg, beaten
¾	cup milk or buttermilk
1	tablespoon treacle or molasses, heated until it runs

Sift together flour, baking soda, cream of tartar, and salt. Pinch in butter with fingers. Add sugar, egg, milk, and treacle. Mix thoroughly and knead for several minutes. Put into greased pie tin and bake at 400 degrees for 40 minutes. It should sound hollow if you tap the bottom. Serve fresh from the oven with sweet butter.

ASSOCIATED HOLIDAYS: IMBOLG, OSTARA, YULE

MAKES 1 LOAF

If you do not want flour,

do not go to the mill.

WELSH PROVERB

◆

Marmalade Loaf

Marmalade is popular throughout the Celtic countries, and even the smallest grocery will carry an assortment of brands to choose from. Favorite flavors include lemon and lime. On my first journey to Ireland, I filled my carry-on luggage with jars of marmalade for family and friends, not realizing it was possible to find them at home.

1	cup strong black tea (not herbal)
2	cups mixed dried fruit
1½	cups brown sugar
1	egg
4	tablespoons orange, lemon, or lime marmalade
4	cups flour
	Salt, nutmeg, and cinnamon to taste

Soak the dried fruit and sugar in tea; cover and let stand overnight. The next morning, stir in the egg and marmalade; mix thoroughly. Sift flour together with spices and add to marmalade mixture. Pour into greased and lined 9 by 5-inch loaf pan. Bake at 350 degrees for 1 to 1¼ hours.

ASSOCIATED HOLIDAYS: IMBOLG, OSTARA, YULE

MAKES 1 LOAF

*Cut your own loaf and
you'll never be hungry.*

SCOTTISH PROVERB

◆

Raspberries and Toast

In the early Christian church, bread was put into the hands of penitents. The clergymen soon discovered that this bread was not always eaten on the spot, but carried home to be used in all sorts of magic charms. Like Hot Cross Buns, the Host was believed to be capable of curing sick children, making fields fertile, increasing the production of milk in cattle, and even putting out or preventing fires.

- 2 cups fresh raspberries
- 3 tablespoons powdered sugar
- 1 cup heavy cream
- ½ cup sherry
- 3 egg yolks, slightly beaten
- 6–8 slices of bread, crusts removed
- 1 stick butter
- 1 teaspoon cinnamon

Sprinkle the raspberries with the powdered sugar. Crush them gently with a fork and set aside. Whip the cream until stiff peaks form. Place the sherry in a bowl and the lightly beaten eggs in another. Dip the bread in the sherry first and then the egg yolks. Melt the butter in a frying pan and when it is hot, fry the bread on both sides until golden brown. Transfer the slices to a warm dish and sprinkle each with a little cinnamon. Cover each slice with raspberries and dollops of whipped cream. Serve immediately.

ASSOCIATED HOLIDAYS: MIDSUMMER, LUGHNASADH, MABON

SERVES 4 TO 6

You'll never plow a field by turning

it over in your mind.

WELSH PROVERB

Johnny-cake

There was an old woman and an old man who lived upon the high road to Inverness with their own little son, Ian. One morning the old woman made an oven-pancake and put it in the old cast iron stove to bake. "You watch the Johnny-cake while your father and I go out to work in the garden," the old woman said to her son.

"All right, Mum," said Ian.

So the old man and the old woman went out and began to hoe radishes, and left the little boy to tend the oven. But he didn't watch it all the time, and all of a sudden he heard a noise. He looked up and the oven door popped open, and out of the oven jumped the Johnny-cake, and went rolling along, end over end, toward the open door of the house. Ian ran to shut the door, but the Johnny-cake was too quick for him and rolled through the door, down the steps, and out into the road long before the little boy could catch him.

Ian ran after him as fast as he could clip it, crying out to his father and mother, who heard the uproar and threw down their long hoes and gave chase, too. But the Johnny-cake outran all three a long way, and was soon out of sight, while they had to sit down, all out of breath, on a bank to rest.

On went Johnny-cake, and by-and-by he came to two well-diggers who looked up from their work and called out, "Where are you going, Johnny-cake?"

"I've outrun an old man, an old woman, and a little boy, and I can outrun you, too!" laughed the Johnny-cake.

"You can, can you now? We'll see about that!" they said, and they threw down their picks and ran after him. But they couldn't catch up with him, and soon they too had to sit down by the roadside to rest.

On ran Johnny-cake, and by-and-by he came to two ditch-diggers. The ditch diggers said, "Where are you going, Johnny-cake?"

"I've outrun an old man, an old woman, and a little boy, and two well-diggers, and I can outrun you, too!"

"You can, can you?" they said. "We'll see about that." And they threw down their spades and ran after him too. But the Johnny-cake soon outstripped them also and, seeing they could never catch him, they gave up the chase and sat down to rest.

On ran Johnny-cake, and by-and-by he came to a bear. The bear said, "Where are you going, Johnny-cake?"

"I've outrun an old man, an old woman, and a little boy, and two well-diggers, and two ditch-diggers, and now I can outrun you!"

"You can, can you?" growled the bear. "We'll see about that!" And he trotted as fast as his legs could carry him after the Johnny-cake, who never stopped to look behind him. Before long the bear was left so far behind that he saw he might as well give up. And so he stretched himself out by the roadside to rest.

On went the Johnny-cake, and by-and-by he came to a fox who lay quietly in a corner by the fence. The fox called out in a sharp voice, but without getting up, "Where are you going, Johnny-cake?"

The Johnny-cake gave a little laugh and said, "I've outrun an old man, an old woman, and a little boy, and two well-diggers, and two ditch-diggers, and a bear, and I can outrun you, too-o-oo!"

The fox said, turning his head from side to side, "I can't quite hear you, Johnny-cake; won't you come a little closer?"

Johnny-cake stopped his race for the first time, and went a little closer, and called out in a very loud voice, "I've outrun an old man, an old woman, and a little boy, and two well-diggers, and two ditch-diggers, and a bear, and I can outrun you, too-o-oo!"

"No," the fox shook his head, "I still can't quite hear you. Won't you come a little closer?"

Johnny-cake came up close, and leaning toward the fox shouted, "I'VE OUTRUN AN OLD MAN, AN OLD WOMAN, AND A LITTLE BOY, AND TWO WELL-DIGGERS, AND TWO DITCH-DIGGERS, AND EVEN A BEAR, AND I CAN OUTRUN YOU, TOO-O-OO!"

"Is that right?" yelped the fox, and he snapped up the Johnny-cake in his sharp teeth in the twinkling of an eye.

◆

Yellow Meal Bread

Yellow is the corn in the glen of Ardkinglas; And yellow is the bracken on the sides of Ben Ima; Yellow is the hair of my loved one, And yellow shall be the dye for her kirtle (Scottish folksong).

1	cup cornmeal (yellow meal)
4	cups flour
1	teaspoon salt, or to taste
2–3	teaspoons sugar, or to taste
1	teaspoon baking soda
1	teaspoon cream of tartar
4	tablespoons butter
2	cups buttermilk

Sieve the dry ingredients. Make a well in the center and pinch in the butter. Pour in the milk all at once and mix to make a soft dough. Turn onto a floured board and knead gently, just long enough to pull it all together. Put on a floured bakesheet, score the surface, and bake at 425 degrees for 30 minutes. Turn off the heat and leave the bread in the oven for another 10 minutes or so. The bread will sound hollow when done.

ASSOCIATED HOLIDAYS: MIDSUMMER, LUGHNASADH, SUN FESTIVALS

MAKES 1 LOAF

Oat Bread

Emigrants sailing to America would often take a few loaves of oat bread with them. It seemed to keep the travelers from becoming ill, and gave them the strength needed for such a long, difficult crossing. The last time I flew to Wales, I brought a loaf of oat bread with me in my backpack as "food for the road." Airplane food is notoriously unsatisfying.

> 2½ cups oatmeal, ground fine
> 2 cups fresh buttermilk
> 2½ cups flour
> ½ teaspoon salt
> 1 teaspoon baking soda

Steep the oatmeal in the buttermilk overnight. The next day, sift the flour, salt, and baking soda together. Stir into the oatmeal mixture. You may add more milk if necessary, but the dough should not be too wet. Put into heavily greased 9 by 5 by 2½-inch loaf pan, turning once to coat all sides. Bake in a preheated 350 degree oven for 1 to 1½ hours. Serve hot with pats of sweet butter.

ASSOCIATED HOLIDAYS: LUGHNASADH, HARVEST FESTIVALS;
ALSO MAKES A GOOD TRAVELING BREAD

Rye bread will do you good,
Barley bread will do you no harm,
Wheat bread will sweeten your blood
Oat bread will strengthen your arm.

IRISH SAYING

Honey Wheat Bread

Give us this day our daily bread, and forgive us our trespasses, as we forgive those who trespass against us (The Lord's Prayer).

The petition for daily bread incorporated into The Lord's Prayer must have originally been a plea to the Goddess, for she has always been the giver of bread, the Grain Mother, and the patroness of bakers, millers, and the hearth. The English title "Lady" comes from the Anglo-Saxon term hlaf-dig, *the giver of bread, while the term "Lord" comes from* hlaf-ward, *guardian of the storehouse.*

2½	cups wheat flour
1	teaspoon baking soda
½	teaspoon salt
1	teaspoon baking powder
¼	teaspoon cinnamon
½	cup light honey
¼	cup vegetable oil
1½	cups buttermilk
½	cup chopped walnuts
1	tablespoon grated orange rind

Mix all ingredients together, beating until well blended. Pour into a greased and floured 9 by 5-inch loaf pan. Let stand 20 minutes. Bake at 375 degrees for 45 to 60 minutes. Turn out onto wire rack and cool.

ASSOCIATED HOLIDAYS: IMBOLG, OSTARA, HARVEST FESTIVALS

MAKES 1 LOAF

Crescent Moon Rolls

Bread was long thought to be the one food essential for survival, and the acts of baking and eating bread often took on a magical significance. This "bread magic" could appear in many forms, from baking bread into all sorts of effigies to speaking charms and exorcisms over bread about to be eaten. Despite the church's objections, women of early Christian Europe baked moon cakes, called croissants (or crescents), for the Queen of Heaven. These rolls, which can also be filled with fruit preserves or a poppyseed filling (see note), are still eaten in honor of the Moon Goddess.

Poppy seeds are used in mixtures to aid sleep, and eaten to promote fertility and wealth. If soaked in wine and drunk, they may render one invisible.

2	packages dry yeast
½	cup lukewarm milk
½	cup plus 2 teaspoons sugar
5	cups flour
1	cup butter, cut in pieces
3	large eggs
¾	cup sour cream
	Juice and zest of 1 lemon
1	tablespoon poppyseeds

Dissolve the yeast in the milk, stir in 2 teaspoons of sugar and allow to foam; set aside. Combine the flour with ½ cup of sugar, and add the butter. Beat in the eggs and add the sour cream, lemon juice, and lemon zest. Add the yeast mixture to the flour mixture. Knead until a soft dough is formed. Shape into a ball and wrap in plastic. Refrigerate overnight. On a lightly floured surface, roll out half the dough into a 12-inch circle; cut into 8 wedges. Spread 1 teaspoon of the filling on each wedge and roll up toward the point. Place each roll on a greased cookie sheet and bend into crescent or moon shapes. Repeat with second ball of dough. Bake at 350 degrees for 20 minutes. Brush with a beaten egg; sprinkle with poppy seeds.

Note: To make a poppyseed filling, pour boiling water over ½ pound of poppy seeds and let stand one hour; drain and repeat. Place the seeds on a towel and squeeze out the excess water. Grind seeds in a food processor. Add ½ cup sugar, 2 tablespoons cream, and 1 egg yolk to seeds. Mix thoroughly.

Associated Holidays: Ostara, Esbat Celebrations

Makes 16 rolls

Dumbcake or Dumb Bread

On St. Mark's Eve (April 24), women along the coast of Wales once prepared a dumbcake with the following traditional ingredients:

>An egg-shell full of salt,
>
>An egg-shell full of malt,
>
>An egg-shell full of barley meal.

When prepared, it's put in a pan for baking. At the proper time, a young man, who is to be the voluntary's husband, comes to turn the cake and retires. Others may witness the ceremony and, if they please, make their cakes in succession. However, all of them must be supperless, and keep a profound silence, whatever may appear; otherwise, they are taught some direful consequence.

Another, in north England, three maidens would make a cake of flour, spring water, salt, and sugar. It was then baked before the fire in a dutch oven, being turned nine times, or three times to each maiden. When thoroughly baked, it was divided into three parts. Each one then took her share and, dividing it into nine slips, passed each one three times through a wedding ring, which had been previously borrowed from a woman who had been married at least seven years. Afterwards, each one ate her nine slips as she undressed herself before retiring to rest, at the same time repeating the following rhyme:

>O good St. Bridgit, be kind tonight,
>
>And bring to me my heart's delight;
>
>Let me my future husband view,
>
>And be my visions chaste and true.

All three must get into a bed with the ring suspended by a string to the bed's headboard, and they will be sure to dream of their future husbands.

◆

Moilean Moire (Mary's Bannock)

The day the Virgin Mary entered heaven is traditionally celebrated on August 15, and is known as the Feast of the Assumption. In Scotland, a special harvest loaf was baked on this day.

To make the flour, one would pick new corn, dry it in the sun, husk it by hand, and grind it into flour. The dough was to be kneaded on a sheepskin, and baked in a fire made of rowan wood (rowan was sacred to the goddess Bridgit, and it was thought to have the power to break evil spells). Each member of the family was to eat a piece of the Moilean Moire while walking sunwise round the fire. The ashes from the fire were placed in a pot and the eldest female member of the family would walk deosil round the fields and pastures to bless both crops and animals.

ASSOCIATED HOLIDAYS: LUGHNASADH, SAMHAIN,
MABON, HARVEST FESTIVALS

I cut me a handful of the new corn,

I dried it in the sun,

I rubbed it sharply from the husk

With my own palms.

I ground it in a quern,

I baked it on a fan of sheepskin,

I toasted it on a fire of rowan

And I shared it round my people.

SCOTTISH FOLKSONG

An Account of the Cailleach

In Scotland, in those places where the crofters' fields are generally of a similar size and near each other, there is a great striving to finish the harvest in time and not to be the last to have the corn cut. It was supposed that he who finished last had to support an invisible hag all the winter long. It was the custom to bind up a handful of straw, the last sheaf of corn cut on the field, and to make it up into the likeness of a woman with docken and ragweed stalks, and tied with threads of various colors. This was called in Argyll, Perthshire, Uist, and other Scottish communities a *cailleach*, or old woman. When a man finished cutting his corn he sent the *cailleach* to a man who had not finished. This was considered a grave insult, and was sometimes reciprocated in bloodshed.

Caution had to be used in conveying the sheaf; usually a young man mounted on a horse passed the neighbor's uncut field at full gallop, as if on urgent business, and threw the *cailleach* into the field without stopping.

Such a man went on horseback in this fashion from Bornish to Milton in South Uist. After placing the *cailleach* he started home, when suddenly two men on horseback set out after him, overtook him, and brought him back to Milton. They shaved his beard and hair and made him "a clipping of bird and of fool," and sent him home.

A crofter would sooner see his best cow dead that see the *cailleach* on his harvest rig. On the Isle of Skye the last sheaf of the harvest is called the *gobhar bhacach*, the halting goat, and dire evil and misfortune were predicted for the man on whom it fell; as Alexander Carmichel writes:

> Cattle-loss, death-loss, and mischance
> will befall the luckless one of the *gobhar bhacach*.

◆

Traditional Scottish Spring Blessing

We shall have flesh.
We should have that,
   we should have that.

The cheek of hen
two bits of barley
That were enough
   That were enough.

We shall have mead,
We shall have spruce,
We shall have wine
We shall have feast.
We shall have sweetness
and milk produce.
Honey and milk,
Wholesome ambrosia,
Abundance of that
   Abundance of that.

We shall have harp,
We shall have pedal,
We shall have lute
We shall have horn.
We shall have sweet psaltery
Of the melodious strings
And the regal lyre
Of the songs we shall have
   Of the songs we shall have.

Corn Dollies

Mechanical reapers and binders have replaced the old hand sickles and have made it unnecessary to have a Lord and Lady of the Harvest who would set the pace for the harvesting work. So, too, without the least superstition—or honor—these same machines cut down the last sheaf of grain.

The cutting of the last sheaf of grain was once an important part of the harvest. There was often a reluctance to be the one to cut the last handful, and the men would sometimes take turns throwing their sickles at it. Others thought it held an evil spirit and trampled it beneath their feet. Many treated it with respect because they believed the corn spirit had retreated into it as a refuge when the rest of the crop was cut. The corn spirit would sleep throughout the winter in the sheaf, whether left in the field or brought into the home.

The corn dolly was a traditional harvest figure made of the last sheaf. Although it was dangerous to cut, afterwards the sheaf could be handled safely. The traditions varied somewhat from region to region, but it was often dressed in women's clothes and bedecked with ribbons, then either left in the field or brought into the farmhouse and set in a place of honor at the harvest supper. Some people brought it to the harvest dance, or placed it on flower-decked funeral pyres, or poured water over it in a fertility ritual. Others kept it all year as a guarantee of fruitfulness in the fields and success with the next year's harvest, or hung them on the ends of the house as a protective charm. Sometimes it was stored away until Yule, when it was fed to the livestock to make them thrive. Some of the grain from the sheaf might be mixed with the seed corn or scattered in the springtime fields among the new plants.

Plough Monday, the Monday following the twelfth night after Christmas, was the traditional start of the farming year. Ploughboys would dress in out-landish costumes, usually as women, blacken their faces, and take to the streets with their ploughs. In some regions they also carried the corn dolly made from the previous harvest. They would laughingly threaten to plough up their neighbor's gardens unless they were paid off with money. Shouts of "Hurrah!" were heard if money was given, or "Hunger, Doom, and Starvation!" if it was not. The money was often drunk in the pub that evening. In towns that still uphold the tradition, a wooden plough and corn dolly are taken to the church to receive a blessing, with the money gathered going to charity.

Depending on the community, the spirit of the corn might be seen as either young or old, and so the corn dolly has many names, among them the Corn Maiden, the Bride, the Kerne Baby, the *Maidhdeanbuain* (shorn maiden), the Mare, the Corn Mother, Harvest Queen, Grandmother of the Corn, Grain Mother, Baba, Hag, *Wrach* (Welsh for hag—rather like the sound a crow makes) or Great Mother. In Scotland she was referred to as the Maiden if cut before Samhain, and as the *Cailleach* (old woman) after the turning of the year. But whatever she was called and however she was envisioned, she was a sacred figure, for she represented the Triple Goddess.

◆

I shall throw the handful far from me,

I shall close my two eyes twice,

Should it fall in one bunch

My stacks will be productive and lasting;

No carlin will come in bad times

to ask a palm bannock from us,

What time rough storms come with frowns

Nor stint nor hardship shall be on us.

Scottish consecration of seed

Pumpkin Bread

Walnuts attract lightning, and people have been struck by a bolt out of the blue when carrying walnuts. Brides have long taken that risk, however, for wearing walnuts in your bodice on your wedding day will prevent pregnancy. Each nut will keep the occurrence from happening for one year.

1	large can pumpkin
1	cup melted butter
¾	cup water
4	eggs
2	teaspoons baking soda
3½	cups flour
2¼	cups sugar
1½	teaspoons salt
2	teaspoons cinnamon
½	teaspoon nutmeg
1	cup chopped walnuts
1	cup raisins

Mix together pumpkin, melted butter, water, and eggs. Blend in baking soda, flour, sugar, salt, cinnamon, nutmeg, walnuts, and raisins. Place batter in a greased and floured loaf pan. Bake at 350 degrees for 1 hour or until top is golden brown.

Associated Holidays: Samhain, Mabon

Makes 1 loaf

Milk, Eggs, and Cheese

A quarrel is like buttermilk:

the more you shake it,

the more sour it grows.

IRISH SAYING

This passage, taken from *The Vision of Mac Conglinne*, shows the love early Celts had for milk and dairy products, and gives us a rare look at their eating habits.

A lake of new milk I beheld

In the midst of a fair plain.

I saw a well-appointed house

Thatched with butter.

As I went all around it

To view its arrangement

I saw that puddings fresh-boiled

were its thatch-rods.

Its two soft door-posts of custard,

Its dais of curds and butter,

Beds of glorious lard,

Many shields of thin-pressed cheese.

Under the straps of those shields

Were men of soft sweet smooth cheese,

Men who knew not to wound a Gael,

Spears of old butter had each of them.

A huge cauldron full of meat

(Methought I'd try to tackle it)

Boiled, leafy kale, browny white,

A brimming vessel full of milk.

A bacon house of two-score ribs,

A wattling of tripe—support of clans—

Of every food pleasant to man,

Meseemed the whole was gathered there.

◆

Buttermilk Cheese

The association of the Great Goddess with the primordial serpent has led to an interesting Welsh belief that certain species, known as "milk snakes," can actually suck the milk of women, cows, and other mammals as they sleep. Likewise, the Cornish once believed that if a snake drank spilled breast milk, it would sprout wings and fly.

Cheese and berries have always gone well together, and this recipe makes a good summertime dish, when fresh fruit and new cheese are plentiful.

4½ cups fresh whole milk
3 tablespoons buttermilk
½ teaspoon rennet
⅓ cup heavy cream
2 pounds strawberries, sliced
Sugar to taste and for sprinkling

In a large bowl mix milk, buttermilk, and rennet. Cover loosely with a cheesecloth and let stand in a warm place until solid. Drain off liquid by placing a strainer lined with cheesecloth over another strainer. Pour the contents of the bowl into the cheesecloth and leave to strain; this will take about 12 hours, so it's best to leave it overnight. Turn the cheese solids into another bowl and mix in the cream and sugar. In a serving dish, layer the cheese and strawberries. Sprinkle each layer with sugar. Top with a layer of cheese and decorate with whole berries.

Variations: Instead of strawberries, try using blueberries, raspberries, or blackberries.

ASSOCIATED HOLIDAYS: BELTAINE, MIDSUMMER, IMBOLG

SERVES 4

Stirabout

The cow is one of the most common totemic images of the Great Goddess. To the Celts, the Milky Way was known as Bothar-bó finne, *The Track of the White Cow. It is surmised that people first domesticated cattle so that they might feed themselves and their children on the milk of the Goddess. The White Cow was commonly depicted as hovering over the moon, and is perhaps the same cow "who jumped over the moon" in the popular nursery rhyme. Later stories of faeries— which in truth are stories of the Goddess in disguise—say that they kept herds of white cattle. Anglo-Celtic names for the Milky Way suggest that they saw it not only as a river, but as a pathway to heaven.*

This is a tasty alternative to the glass of milk before bedtime.

2	cups whole milk
1	teaspoon flour
1	teaspoon sugar, or to taste
¼	teaspoon cinnamon or nutmeg
2	tablespoons cold milk

Heat the milk to near boiling. Sift together the flour, sugar, and cinnamon or nutmeg and mix with two tablespoons of cold milk. Stir the flour mixture into the hot milk.

Variation: Try stirring in mashed bilberries or blueberries.

ASSOCIATED HOLIDAYS: IMBOLG, ANYTIME YOU NEED A PICK-ME-UP

SERVES 1

The Milkmaid and the Sailor

Long ago, the women and girls of Cardiff would go to the harbor to sell buttermilk to the sailors who had been out to sea. Oftentimes there would be a dozen or more churns of the chilled milk for sale on the docks, such was the demand for it.

Among the girls selling milk one day was a young lass from Caerphilly, who had traveled the long miles with her churns in the back of her horse cart. Bronwen Dafis, for that was the girl's name, was standing in her cart, singing to the passersby of the quality of her wares. "Fresh buttermilk! Come and try my cream and butter, my milk and cheese! Who will buy my fresh buttermilk?" She had a charming voice and a lovely face and figure, and many was the sailor who stopped to buy her buttermilk.

Below at the pier, a ship from Ireland was tied up while her cargo was being unloaded. One of the sailors heard Bronwen's voice, and came to ask the price of her buttermilk.

"A penny a quart," said she, and glanced down with a smile. "A better deal you will not find."

"You may be right," he laughed. "I'll try some. Give me a whole quart of it, for I've missed the taste of buttermilk at sea and I'm terribly thirsty." He drank deeply of the milk while Bronwen looked on. When he finished, he handed the jar back up to her. As he was standing near the cart just below her, he reached up and wiped his mouth with a corner of her apron. "Thank you." He bowed and turned to go.

Instead of crying out in anger, as was her right, Bronwen merely jumped from her cart and followed the strange sailor down the street. She left her horse and her cart and her churns behind her. The other milkmaids tried to stop her, but it was no use. Wherever the sailor went Bronwen followed, whether it was to the fruitseller's, the butcher's, or the public house.

Word of the incident finally reached Bronwen's brother, who was working on the docks. He went along the street and into the public house where his sister stood quietly behind the sailor at the bar. "Bronwen, come over here at once," he called.

The girl did not answer. She did not even turn her head.

"Bronwen, it's me, Owain. I've come to take you home."

Still the young milkmaid did not answer. Finally her brother went up behind her, took out his knife, and cut the string of the apron.

No sooner did the apron fall to the floor than the girl looked about her with surprise and confusion. "O-Owain," she said. "What are you doing here? What am I doing here?"

Without a word Owain picked up the apron, took it over to the stove, and shoved it through the door. He stood there and watched it until it was burned through and nothing remained but a pile of ashes. Then he turned to deal with the sailor, but the mysterious man was gone. Nor did any see him leave.

May the Lady guard us all from such danger!

An Irish May Day Custom

Description of West Meath, 1682:

On May Eve, every family sets up before their door a green bush, strewed over with yellow flowers, which the meadows yield plentifully. In countries where timber is plentiful, they erect tall slender trees, which stand high, and they continue almost the whole year; so as a stranger would go nigh to imagine that they were all signs of ale-sellers.

A type of milk drink is made of whatever they have, which some call stirabout, or hasty pudding, that is flour and milk boiled thick; and this is holden as an argument of the good wife's good huswifery, that made her corn hold out so well as to have such a dish to begin summer fare with; for if they can hold out so long with bread, they count they can do well enough for what remains of the year till harvest; for then milk becomes plenty, and butter, new cheese and curds and shamrocks, are the food of the meaner sort all this season. Nevertheless, in this mess, on this day, they are so formal that even in the plentifullest and greatest houses, where bread is in abundance all the year long, they will not fail of this dish, nor yet they that for a month before wanted bread.

Egg in a Cup

According to Moira Dunne of Dublin, a good way of preserving eggs for a short period of time requires that you gather them straight from the nest and rub their shells with a thin layer of butter. This will seal in the freshness and keep the albumen soft when the eggs are cooked. Moira's mother used to make eggs in a cup as an after-school snack.

1   **egg, the fresher the better**
     White breadcrumbs
     Pat of butter
     Salt and pepper to taste

Bring a small pot of water to a rapid boil and carefully slip the egg in so that the shell does not crack. Return the water to a boil and cook the egg for 4 to 6 minutes, according to taste (a 4-minute egg will be rather soft, while a 6-minute egg will produce a soft yolk and solid white). In the meantime, warm a teacup. Remove the top of the egg and spoon the matter into the dry teacup. Scramble with a spoon and add the breadcrumbs, butter, salt and pepper.

ASSOCIATED HOLIDAYS: OSTARA, BELTAINE, NAME DAY/
BIRTHDAY BREAKFASTS

SERVES 1

May the blessing of light be on you,

Light without and light within.

May the blessed sunlight shine on you

and warm your heart till it glows

like a great peat fire,

so that the stranger may come

and warm himself at it,

and also a friend.

CELTIC BLESSING

Scotch Eggs

Still found in pubs, Scotch eggs make a wonderful snack. My mother used to make them during the school year, and pack them in our lunches. The only way to eat them is with your fingers, so be sure to have lots of napkins close at hand! You can eat them while still hot, but they tend to fall apart. Traditionally they are served either cold or at room temperature.

10	hard-boiled eggs, chilled
	Flour for dusting
2	pounds pork sausage
1½	cups fresh breadcrumbs
2	teaspoons mace or minced parsley
½	teaspoon salt
½	teaspoon pepper
2	eggs, beaten
	Oil for deep frying

Remove the shells from the hard-boiled eggs and dust with flour. Set aside. Roll out the pork sausage on a flat surface. In a shallow bowl, mix the breadcrumbs with the mace, salt, and pepper. Take each hard-boiled egg and dip into the beaten eggs, then wrap it in the sausage meat until it is completely covered. It is easiest to do this with your fingers. The meat should be about ½ inch thick around each egg.

Once the egg is completely covered, roll it in the breadcrumb mixture. When all the eggs have been prepared this way, heat the oil about 4–5 minutes to 350 degrees and deep fry the eggs, one at a time, until golden brown.

ASSOCIATED HOLIDAYS: OSTARA, BELTAINE,
DINNER AT YOUR FAVORITE PUB

SERVES 4

*The cocks crow but
the hens deliver the goods.*

SCOTTISH PROVERB

Berneen of the Flaming Hair

There once was a girl named Berneen Ahearne who was on her way to the market to sell her basket of eggs.

"If the price of eggs be up," she mused, "I'll be earning a handful of coins, I will; yet if the price be down, why, I'll not do too poorly there, either, for I have food for a week."

And with those words she saw a wee man sitting down by the hedge, working away at a tiny leather brogue. Why, she thought, me luck is getting better all the time. If I had a hold of that wee lad, I'd make him tell me where his treasure is—for the like of such a creature knows where gold does be hid. I'll be the richest woman in all the village, and will have servants to sell my eggs.

And so Berneen crept up behind the tiny shoemaker, like a cat would stalk a bird, and with a shout grabbed him around his neck.

Well, the leprechaun let out a howl to be sure, for he was terribly surprised. In all his hundred years he had never been caught so. It was downright humiliating.

"I have you now, my dear own!" crowed Berneen.

"Oh, surely you have, my lady, indeed, yes you do." The leprechaun tried to smile. "The strength of your thumb is destroying my windpipe to be sure."

"Never mind that," said Berneen, giving the little fellow a shake. "Show me your treasure!"

"I'd have you to know," he said, his face turning red, "that the pot of gold I could give you is guarded by a fierce serpent."

"What care have I for the creeping beasts of the world?" said Berneen. "A serpent couldn't scare me at all. Besides," she added, her eyes narrowing dangerously, "you know as well as meself that there are no snakes in Ireland."

"Why, you're a brave girl," said the leprechaun. "A clever and wise and handsome one too, might I add. I've travelled quite far, if truth be told, and I've never seen one to your equal."

"Go on with your prattle," said Berneen, pleased all the same.

"I'm not as young as I used to be," said the leprechaun, "and I couldn't keep up with such a comely lass as yourself. But it's light in the body I am, and I could perch on your basket handle, and you can carry me to the gold, if you don't mind. I'll show you the way."

Berneen paused to consider this but a moment and said, "All right, I'll carry you; but mind now, I'll put you down to walk by my side if I find you are lying."

The leprechaun had not lied, and she didn't feel the burden of carrying him at all, but Berneen was no fool, either, and she kept a tight hold of the little shoemaker's ear.

Yet what did the wee lad do but reach down into the basket and begin to toss out the eggs! She twisted his ear painfully, but the harder she beat him the faster he tossed out the eggs! "Ow! Ow! Why are you beating me, Berneen of the flaming hair? I'd have you know when I spill an egg on the ground a full-grown chicken leaps out!"

"Flattery will get you nowhere," fumed Berneen. "So quit your silver-tongued ways!"

"If you doubt me," cried the leprechaun, "turn around and have a look at the chickens that are flocking behind."

With that Berneen turned, and the leprechaun slipped from her grasp. He made one spring from the basket and leaped over a stone wall, vanishing quickly away.

"That tricky creature had me fooled entirely." Berneen shook her head. "And my beautiful eggs, all destroyed! Still and all," she considered, "I can't see it clear to be mad at him. I am the finest woman he's seen, and that is a good thing to know!"

Woman, if you come to my bright people,
you will have a crown of gold for your head;
honey, wine, and fresh milk to drink
you will have with me there, beautiful one.

THE WOOING OF ÉTAÍN

Tossed Eggs with Shallots

Where you see shells you may guess eggs (Irish proverb).

3	shallots, chopped
¼	cup chopped bell pepper
2	tablespoons butter
4	eggs, beaten
¼	teaspoon fresh marjoram
¼	teaspoon fresh dill weed
¼	teaspoon fresh thyme, minced
	Pinch of cayenne pepper
	Salt and black pepper to taste
⅓	cup cheddar cheese, shredded

Sauté shallots and bell pepper in butter over medium heat until soft. Combine eggs, marjoram, dill weed, thyme, cayenne pepper, salt, and pepper. Whisk until fluffy. Pour mixture into the pan with onions and pepper. Blend in cheese. Scramble over medium heat, stirring frequently.

Variation: Instead of shallots and bell pepper, try chopped onion and ham.

Associated Holidays: Ostara, Beltaine,
Name Day/Birthday Breakfasts

Serves 2

Bread and Cheese Throwing

In Gloucestershire, following Whit Sunday evensong, basketfuls of bread and cheese are thrown from a wall near the old castle. It is not known how old this custom is, but bits of bread are preserved by locals who think they are good luck, and will use them in much the same manner as hot cross buns in home medicine. Other people bury them in the fields to ensure good crops.

✦

Shirred Eggs

Butter is said to arrive at the moment when the cream begins to clot. The charm to hasten it, said in the Highlands, is: "Churn, butter, dash; Cow's gone to the marsh. My children sit by the garden gate, beggin' for butter to butter their cake. Come butter come."

6   custard cups
     Butter or margarine
6   eggs
     Salt and pepper to taste
2   tablespoons light cream or milk
6   tablespoons shredded mild cheddar cheese (optional)

Butter a custard cup for each egg. Carefully break eggs into the prepared custard cups; sprinkle with salt and pepper. Add 1 teaspoon of the light cream to each egg-filled cup. Set cups in a baking pan; place on oven rack. Pour hot water around the cups in the pan to a depth of 1 inch. Bake at 325 degrees for 20 minutes, or until the eggs are firm.

If desired, top each egg with 1 tablespoon of the cheddar cheese 15 minutes into the baking. Bake an additional 5 to 10 minutes or until the eggs are cooked and the cheese is thoroughly melted.

ASSOCIATED HOLIDAYS: IMBOLG, OSTARA, BELTAINE

SERVES 3

Name Day Breakfast

Such an elaborate breakfast is good for special days, such as name days or birthdays.

¼ cup onion, chopped fine
¼ cup bell pepper
¼ cup butter
2 potatoes, peeled and chopped fine
¼ teaspoon salt, or to taste
1 teaspoon water
5 jumbo eggs
2 tablespoons milk
   Salt and pepper to taste
1 cup cooked ham, diced
2 slices cooked bacon, crumbled

Sauté onion and bell pepper in butter until tender. Add potatoes, salt, and water. Cover and cook over medium heat for about 10 minutes or until potatoes are tender. Beat together eggs, milk, salt, and pepper. Stir in ham and bacon. Pour over potato mixture. Cook, without stirring, until mixture begins to set on the bottom and around the edges. Lift and fold with a spatula so uncooked portion flows underneath. Continue cooking about 5 minutes or until eggs are cooked throughout but still glossy and moist. Serve immediately.

Associated Holidays: Name Days/Birthdays

Serves 4

The thieving pig's ear can hear

the grass growing.

Welsh Proverb

Cooper's Hill Cheese Rolling

The cheese rolling competition in Gloucester is perhaps one of the most spectacular and dangerous of ancient British customs. It takes place in the evening early in springtime, and is open to all and sundry. There is a master of ceremonies, dressed in a white coat and beribboned hat. On the count of three, the first cheese is rolled down the hill; on the count of four the runners throw themselves after it. The winner is the first one who seizes the cheese.

At the top of the hill is a permanent maypole marking the starting place, and the hill is thickly wooded except for where the cheese is rolled. A popular theory of its origin suggests that the cheese represents the sun. Winter was often considered to be a dangerous enemy, particularly in the far north, threatening food supplies as well as the lives of the very young and very old. By rolling miniature "suns" down the hill, the Celts and Saxons were perhaps imitating the sun's course through the sky, and urging summer along. Similar customs abound throughout continental Europe, where people roll flaming wheels down snowcovered hills at Midwinter.

Garland Dressing

In Oxfordshire, there is a unique remnant of Beltaine. The garland, which stands permanently on the rood screen of the local church, is a large cross decorated with greenery. It is human in form, with a narrow waist and skirt, leafy head and arms, and is often referred to as "The May Lady." On May Day the garland is taken down and dressed with fresh greens of elder, box, and yew. The village children make a procession to the church carrying homemade crosses decorated with flowers. The flowers are left beneath the garland.

At one time, according to the local vicar, there used to be a statue of the Virgin Mary on the screen.

Welsh Rabbit

The Easter Bunny has his origins in the festival of the Goddess Eostre, when it is said that her totem, the Moon Hare, would lay eggs for good children to eat. The Easter Bunny still brings eggs to children, although they are now made of chocolate. The Celts did not see a man's face, but rather the image of a rabbit, when they gazed at the Full Moon.

1½	cups shredded cheddar cheese
¾	cup milk
1	teaspoon dry mustard
1	teaspoon Worcestershire sauce
	Dash cayenne pepper
1	beaten egg
4	slices toasted bread or 4 poached eggs

Combine cheddar cheese, milk, dry mustard, Worcestershire sauce, and cayenne pepper in a medium saucepan. Cook over low heat, stirring constantly, until the cheese melts. Slowly stir about half of the hot cheese mixture into the beaten eggs. Return the cheese and egg mixture to the pan.

Cook and stir over low heat until mixture thickens and begins to bubble. Serve at once over toast or poached eggs. If desired, you may place the slices under the broiler until the cheese is bubbling and brown.

Variation: To make Beer Rabbit, substitute ¾ cup ale or lager for the milk. Top each serving with several slices of crispy bacon.

ASSOCIATED HOLIDAYS: OSTARA, BELTAINE, MIDSUMMER

SERVES 4

An egg today is better than

a roasted ox tomorrow.

WELSH PROVERB

Bugloss Cheese

Bugloss, or borage as it is more commonly known, frequently was used to enhance the flavor of soups and cheese, while its flowers were crystallized and used as decorations. It has a light, green taste, rather like a cucumber.

From The Treasurie of Hidden Secrets and Commodius Conceits, *1586: "The vertue of the conserve of borage is especially good against melancholie, it maketh one merrie."*

If you don't wish to brew borage as a tea or boil it into jam, you may do as people in the last century did, and simply toss a few leaves and flowers into a glass of wine and drink it down.

1 dozen young bugloss (borage) leaves
1 (8-oz.) container cottage or farmer's curd cheese
Pinch of pepper
Fresh borage flowers for garnish

Wash and dry borage leaves, cut fine. Drain cottage or farmer's cheese and place in serving bowls. Add a pinch of pepper if desired, and mix in the chopped leaves. Garnish with fresh borage flowers and serve.

ASSOCIATED HOLIDAYS: BELTAINE, MIDSUMMER, LUGHNASADH

Borage give always courage.

ENGLISH PROVERB

Bell Talk

If you ever travel through the English countryside, you can't help but hear the bells from various churches and castle towers. If you listen carefully, each bell has its own unique voice. The most famous is the St. Clements Church in London, which seems to say, "Oranges and Lemons." It is not unusual for these bells to always be discussing food:

A nut and a kernel
Say the bells of Acton Burnell.
A pudding in the pot
Say the bells of Acton Scott.
Roast beef and mutton,
Say the bells of Church Stretton.
You're too fond of beer,
Say the bells of Ellesmere.
Buttermilk and whey
Say the bells of Hopesay.
Roast goose and gander,
Say the bells of Langor.
White bread and red wine
Say the bells of Leintwardine.
Three golden pickles
Say the bells of St. Michaels.
A boiling pot and stewing pan,
Say the bells of St. Julian.
Pancakes and fritters,
Say the bells of St. Peter's.
Where must we fry them?
Say the bells of Cold Higham.
In yonder land thurrow,
Say the bells of Wellingborough.
You owe me a shilling,
Say the bells of Great Billing.
Ivy, holly, and mistletoe,
Say the bells of Wistanstow.

◆

Floral Cheese Pie

In the English countryside, from times long ago, it has been the custom at Imbolg to take three large cheeses and decorate them with flowers. The cheeses are placed on litters—also decorated with flowers and greenery—and carried through the village. A crowd of people follow behind the cheeses, singing, dancing, and playing instruments. The cheeses are carried to the church, are rolled three times deosil (sunwise) around the church, blessed, and broken up to distribute among all those gathered.

Elders are generally in bloom in late June or early July; their delicate blossoms make a very nice flavoring for this simple cheese pie.

6	cups farmers cheese (cottage cheese may be substituted)
6	egg yolks
1½	cups powdered sugar
1½	cups cream
1	cup candied fruit
½	cup slivered almonds
½	teaspoon grated lemon zest
2	sticks butter
3	teaspoons vanilla
¾	cup fresh elder blossoms
1	small flowerpot

Do not pick your blossoms until you are ready to prepare the pie; otherwise they are apt to wilt. Drain the cheese through cheesecloth and add curds to a large bowl. Beat in eggs one at a time. Add the sugar and blend well. In a large saucepan, heat the cream until near boiling and add the cheese mixture. Cook over low heat, stirring constantly, until thick. Do not let it boil. Add the fruit, almonds, and lemon zest and set aside to cool. Cream together butter and vanilla and stir into cheese mixture. Fold in the elder blossoms. Line the flowerpot with cheesecloth, leaving enough of the cloth to fold over the batter. Fill the pot with the cheese mixture and cover. Refrigerate for several days. The whey will drip out the bottom of the pot, so be sure to place a pan underneath it to catch the liquid. When drained, carefully unmold the pie with a knife. Remove the cheesecloth and smooth the side with a hot knife. Serve.

Variation: Roses, marigolds, or other edible flowers may be used.

Associated Holidays: Imbolg, Beltaine, Midsummer

Makes 1 pie

Carrageen Moss Blancmange

In Scotland, there is a ring of stones said to mark the spot where fair Janet rescued Tam Lin from the Faerie Queen. Offerings of fresh milk are still poured on such sites as tokens of regard to the Queen and her people.

- 1 cup dried carrageen moss
- 3 cups whole milk
- 1 tablespoon sugar
- ½ teaspoon lemon zest

Place the carrageen moss, milk, sugar, and lemon zest in a pan and simmer over medium heat until the carrageen has almost dissolved. Strain and pour into a wetted jelly mold. Set to cool and turn it out when set. Serve with fresh or stewed fruit.

ASSOCIATED HOLIDAYS: BELTAINE, MIDSUMMER, LUGHNASADH

SERVES 4

Egg Cheese

There was once an old British custom of creeping to the cross with apples and eggs, where penitents (including kings) would crawl toward the Easter altar carrying these ancient fertility symbols of the goddess.

- 2 quarts milk
- 4 eggs
- 2 cups buttermilk
- ¼ cup sugar
  Honey
  Fruit

Heat the milk in a double boiler. Combine the eggs, buttermilk, and sugar and add to the milk on the stove. Simmer over low heat for 30 minutes, stirring every once in a while to keep it from sticking. Strain into a bowl and chill for 3 hours or so. Serve with honey and fruit.

ASSOCIATED HOLIDAY: OSTARA

SERVES 6 TO 8

Junkett or Curds and Whey

When it is raining buttermilk, the beggars have no cups (Manx proverb).

5	cups buttermilk or soured milk
2½	cups whole milk
½	teaspoon ground cinnamon
1	teaspoon caraway seeds
1	tablespoon sugar, or to taste

Put the buttermilk in a large mixing bowl. Scald the whole milk in a saucepan by heating to just below the boiling point. Quickly add it to the buttermilk in the bowl; stir thoroughly. Allow this mixture to stand until it is cool; drain through a cheesecloth, reserving whey. Squeeze the curds from time to time while draining.

Mix the cinnamon and caraway seeds into the cheese curds; sweeten with sugar. Turn curds into small dessert dishes. Mix a little sugar with 5 tablespoons of the whey and pour over the curds. Serve.

ASSOCIATED HOLIDAYS: OSTARA, BELTAINE, MIDSUMMER

SERVES 2

The Groaning Cheese

Because it is a milk product, cheese has a long association with the mysteries of birth and lactation. Until the beginning of this century, christening customs of rural Britain included passing the child through a hole in the center of a large cheese, known as the groaning cheese. The groaning cheese was rather large, often a cheddar, and would be distributed to everyone in the house as soon as the new life entered the world. It was considered good luck, and many people would keep their share and take it home to plant in the fields.

The method of the cutting varied from location to location, but was sometimes done by the doctor, if one were present, and more often by the husband. The cut would begin in the middle, and gradually form a ring that the baby could be passed through. What is not eaten on the day of birth would be given to visitors up until the child's baptism. It was unlucky to refuse to take your share. It is interesting to note that in parts of England a woman's time of labor is still called "a groaning."

◆

Bainne Clabair (Bonnyclabber or Thick Milk)

In the twelfth-century *Vision of MacConglinne*, there are references to "a delectable drink of very thick milk, of milk not too thick, of milk of long thickness, of yellow bubbling milk the swallowing of which needed chewing." References to such types of milk abound in early Celtic writings, and continued until very recently. The British called these drinks "clabber," and there are many ways of souring milk, called clabbering. The juice of plants, such as butterwort, was sometimes used. Before the mechanical separation of milk and cream, the milk was usually set in large containers near the fire. The cream rose to the top and was skimmed off. The residue was soured into a sort of jelly and taken as a delicious drink.

Wroth Silver and Rum Milk

The payment of wroth silver is one of the oldest continuing customs of Britain. It takes place at dawn in mid-November, on St. Martin's Day, when representatives of the twenty-five parishes of the Hundred of Knightlow are summoned to the lord of the manor to pay wroth silver before sunrise. As each parish is named, the representative steps forward and places money in a hollow stone, repeating the words "wroth silver." The parish representatives all retire to the Dun Cow Inn for a breakfast including the traditional drink of rum and hot milk.

Wroth silver is money paid to the lord in lieu of castleward, a feudal obligation for protection, and to preserve the right of people to drive cattle across the Duke of Buccleuch's land. Long ago, the roads were in wretched shape and dangerous to travel on, so this privilege was an important one. It is believed the custom has survived from the time of the Celts. Defaulters of the wroth silver were to make a forfeiture of a white bull with red ears and red nose. Such an animal would be almost impossible to obtain, and points to legends of fairy white cows with red ears who wandered around Britain supplying an unlimited amount of milk.

◆

To Dress Sorrel with Eggs

From a sixteenth-century Anglo-Irish Cookbook:

"Put two handfuls of Sorrell clean pick'd and washed into a saucepan, with a bit of butter, a pinch of flour, a little salt, pepper, and nutmeg, stew it, and a quarter of an hour before you use it, pour in two or three spoonfuls of drawn butter. Garnish with hard-cooked eggs, cut in quarters, laying one end on the sorrel, and the other on the side of the plate, with the yolks uppermost, and serve it up, either for a course at Dinner, or else for a supper."

Parsley, Sage, Thyme, Savory, and Lemon Thyme Butter

A seventeenth-century recipe:

"Clarify your butter, then mix it with a little oil of any of the herbs, till the butter is strong enough to your taste or liking. Then mix them well together. This is a great rarity and will make the butter keep a long time. This will be better than eating the plants with bread and butter by taking butter newly made and working it well from its water milk and wheyish parts before you put in the oils."

Homemade Herbal Butters

Not all people are gifted at buttermaking, and they sometimes resort to spellcraft to produce butter in the churn. The most productive method, and the most horrifying, was to stir the milk round with the dead hand of a hanged criminal.

Making butter by means of an ordinary rotary churn turned by hand was always a somewhat uncertain task, often made doubly difficult when the butter refused to come. If a churn was made of rowan wood, you would stand a better chance of nullifying an evil witch's power. A silver coin thrown into the cream or three white hairs from a black cat would also take away a witch's curse.

Before the establishment of local creameries, every farmhouse had its own churn to make butter. Butter was an important commodity, and as such there were many superstitions about buttermaking. Evil spirits or a spiteful neighbor could jinx the entire project. A good buttermaker, therefore, knew a whole stock of prayers, charms, and incantations to say during the churning. The following charm from the Highlands of Scotland calls on St. Bridgit. However, it is apparent from the references that the charm is older, and was originally a prayer to the Goddess:

Come, great Bridgit, handmaid calm,

hasten the butter on the cream;

see my children, waiting yonder,

waiting for buttered bannocks and fresh cream.

Come ye rich lumps, come!

Come ye rich lumps, come!

Come, ye rich lumps, masses large,

Come ye rich lumps, come!

You who put the beam in moon and sun,

You who put the food in field and herd,

You who put fish in stream and sea,

Send the butter up to me!

Butter was probably first enhanced with herbs in the early Middle Ages, when it was wrapped in sorrel leaves and stored in clay pots filled with saltwater. The sorrel was used to keep the butter fresh and sweet, but it no doubt lent its lemony taste to the butter in the process.

The basic recipe for making herb butters is simple. You start with unsalted sweet butter and cream it until it is light and fluffy. Chopped herbs, flowers, and seeds are blended into it, along with lemon juice, lemon zest, salt, and pepper. For holidays and other festive occasions, you can pack the soft butter into a wooden butter mold, chill until solid, then turn out with the design face up. These can be found in antique shops and speciality stores; I have several handed down to me by my grandmother. Or you may try ice cube trays or candy molds to create fun and decorative shapes. The simplest way to present your butter might be to roll it between two pieces of waxed paper about ¼ inch thick, chill, and use cookie cutters to shape the butter into suns or crescent moons. You may try decorating the butter or the plate with sprigs of fresh herbs or flowers to make an easy and attractive centerpiece.

Herbal Butter Recipe

Try your own combinations. Well-flavored herbs to experiment with include thyme, rosemary, sage, salad burnett, parsley, tarragon, garlic, chives, chervil, and mint.

2	sticks unsalted butter, softened (see note)
4–6	tablespoons chopped fresh herbs, flowers or seeds or
4–6	teaspoons dried herbs
	Juice and grated zest of 1 lemon
	Salt and pepper to taste or
	try dry mustard or paprika for a zesty kick

Cream the butter until light and fluffy. Chop the herbs and flowers very fine or pulverize the seeds and blend them into the butter. Spoon onto a sheet of waxed paper and roll it up so that the butter is about ½ inch in diameter. Refrigerate until ready and cut into slices.

for meats and fish	Garlic and ramson
for fish	Lemon balm and lemon juice
for meats	Mint, parsley, and cayenne pepper
	Parsley, chives, chervil, tarragon, and shallots
for toasted bread or biscuits	Scented geranium leaves, rose petals, or pinks
	Grated orange zest and sugar
	Roses and lavender
	Cinnamon, nutmeg, and mace
	Orange water, orange zest and cinnamon
	Honey and lemon zest
	Marjoram, thyme, and minced garlic
	Chopped almonds and rose petals
	Rose water and fresh rose petals
for chicken, eggs, or vegetable dishes	Marigold petals, chives, and parsley
for potatoes or fish	Parsley, lemon juice, and savory
for chicken, lamb, or vegetables	Mint, garlic, and parsley
for beef or burgers	Dry mustard and pepper
for vegetables	Thyme, parsley, and sage

for fish, beef, chicken, or vegetables	Lemon juice, grated zest and tarragon
for bread and meat	Parsley, chives, and lemon
for fish, bread, and vegetables	Basil, thyme and parsley
for pork or chicken	Ginger and orange zest
for lamb, chicken, or fish	Basil and garlic
for seafood or vegetables	Mint and chives

Note: For an herbal cheese, select a soft cheese and substitute it for butter in the above recipe to make a flavorful spread for bread, crackers, and toast. Herbs that work especially well with cheese include caraway, chervil, chives, dill seed, sage, rosemary, fennel, marjoram, mint, savory, and thyme.

Almond Butter

From Delights for Ladies, *1594:*

Blanch your almonds, and beate them as fine as you can with faire water, two or three hours, then strain them through a linen cloth, boil them with rose water, whole mace, and aniseeds, till the substance be thick: spread it upon a faire clothe, dressing the whey from it, after let it hang in the same cloth some houres, then strain it and season it with rosewater and sugar.

Faerie Butter

From The Receipt Book of Elizabeth Cleland, *1759:*

4 egg yolks
2 cups sugar
2 tablespoons orange-flower water
2 sticks butter, softened

Beat together egg yolks and sugar; blend in the orange-flower water and butter. Force it through a cookie press to form decorative shapes, and serve on a plate at supper.

Milk, Egg, and Cheese Pottage

From The Reign of Bres: *"Bres ordered a tax on every house in Ireland to be paid with the milk of hornless dun cows. At one time, to deceive him, Nechtan singed all the cows of Ireland in a fire of fern, and then he smeared them with the ashes of flax seed, so that they were all dark brown. And another time he made 300 cows of wood with dark brown pails in place of udders, and the pails were filled with black bog stuff. Bres came to look at the cows and to see them milked before him, and when they were milked it was bog water that was squeezed out. Bres took a drink of it thinking it to be milk, and he was not the better of it for a long time."*

- 6   hard-boiled eggs, separated
- 3   cups whole milk
- ¾   cup bread crumbs
- 1   teaspoon ground almonds
- 1   teaspoon sugar
- ¼   teaspoon saffron
- ½   teaspoon salt, or to taste
- ¾   cup cheddar cheese, grated

Mash the egg yolks and beat together with milk, bread crumbs, ground almonds, sugar, saffron, and salt. You may use a blender to make a smoother mixture, but this is not necessary. Cook over medium heat until thick and bubbly. Add the egg whites, chopped, and the grated cheese. Stir for a few minutes and then serve hot with slices of fresh bread.

ASSOCIATED HOLIDAYS: OSTARA, BELTAINE, NAME DAYS/BIRTHDAYS

SERVES 2 TO 3

He who drinks milk lives long.

GALICIAN PROVERB

Soups and Stews

You don't know what is in the pot

until the lid is lifted.

IRISH PROVERB

The Sacred Herb

For centuries sage has been praised for its health-giving properties. It is said that sage will prolong your life when planted in a garden. (If it prospers well in the garden, it is a sign that the woman rules the house.)

The best time of year to eat sage or drink sage tea is in springtime, and it makes a wonderful tonic to clear the body of impurities. People once ate it with bread and butter, and one of the most popular uses was as a spice in soups. If you pluck and eat twelve leaves at noon on St. Mark's Day, you will see your future mate. In *The Virtues of British Herbs,* 1772, it is written:

> There is a woman of the little town of Starground, so old that for that reason only she has been called a witch. About five square yards of ground, enclosed by a mud wall, before the door of her little habitation, was planted with sage. Her exact age could not be known, for she was older than the register, but the people in general remark their fathers called her the old woman.

◆

How can a man die

who has sage in his garden?

ENGLISH PROVERB

Chicken Stock

Chicken stock is still a cure-all in many Celtic homes. It can be eaten plain, with bread and butter floating on the surface, or as a base for other soups. This particular recipe is enhanced by potent herbs.

Bay trees are said to be immune from lightning strikes, and if a person stands under one during a storm they will never be struck. It is therefore wise to plant one beside your house to protect it during thunder storms. Bay trees have the added advantage of keeping out plague and pestilence.

A Cornish belief states that to eat cloves will attract wealth.

Bones and leftover carcass of at least two cooked chickens
Chicken giblets
1 carrot, sliced
2 sticks celery, sliced
1 medium-sized onion, stuck with several cloves
Pinch of sage
2 tablespoons parsley
1 teaspoon thyme
1 bay leaf
1 teaspoon salt
6 peppercorns
12 cups water
1 chicken bouillon cube (optional)

Put all the ingredients in a large soup pot. Bring to a boil and skim off any fat. Cover and simmer over very low heat for at least 2 hours. If you desire a stronger flavor, boil down the liquid.

Strain the liquid into a sterilized jar. Allow the stock to cool and remove any fat before using. The stock should be refrigerated until needed. It should not be kept in the refrigerator for more than a few days but it can be frozen for up to 6 months.

ASSOCIATED HOLIDAY: SAMHAIN

MAKES 8 CUPS

It is a bad hen that
will not scratch herself.

IRISH PROVERB

Beef Stock

From the Boke of Secrets, 1560, it is written: "This herb (sage) yf left to putrify with the blood of a serpent or a bird like an oysell, if it be touched on the brest of a man, he shall lose his sence of felynge the space of fifteen days or more. And if the foresaid serpent be burned and the ashes of it put in ye fyre, anone shall there be a rainbowe with an horible thunder. And yf ye aforesaid ashes be put in a lamp, and be kindled, it shal appeare that all the house is full of serpints and this hath been proved of men of late tyme."

Beef stock, enhanced with fresh sage, also makes a good base for a variety of other soups.

- 3 pounds beef bones
- 3 sticks celery, sliced
- 2 medium-sized onions, stuck with several cloves
- 1 carrot, sliced
- 1 small potato, peeled and sliced
  Pinch of sage
- 2 tablespoons parsley
- ½ teaspoon thyme
- 1 bay leaf
- 8 peppercorns
- 8 cups water
- 1 beef bouillon cube (optional)

Put all the ingredients in a large soup pot. Bring to a boil and skim off any fat. Cover and simmer over very low heat for at least 2 hours. If you desire a stronger flavor, boil down the liquid.

Strain the liquid into a sterilized jar. Allow the stock to cool and remove any fat before using. The stock should be refrigerated until needed. It should not be kept in the refrigerator for more than a few days but it can be frozen for up to 6 months.

ASSOCIATED HOLIDAYS: SAMHAIN, YULE

MAKES 6 CUPS

Kidney Soup

You cannot eat soup with a fork (Breton proverb).

½ beef kidney
1 quart beef stock
1 medium-sized onion, sliced
½ turnip, sliced
1 carrot, sliced
1 stalk celery, chopped fine
1 tablespoon ground rice
Thyme to taste
Salt and pepper to taste
Chopped parsley and croutons to serve

Skin the kidney and cut into pieces; bring to a boil in the beef stock. Add the onion, turnip, carrot, and celery. Simmer for 1½ hours. Blend the ground rice in a little of the stock; add to the soup and boil another fifteen minutes. Strain the soup through a sieve, rubbing through the vegetables and kidney, or use a blender to smooth. Reheat soup; season to taste and serve hot with parsley and croutons.

ASSOCIATED HOLIDAYS: SAMHAIN, YULE

SERVES 4

Don't break your shins on
your neighbor's pots.

WELSH PROVERB

◆

Scotch Broth

An English belief says that to wear a sprig of thyme in your hair is to become irresistible to the opposite sex, while an old Manx belief proclaims if you carry a branch of thyme into the home of one who is old and ailing, they will surely die.

1½	pounds stewing beef, cut into pieces
8	cups water
4	tablespoons pearl barley
3	turnips, sliced
3	carrots, sliced
1	potato, peeled and cubed
2	leeks, trimmed and sliced
2	stalks celery, chopped fine
1	medium-sized onion, chopped fine
1	cup red cabbage, chopped fine
¼	teaspoon each salt and pepper, or to taste
¼	teaspoon lemon thyme
	Fresh parsley, chopped, for garnish

Trim any fat off the meat and put it in a large soup pot. Cover with water and bring to a boil. Skim off any fat, and add the barley. Cover and let simmer for 1 hour. Add turnips, carrots, potato, leeks, celery, and onions and simmer for an additional hour. Add the cabbage and season to taste with salt, pepper, and thyme. Simmer for an additional 15 minutes and serve with parsley sprinkled on top.

ASSOCIATED HOLIDAYS: SAMHAIN, MABON, YULE

SERVES 4 TO 6

The first drop of broth

is the hottest.

SCOTTISH PROVERB

◆

Elder and Nettle Pottage

Taking feverfew prevents sickness, and is a cure for many types of headaches. Herbalist John Hill wrote, "A lady of greate worth and virtue told me that having in the younger part of her life a very terrible and almost constant headache, fixed in one small spot and raging all times almost to distraction, was at length cured by a maid servant with this herb."
From T. Tryon, 1692:

Take elder buds, nettle tops, feverfew, clivers, and watercress, and what quantity of water you please proportionable to your quantity of herbs, add oatmeal according as you would have it in thickness and when your water and oatmeal is just ready to boyl, put your herbs into it, cut or uncut as you like best. Take a ladle and lade it, and then you may eat it with the herbs or strain it adding a little butter, salt, and bread. The best will be not to eat it till it is somewhat cooled, and not past as hot as milk from a cow. You are to remember not to let it boyl at all. This is a brave, wholsom, cleansing sort of pottage far beyond what is commonly made.

ASSOCIATED HOLIDAYS: BELTAINE, MIDSUMMER

In pottage without herbs there is neither goodness nor nourishment.

IAGO AB DEWI

◆

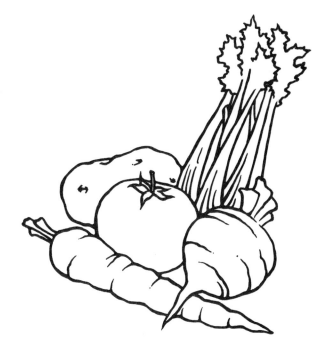

The Soup Contest

The faeries of Wales, known as *Y Tylwyth Teg,* the "fair people," play a dominant role in Welsh folk tales. They are not the small, airy creatures of popular belief, but are almost human in form. In fact, many of their women marry mortal men and bear their children. They live in villages, and most are friendly toward humans. There are some, however, who are evil-minded and intent on causing harm to all who cross their path. Maelor was one such creature.

There was once a farmer who lived in Cardiganshire with his two sons and his young daughter, Maggi. Although he was old and feeble, his sons wouldn't turn their hands to anything resembling work, and despite the best efforts of his daughter, the farm soon fell into disrepair.

A large, vast forest rose behind the farm, and one day the father said to his sons, "Go out and chop some wood. Perhaps we can sell it to pay off some of our debts."

Well, after much cajoling and shouting, the farmer convinced his oldest son, Dewi, to go first. But when Dewi had gotten far into the forest, and began to chop at a scraggly old oak tree, what should he see coming up to him but a great, fearsome giant!

"I am Maelor and this is my forest," he roared. "If you chop down the trees in my forest, I will kill you."

When Dewi heard that, he tossed aside his axe, and ran off towards home as fast—aye and faster—than a rabbit. He came in quite out of breath, and panted, "Father, father, there is a giant in the forest! He threatened to kill me!"

"What?" scoffed the old man. "You're a miserable excuse for a son. Why, when I was younger, no giant would have ever scared me from cutting trees on my own land."

So the next day the farmer sent his second son into the forest, and he fared no better. Edren had hardly struck the scraggly oak tree three times when the giant appeared from nowhere and roared, "I am Maelor and this is my forest. If you cut down any trees in this wood of mine, I will have to kill you."

Like his older brother, the second son threw down his axe and beat a path for home. When he arrived, his father was very angry, and said, "No giant would have ever scared me when I was young."

On the third day, Maggi wanted to set off.

"You?" asked the older brothers. "Indeed! Whoever heard of such a marvel? You'll do it bravely, no doubt, and well—you who have never been beyond the front gate!"

Maggi ignored her brothers' cruel teasing, and simply asked for a good store of food. Since her father had no cheese curds, she hung a pot over the fire to make herself some, and she put it into her knapsack and set off into the forest. Her brothers' laughter rang in her ears long after the farm was out of sight.

Maggi found a fine oak tree, and after chopping at it for a while she saw the giant come up to her. "If you chop the trees in my forest, little girl, I'll kill you," said the giant.

Maggi was young, but she was clever; and although fear pounded in her heart, she pulled her cheese out of her knapsack, and squeezed it till the whey spurted out. "Watch how you speak to me, you hairy, over-sized oaf, and mind your manners!"

"Ho!" laughed the giant. "A feisty one, but what harm can you bring me."

"You'll go back where you came from and leave me alone or I'll squeeze your head like I'm squeezing the water out of this stone!" shouted Maggi.

The terrified giant quickly backed down, his eyes near to popping from their sockets. "No! Don't hurt me! If you spare my life, mighty one, I'll help you chop wood."

"Well . . ." Maggi pretended to think the deal over. "I suppose that I can strike that bargain." The giant helped Maggi chop down the trees, and by nightfall they had several cords of wood to sell at market.

When evening drew near, the giant said, "My home is no doubt closer than yours. You'd better come back with me."

Maggi was willing enough, for she was awfully tired, and when they reached Maelor's home the giant made up the fire. Maggi went to fetch water for their soup. Two iron pails stood by the fireplace, and they were so big and heavy, that she couldn't so much as lift them from the ground, much less get them to the well to fill with water.

"Bah!" said Maggi. "It's not worth my while to touch these finger-bowls. I'll just go and fetch the spring itself."

"No, no, little girl," said the giant hastily. "I can't afford to lose my spring water. Just tend to the fire, and I'll go get the water."

When the giant came back, they cooked a large pot of soup.

"Let's have an eating match," the girl challenged Maelor. The huge giant eagerly agreed, for he knew he could hold his own in an eating contest against a wee wisp of a girl. So they sat down; but the lass took her knapsack unawares to the giant, and hung it before her, and so she spooned more into the bag than she ate herself; and when the knapsack was quite full, she took out her knife and made a slit in the leather. When they had eaten a while longer, Maelor laid down his spoon, saying, "No, girl! I'm done. I can't manage a morsel more!"

"You must eat," encouraged Maggi. "Why, I'm not even half-full yet! My stomach nearly roars from hunger. Do as I did and cut a hole in your stomach so you can keep eating as much as you want!"

"But doesn't it hurt you cruelly?" the giant asked doubtfully.

"Nothing to speak of," shrugged the girl. "It doesn't even tickle."

So the giant cut a gash in his hairy belly and, of course, he died. The girl gathered up all of the gold and silver that she found in the hillside and went home with it, and you may be glad to hear that it went a great way to pay off the debt.

◆

A Marriage Divination

A maiden stands on something on which she never stood before, holding a pot of cold broth in her hand, repeating the following lines. She then drinks nine times, goes to bed backwards, to dream of her partner:

> Hot broth or cold broth, I drink to thee;
>
> If ever I marry a man, or man marry me,
>
> I wish this night I may him see,
>
> Tomorrow may him ken,
>
> In church, fair, or market,
>
> Above all other men.

◆

Chestnut Soup

Hunger will conquer a lion (Breton proverb).

> Lightly salted water for boiling
> 1 pound chestnuts
> 5 cups chicken stock (page 149)
> 1 small onion, chopped
> 2 cups fresh milk
> ¼ teaspoon nutmeg, or to taste
> ¼ teaspoon ground mace, or to taste
> Salt and pepper to taste
> Croutons to garnish

To skin the chestnuts, make a cut along the flat side of each chestnut and drop them into a pan of boiling, salted water. Boil for about 5 minutes. Chestnuts must be peeled while hot, so only take out a couple at a time. Remove both the outer shells and inner skins. In a fresh pan of water, simmer the peeled chestnuts for about 15 minutes until they are tender. Be careful not to overcook them, or else they will fall apart. Discard the water and purée the chestnuts in a blender, then return them to the soup pot. Sauté the onion until soft and add to the pot along with stock, milk, nutmeg, and mace. Season to taste with salt and pepper. Reheat and serve with croutons for garnish.

Variation: Add bay leaf, cloves, thyme, 1 slice chopped onion, and ¼ cup of sherry when adding chestnut purée soup to the pot. Heat through and serve.

ASSOCIATED HOLIDAYS: YULE, NEW YEAR'S EVE, WINTER CELEBRATIONS

SERVES 4 TO 6

Partan Bree

"Partan" is the Gaelic word for crab and "bree" comes from brigh, *which means "broth." This rich and creamy crab soup is a favorite in Scotland.*

3 cups milk
1 cup uncooked rice
1 potato, peeled and cubed very small
4 anchovy fillets
½ pound fresh cooked crabmeat
2 cups water or chicken stock (page 149)
Salt and pepper to taste
¾ cup heavy cream
Parsley or croutons for garnish (optional)

In a heavy-bottomed soup pot, bring the milk to near-boiling. Add the rice, potato cubes, and anchovy fillets. Simmer over medium heat until the rice and potatoes are well done. Remove from the heat and add the crabmeat. Purée the soup in a blender or food processor, then return soup to a large soup pot and gradually stir in the chicken stock. Season with salt and pepper to taste. Add swirls of the fresh cream just before serving. Serve hot or cold, and garnish with parsley or croutons.

Variation: Start with 1 can of condensed celery soup and blend with an equal amount of tomato juice in a pot. Heat to near-boiling. Turn off heat, blend in ½ cup cream, 1 cup cooked crab, and ¼ cup dry white wine. Return to heat and simmer over low to heat crab meat through. Season to taste with salt and pepper.

ASSOCIATED HOLIDAYS: IMBOLG, BELTAINE

SERVES 4 TO 6

Talk does not fill the stomach.

SCOTTISH PROVERB

◆

Mutton Soup

Eating foods spiced with mace increases psychic powers (Celtic belief).

2 pounds mutton, including bone
2 quarts water
6 tablespoons pearl barley
   Salt and pepper to taste
   Worcestershire sauce
1½ cups chopped carrots
1 cup chopped turnips
1 medium-sized onion, chopped
½ teaspoon chopped parsley
1 cup chopped celery
1 large clove garlic, chopped

Boil the mutton pieces in water for 10 to 15 minutes. Scrape the scum off the surface and add barley, salt, pepper and Worcestershire sauce. Cover and simmer for 1½ hours. Add the rest of the ingredients, cover, and simmer one hour. Add more water if needed. Remove the bone and serve.

ASSOCIATED HOLIDAY: LUGHNASADH

SERVES 6

Don't put wool on a sheep's back.

IRISH PROVERB

Brotchan Foltchep (Leek and Oatmeal Soup)

Legend has it that St. Patrick once tended a dying woman who said that she had seen a vision of an herb, and that she would die unless she had it. St. Patrick asked her what this herb looked like, and she said, "Like rushes." Patrick blessed the rushes so that they became leeks. The woman ate them, and was well once more. The nettle soup variation is also said to be a favorite dish of St. Colmcille.

Oatmeal may seem like an odd choice if you are used to using flour, starch, or pureed vegetables to thicken a soup.

1	tablespoon melted butter
¼	cup oatmeal, uncooked
5	cups whole milk or beef stock (page 150)
	Salt and pepper to taste
	Pinch of ground mace
3	cups sliced leeks
1	tablespoon fresh parsley and croutons to garnish

Heat the butter in a pot and add the oatmeal; stir over low heat until it begins to brown and smell toasted. Add the milk or beef stock and season with salt, pepper, and mace to taste. Add the leeks and simmer gently for 45 minutes. Stir in the chopped parsley before serving.

Variation: A springtime version can be made when nettle-tops are young. Simply substitute 3 cups of nettle-tops and three chopped scallions for the leeks.

ASSOCIATED HOLIDAYS: BELTAINE,
LUGHNASADH

SERVES 4

Yarrow and Onion Soup

Yarrow, like borage, provides courage to one who needs it. I am still somewhat shy about public speaking, and will keep a pinch of dried yarrow leaves in my pocket.

It is said that eating yarrow or using an infusion as a hair rinse will prevent baldness. If you're already going bald, however, it will not be of any help.

Most men say that the green leaves of yarrow, if chewed, are a remedy for toothache (John Gerard, 1597).

A maiden wishing to see her future husband must take one of the serrated leaves of the yarrow, and with it tickle the inside of the nostrils, repeating, "Yarroway, yarroway, you bear a white blow, if my love loves me, my nose will bleed now."

The old name for yarrow was nose bleed because the leaves of the plant were used to make the nose bleed to ease the pain of a migraine. Other medieval herbals, on the contrary, say that yarrow will staunch a nosebleed.

3	cups yarrow leaves, somewhat packed down
2	tablespoons butter
1	small onion, chopped fine
1	tablespoon flour
2	cups chicken stock (page 149)
	Salt and pepper to taste
1½	cups milk or light cream
1	tablespoon heavy cream
	Grated nutmeg
	Pinch of cinnamon
	Parsley to garnish

Wash leaves thoroughly and place in a pan of ¼ cup boiling water. Cook over low heat for 8 to 10 minutes. Drain. Melt butter, sauté onion. Add flour slowly and stir to keep from sticking. Add stock and stir to thicken. Return yarrow to the pot and season to taste with salt and pepper. Cover and let simmer 10 minutes. Rub through a sieve or purée in a blender and return to pot. Heat milk or light cream and stir into soup. Add nutmeg and cinnamon to taste, swirl in cream, and garnish with parsley.

ASSOCIATED HOLIDAYS: MIDSUMMER, LUGHNASADH

SERVES 2

Cullen Skink (Smoked Haddock Soup)

Irish fishermen consider it lucky to catch fiddle fish which, though themselves are inedible, bring good luck to the boat and her crew. It is customary to attach the fiddle fish to the prow of the ship and leave it there until it finally falls to pieces on its own.

1½	pounds smoked haddock fillets
2	cups cream
1	onion, finely chopped
4	cups water
1	large potato, peeled and diced
3	tablespoons butter
1	cup fresh cream
	Salt and pepper to taste
¼	teaspoon paprika
	Homemade bread for dipping

Put the smoked haddock in a large, shallow pan with the milk, onion, and water. Bring slowly to a boil, then remove from the heat. Remove the fish from the pan, skin and bone it, then flake it into small pieces. Set flaked fish aside. Place the skin and bones in a soup pot with the cooking liquid and the onion. Add the potato; cover and simmer for one hour. Strain the stock through a sieve and return the liquid to the soup pot. Add the fish, butter, and cream, and season to taste with salt, pepper, and paprika. Mop up the soup with hearty slices of freshly baked bread.

ASSOCIATED HOLIDAYS: IMBOLG, BELTAINE

SERVES 4

Arise, arise, ye dairy maids,

Shake off your drowsy dream.

Step straight into your dairies

and fetch us a bowl of cream!

SCOTTISH FOLK SONG

Traditional Irish Stew

An Irish belief says to keep a sprig of thyme in your pocket while passing a faerie mound. It will protect you from mischief and enable you to see the faeries.

3   pounds lamb neck chops, trimmed of fat, bone, and gristle
2   pounds potatoes
1   pound onions
½   tablespoon chopped parsley
½   tablespoon fresh thyme
2   cups water
    Salt and pepper to taste

Cut meat into pieces. Peel and slice potatoes and onions. Layer half of the potatoes in saucepan, then half of the meat and herbs, and finally half of the onion. Season each layer to taste and repeat the process. Pour water over, cover with a sheet of foil as well as the lid, and simmer gently for about 2 hours, occasionally shaking the pan to prevent sticking. Add liquid if it seems too dry, but a good Irish stew should be thick and not like a soup.

ASSOCIATED HOLIDAYS: ST. PATRICK'S DAY, SAMHAIN, MABON, YULE, ESBAT CELEBRATIONS, WINTER DINNERS

SERVES 4

A stew boiled

is a stew spoiled.

IRISH PROVERB

Oatmeal Herb Pottage

Women in their third trimester of pregnancy should carry in their purse a tiny packet of strawberry leaves to ease the discomforts of childbearing.

- 1 tablespoon melted butter
- ¼ cup oatmeal, uncooked
- 5 cups whole milk or beef stock (page 150)
  Salt and pepper to taste
- 1 handful each of fresh spinach, parsley, marigold flowers, succory, strawberry leaves, violet leaves
  Croutons to garnish

Heat the butter in a pot and add the oatmeal; stir over low heat until it begins to brown and smell toasted. Add the milk or beef stock and season to taste with salt and pepper. Mince the herbs fine, and add to the pot and simmer gently over low heat for 45 minutes. Garnish with croutons.

ASSOCIATED HOLIDAYS: LUGHNASADH, MIDSUMMER

SERVES 4

Carrot Soup

Carrots are often eaten to promote lust, cure impotence, and help women conceive.

- 2 pounds carrots, peeled
- 1 tablespoon butter
- 2 cups white wine
  Salt, cinnamon, and sugar to taste
- ¼ cup dates
- ¼ cup currants
  Sugar to garnish

Boil carrots and purée in a blender or, more traditionally, beat them in a mortar. Return them to the pot and add butter, white wine, salt, cinnamon, and sugar to taste. Shred dates and add to soup with currants. Simmer gently until heated through. Dish out into bowls, sprinkle with sugar, and serve with hard-boiled eggs.

ASSOCIATED HOLIDAYS: MIDSUMMER, LUGHNASADH

SERVES 2

County Wexford Irish Stew (A Variation)

People once referred to tomatoes as love apples because they were used in many love spells. Few people, including my great grandmother, would eat them because they were believed to be poisonous.

- 2 pounds mutton
- 2 pounds potatoes, sliced
- 2 onions, peeled and chopped
- 1 carrot, sliced
- 1 tomato, sliced
- 2 mushrooms, sliced
- 1 turnip, peeled and sliced
  Salt and pepper to taste
- 2 cups water
- 1 teaspoon chopped fresh parsley

Cut the meat into bite-sized pieces. Put the meat in the bottom of a heavy saucepan; add vegetables. Season with salt and pepper to taste. Add the water and bring to a boil. Skim, then simmer for an hour. Serve the meat in the center of a hot platter. Arrange the vegetables around it and pour a little of the sauce over it. Garnish with parsley.

ASSOCIATED HOLIDAYS: SAMHAIN, MABON, YULE,
ESBAT CELEBRATIONS, WINTER DINNERS,
ST. PATRICK'S DAY

SERVES 4 TO 6

Cockle Soup

Dried pieces of seaweed kept above the fireplace are a charm to keep the house safe from fires. Likewise, seaweed should be carried aboard a ship at sea, for one of the greatest dangers a sailor faced was if his boat caught fire (Sailor's belief).

Salted water for cooking
4 dozen cockles or mussels
2 heaping tablespoons butter
2 heaping tablespoons flour
4 cups cockle stock
2 cups whole milk or cream
2 tablespoons chopped parsley or seaweed
½ cup chopped celery
Salt and pepper to taste
Cream

Scrub the cockles well to clean off sand and grit. Put them into a large saucepan; cover with salted water. Bring water to a boil; all cockles should open. Do not continue cooking. Remove cockles to cool, reserving liquid. Remove cockles from shells. Melt the butter in a saucepan, and stir in the flour. Add the strained cockle juice and milk, stirring all the time until it is smoothly blended. Put in the chopped parsley, celery, and seasoning. Cook for 10 minutes. Finally, add the cockles, heat, and serve with a dollop of cream on each portion.

ASSOCIATED HOLIDAY: IMBOLG

SERVES 4

In Dublin's fair city,

Where the girls are so pretty,

I first set my eyes on sweet Molly Malone.

She wheeled her wheelbarrow,

through streets broad and narrow,

Crying, "Cockles and mussels, alive, alive oh!"

IRISH FOLKSONG

Cardiwen's Cauldron

Cardiwen (or Cerridwen) is one of the Celtic names for the Triple Goddess, although in the following tale she is disguised as a witch. Tegid Foel was the Goddess' consort and the father of Afagddu, the world's ugliest man, and of Morfan, a warrior so ugly that no man would fight him at Camluan (the battle where Arthur and Mordred were slain). The Welsh bard Taliesin is said to have been born of Cerridwen and gained his poetic inspiration from her mystical cauldron.

In times past there were enchanted islands in the Atlantic Ocean, off the coast of Wales, and even now the fishermen sometimes think they see them. On one of these there lived a man named Tegid Voel and his wife called Cardiwen. They had a son, the ugliest boy in the world, and Cardiwen formed a plan to make him more attractive by teaching him all possible wisdom.

Cardiwen was a great magician and resolved to boil a large cauldron full of knowledge for her son, so that he might know all things and be able to predict all that was to happen. She thought people would begin to value him in spite of his ugliness if he were wise. But the spell was a long time in the making, and the cauldron had to burn a year and a day without ceasing, until three blessed drops of the water of knowledge were obtained from it.

So Cardiwen ordered a boy named Gwion to stir the cauldron and a blind man named Morda to feed the fire; and she made them promise never to let it cease boiling for a year and a day. Cardiwen herself continued to gather herbs to add to the broth.

One day, when the year was nearly over, it chanced that three drops of the broth bubbled up out of the cauldron and fell on the finger of Gwion. They were fiery hot, and he put his finger to his mouth to soothe the pain. The instant he tasted them he knew that they were the enchanted drops for which so much trouble had been taken. By their magic he at once foresaw all that was to come, and especially that Cardiwen the enchantress would never forgive him.

Gwion fled. The cauldron burst in two, and all the broth flowed forth. Cardiwen came in and saw the toil of the whole year lost. She seized a stick and threatened Morda, but all he said was, "I am innocent. It was not I who did it."

"True," said Cardiwen. "I see it now. It was the boy Gwion who robbed me." She rushed to pursue him. He saw her and fled, changing into a hare. But she became a greyhound and followed him. Running to the water, Gwion became a fish. But she became another and chased him below the waves. Gwion turned himself into a bird, and she became a hawk and gave him no rest in the sky. Just as Cardiwen swooped on him, he espied a pile of winnowed wheat on the floor of a barn, and dropping upon it, he became one of the wheat grains. Cardiwen changed herself into a high-crested black hen, and scratched him up and swallowed him. Then she changed back into the form of a woman, and Gwion found himself in the darkness of her womb.

When the child was reborn, Cardiwen found him so beautiful that she could not kill him outright, but wrapped him in a leather bag and cast him into the sea, committing him to the mercy of the waves.

Now a certain king named Gwyddno had a weir for catching fish on the sea-strand near his castle. Each morning would find him at the water's edge, and he was known to take a hundred pounds' worth of fish each time.

But on this particular occasion he sent his son Elphin to the salmon weir. Elphin was always an unlucky one, and the king hoped that he would be able to find something of value.

"Oh, Dafi," the prince called to the man tending the weir. "What has the sea brought us this day?" "Nothing of value," he replied. "There is nothing in the weir but a leather bag which is caught on one of the poles."

"How do you know that it has no value?" questioned Elphin. "Perhaps it contains gold." Taking up the bag, he opened it, and to his great sadness he saw that it did not contain any wealth, only a small boy.

"What a radiant brow he has," exclaimed Dafi.

"Then let him be called Taliesin, which means radiant brow," declared Elphin. He lifted the boy and placed him before him on his horse, and together they rode back to the castle. On the way, Taliesin made up a song.

> Never in Gwyddo's weir
>
> was there such good luck as this night.
>
> Fair Elphin, dry your tears!
>
> Being too sad will not avail,
>
> Although you may think you have gained nothing.
>
> Too much grief will do you no good—
>
> Do not doubt the miracles of the one most high.
>
> Although I am but little, I am highly gifted.

From seas, and from mountains,

and from the depths of rivers,

wealth comes to the fortunate man.

Elphin of lively qualities,

your resolution is unmanly.

You must not be oversorrowful.

Better to trust in God than to forebode ill.

Weak and small as I am

on this foaming beach of the ocean,

in the day of trouble I shall be

of more service to you than three hundred salmon.

Elphin of notable qualities,

be not displeased at your misfortune.

Although I seem weak here in my bag,

there lies virtue in my tongue.

While I continue as your protector,

you'll have no reason to fear.

Elphin stared at him in amazement, and he asked, "Are you man or spirit?" In answer the boy sang to him of his flight from Cardiwen:

I have fled with vigor, I have fled as a frog,

I have fled in the semblance of a crow scarcely finding rest;

I have fled vehemently, I have fled as a chain of lightning;

I have fled as a roe into an entangled thicket;

I have fled as a wolf cub, I have fled as a wolf in the wilderness;

I have fled as a fox used to many swift bounds and quirks;

I have fled as a martin, which did not avail;

I have fled as a squirrel that vainly hides;

I have fled as a stag's antler, or ruddy course;

I have fled as a spear-head, of woe to such as have a wish for it;

I have fled as a fierce bull bitterly fighting;

I have fled as a white grain of pure wheat.

Into a dark leather bag I was thrown

and on a boundless sea I was sent adrift.

To me it was an omen of being tenderly nursed.

And the Lord God then set me at liberty.

Elphin came with Taliesin to the house of his father, and Gwyddo asked him if he had a good haul at the fish weir.

"I have something better than fish," Elphin proudly declared.

"Better than fish?" asked his father. "Whatever do you mean?"

"I have a bard," said Elphin.

Gwyddo looked at the small boy critically. "Alas, what will he profit you, Elphin?"

It was Taliesin who said, "I will profit him more than the weir ever profited you."

Gwyddo's eyebrows shot up in surprise. "Are you able to speak, and so little a boy?"

"I am better able to speak than those who question me," replied Taliesin.

From that time on Elphin prospered, and he and his wife cared for Taliesin tenderly and lovingly, and the boy dwelt with them until he was thirteen years old.

That winter Elphin went to pay a visit to his uncle Maelgwyn, who was a great king and held open court. There were four and twenty bards there, and all of them proclaimed that there was no king who had a wife as beautiful as Maelqwyn's queen.

Elphin, well into his cups, called out, "I myself have a bride prettier than yours, Maelgwyn, and what is more, I have a bard who is the wisest in all the land."

"Than he should have better counseled your words, Elphin," said the king coldly, and he locked the boastful young man in prison.

Taliesin learned of the matter, and he set forth at once to try to free his adoptive father.

In those days it was the custom of kings to sit in the hall and dine in royal state with lords and bards about them who should keep proclaiming the greatness and glory of the king and his knights. Taliesin placed himself in a quiet corner, waiting for the four and twenty bards to pass, and as each one passed by, Taliesin made an ugly face, and gave a sound with his finger on his lips, like so: "Blerwm, blerwm!" Each bard went by and bowed low before the king, but instead of chanting his praises, each could only say "Blerwm, blwerwm!" The king thought they were intoxicated, and he had the squire strike the chief bard with a broom.

The chief bard came to his senses, shook his head, and said, "There is a spirit which sits in the corner of your dun, in the form of a child. It was he that enchanted us." The king asked that Taliesin be brought forward, and he demanded to know who he was.

> Primary chief bard am I to Elphin,
>
> And my native land is the region of the summer stars.
>
> I am a wonder whose origin is not known.
>
> I have been fostered in the womb of Cardiwen,
>
> I have been teacher to all intelligences,
>
> I am able to instruct the whole universe.
>
> Before that I was little Gwion,
>
> Now I am Taliesin.

When he was done speaking, silence reigned in the hall. Maelgwyn was the first to speak. "A fine song, indeed, little man," he smiled. He looked at his chief bard and said, "And what will you sing for us?"

The chief bard nervously lifted his harp and struck an opening cord, but as before all he could sing was "Blerm, blerm, blerm."

"Charming," frowned the king. He turned to Taliesin and asked, "Will you sing for us again?" Taliesin took a deep breath, feeling the power of the cauldron coursing through his veins. He sang:

> Discover what it is,
>
> the creature from before the flood.
>
> Without flesh, without bone,
>
> without vein, without blood,
>
> without head, without feet.
>
> It will neither be older nor younger
>
> than at the beginning.

How the sea whitens

when first it comes!

It is in the field,

it is in the wood,

Without hand and without foot.

Without signs of old age.

It is as wide

as the surface of the earth.

It was not born,

nor was it seen.

It will cause consternation

wherever God wills it.

On sea and on land

it neither sees, nor is seen.

Its course is devious,

and it will not come when desired.

On land and on sea

it is indispensable.

It is without equal.

It is many-sided.

It is not confined.

It is incomparable.

It comes from four quarters.

It is noxious, it is beneficial,

It is yonder, it it here,

It will destroy

but it will not repair the injury.

It will not suffer for its doings,

seeing it is blameless.

One Being has prepared it
out of all creatures
to wreak vengeance
on Maelgwyn Gwynedd.

And while Taliesin sang, there came suddenly a mighty storm of wind, so that the king and all his nobles thought the castle would fall on their heads. They saw that the young boy had not merely been singing the song of the wind, but seemed to have power to command it.

The king grew pale, and he hastily ordered that Elphin should be brought from his dungeon and placed before the young bard. Taliesin spoke a few words in an ancient language, and the chains came loose from Elphin's feet, and he was free. Together they mounted upon their horses and rode back home, leaving the evil king and all his court in fearful awe.

◆

Scottish Pheasant Soup

The Celts once considered parsley a magical plant associated with the dead and capable of laying restless spirits. It was used as a garnish for meat to mollify the spirit of the butchered animal, and the spoken word was thought an effective protection against evil spirits.

Bay leaf has a long history of aiding psychic powers, purifying the home, and granting wishes. Keep it in the house to protect against lightning strikes, sicknesses, and harmful magic. If a bay tree withers, it is a sign that the lord of the manor will die. Do not burn the wood, as it is unlucky.

Because salt is incorruptible and preserves other things from decay, it is a symbol of eternity and immortal life for many cultures. The Scots once swore oaths over it, and in England if you sat "above the salt," at the table, you were pretty honored, indeed. In the Outer Hebrides, shepherds would rub it on their cattle before transferring them to another field, and milkmaids would put a pinch of it into their pails to keep the milk safe from witches.

2   pheasant carcasses and their giblets or
    2 pounds pheasant or other game bird meat
2   tablespoons oil
2   tablespoons butter
2   carrots, sliced
3   celery sticks, sliced
1   small parsnip, peel and diced
1   leek, washed, trimmed and cut in pieces
3   cloves garlic, peeled and minced
4   cups chicken stock (page 149)
3   cups peeled, crushed tomatoes
6   tablespoons parsley
1   tablespoon fresh rosemary
1   bay leaf
¼   teaspoon allspice
    Salt and pepper to taste
1   cup sherry

Heat oil and butter in a soup pot. Add carrots, celery, parsnip, leek, and garlic. Cover and cook over medium heat for 20 minutes. Add chicken stock, tomatoes and pheasant meat/giblets. Simmer another 15 minutes. Add parsley, rosemary, bay leaf, allspice, salt and pepper. Stir and simmer, covered, for 30 minutes. Add sherry and adjust seasonings. Serve.

ASSOCIATED HOLIDAYS: SAMHAIN, MABON

SERVES 4

Cawl Mamgu

The leek is the national emblem of Wales, and on St. David's Day the Welsh traditionally wear leek leaves pinned to their clothes. St. David is said to have lived only on leeks, bread, and water during his meditation periods. The story is apocryphal, however, as there is no St. David. He was probably invented to "canonize" a local deity, Dewi, a sea spirit who has also become associated with the red dragon of Wales. This sea god bore the title Waterman, which monks took to mean that St. David only drank water. The leek was perhaps sacred to early Welsh tribes who used it as a staple vegetable.

There is an old Welsh custom, known as cymhortha, *that took place whenever farmers got together for a communal task. There would be a shared meal, and everyone would bring leeks to make the soup—nothing else would be added.*

Because leeks are sometimes difficult for people to acquire, they will instead wear daffodils pinned to their clothing on March 1, as the flowers are also associated with the saint.

If leeks grow on the roof, your home will never be struck by lightning.

4	medium-sized leeks, washed, trimmed, and cut into small cubes
2	large onions, peeled
4	carrots, peeled and slice in small cubes
3	parsnips, peeled and sliced in small cubes
1½–2	pounds mutton, sliced
½	cup uncooked rice
1	small potato, peeled and cubed
	Salt and pepper to taste
	Water to cover
	Fresh herbs for garnish

Make a flavoring bundle by wrapping the leaves of the leeks, the parsley stalks, and the onion skins in cheesecloth. Tie bundle with string and add to the soup pot along with the vegetables, meat, and rice. Add a little salt and pepper to taste and cover with water. Bring the soup slowly to a boil, skim off the fat, then cover and simmer over low heat for 2 hours. Remove the meat bones and the flavoring bag. Sprinkle the herbs on top just before serving.

ASSOCIATED HOLIDAYS: LUGHNASADH, ST. DAVID'S DAY

SERVES 4

Formorian Hospitality

From *The Ballad of Magh Tuireadh:*

The Dagda went to the camp of the Formor, and they made broth for him, for they heard he had a great love of broth. They filled the king's cauldron with four times twenty gallons of new milk, and the same of meat and fat, and they put in goats and sheep and pigs along with that, and boiled it all together. Then they poured it all out into a great hole in the ground, and they called the Dagda to it, and told him to eat his fill so that they would not be reproached for their hospitality. "We will make an end of you if you leave any part of it," they warned him.

So the Dagda took the ladle, it being big enough for a man and a woman to lie in the bowl of it, and he took out bits of the soup; the half of a salted pig and a quarter of lamb a bit would be, too.

"If the broth tastes as well as the bits taste, this is good food," he said. And he went on putting the full ladle into his mouth till the hole was empty; and when all was gone, he put down his hand and scraped up all that was left among the earth and gravel. Sleep came upon the Dagda after eating the broth, and the Formor laughed at him, for his belly was the size of the cauldron of a great house.

Mugwort

Yf this herb be within a house there shall no wyches, spyryte abyde (*The Grete Herball,* 1539).

Mugwort is a popular herb once used by the Celts in tea and to season vegetables, but now it is mostly used in magic. If rubbed on a crystal ball, scrying bowl, or magic mirror, it will increase the strength. William Coles, in *The Art of Simpling,* said, "If a footman take mugwort and put it into his shoes in the morning, he may goe forty miles before noon and not be weary."

Mussel and Onion Stew

If onion's skin is very thin, a mild winter's coming in; if onion's skin is thick and tough, the coming winter's cold and rough (Scottish saying).

- 5 pints mussels
- ⅔ cup white wine
- 6 small onions, sliced
- ¼ cup butter
- 4 shallots, chopped
- 6 cloves of garlic
- 2 carrots, chopped
- 4 potatoes
  Fresh parsley, thyme, and bay leaf, tied together
  Chopped parsley
  Black pepper

Scrub and "debeard" the mussels. Discard any that remain open after tapping; shellfish should be alive before cooking. Place them in a large saucepan with the white wine. Cook on high heat until the mussels are open. Again, throw away any that remain closed. Remove the mussels; strain the liquid and reserve. In another pan, sauté the onions in butter or olive oil. Add the shallots, garlic, and chopped carrots. Peel and slice the potatoes. Put them in a pan with the herbs, chopped parsley, and reserved liquid from the mussels. Season to taste with pepper. Simmer for about one hour. Shell the mussels and, if desired, save shells. Take a ladle of the vegetable broth, making sure to include potatoes, and purée in a blender, food processor, or food mill. Add to the rest of the vegetables again and put all the mussels into the pot. Simmer until the mussels are hot. Remove and discard bay leaf. The shells may be added for decoration. Serve with white wine and slices of garlic bread.

ASSOCIATED HOLIDAYS: HARVEST FESTIVALS

SERVES 4 TO 6

Watercress Soup

Legend states that St. Brendan the Navigator, who sailed to North America, lived to the ripe old age of 108 by eating watercress soup. This pale green soup can be served either hot or cold.

1   pound carrots, sliced into ¼ inch pieces
1   stalk celery, chopped
1   cup chopped watercress
2   medium-sized potatoes, peeled and diced
2   large onions, finely chopped
1   bay leaf
5   cups chicken stock (page 149)
1   cup heavy cream or milk
1   cup sweet sherry or port
    Salt
    Freshly ground black pepper
    Sprigs of watercress to garnish

Put the carrots, celery, watercress, potatoes, onions, bay leaf, and chicken stock into a good-sized soup pot. Cover and cook over a medium flame until all vegetables are tender. Remove and purée soup in blender until smooth, and return to pot. Add the cream, sherry, salt, and pepper. Milk may be added to thin the soup. Garnish with sprigs of fresh watercress.

ASSOCIATED HOLIDAY: MIDSUMMER

SERVES 4 TO 6

Oxtail Soup

Tarragon can cure snakebites when eaten or rubbed on a wound (British folk belief).

2	pounds meaty oxtails, cut into 2-inch pieces
¼	cup flour, seasoned if desired
½	stick butter for browning
1	celery stalk, chopped
1	large onion, peeled and chopped
3	carrots, sliced
¼	teaspoon thyme
¼	teaspoon tarragon
1	bay leaf
2	teaspoons salt, or to taste
¼	teaspoon pepper
5	cups beef stock (page 150)
5	cups water
½	cup watercress
1	cup port

Dredge the oxtail pieces in flour. Brown the meat and all the vegetables in the butter for about 5 minutes. Transfer ingredients to a large soup pot and add the thyme, tarragon, bay leaf, salt, beef stock, and water. Bring to a boil and skim the fat from surface of the soup.

Cover soup and simmer over low heat for about 4 hours. Remove from heat and strain into a bowl. Remove the meat and, when it has cooled, separate it from the bones and remove the fatty skin. Return the meat to the soup. If desired, purée the vegetables in a blender and return them to the soup, or else leave them whole. Transfer soup to a new soup pot and heat to just below the boiling point. Add the watercress and cook over medium heat 4–5 minutes. Add the port; season to taste and serve.

ASSOCIATED HOLIDAYS: HARVEST SUPPERS, YULE

SERVES 4 TO 6

See the cow, buy the sheep, but

never be without the horse.

WELSH PROVERB

Osian's Mother

From *The Fionn Cycle:*

It happened one time when Fionn and his men were coming back from the hunt. A beautiful fawn leapt up before them, and they followed after it, men and dogs, until at last they were all tired and fell back. All but Fionn himself, that is, along with Bran and Sceolan, his favorite hunting dogs.

As they were going through a valley, the fawn suddenly stopped and lay down on the smooth grass. Bran and Sceolan scamped up to it, and they did not haw it at all, but went playing about the fawn, licking its face.

Fionn was amazed when he saw his fierce hunting dogs frolicking with the deer, and when he went in for the kill his own dogs turned and growled at him. So the great leader of the Fianna had no choice but to return to Almhain, his home, with the fawn and his hounds following close behind.

When Fionn was alone that evening, a beautiful young woman approached him. She was dressed in a costly green gown and wore a torque of purest gold around her neck. "I am the fawn that you were hunting today," she said simply.

"What do you mean?" asked Fionn.

"For refusing the love of Fear Doiche, the Dark Druid, I was put into that shape. And for three years I have lived the life of a wild deer in a far part of this land, and I was hunted like a wild deer. But I learned that if I could reach the dun of the Fianna, the druid would have no more power over me. So I made away, and I never stopped until I saw Bran and Sceolan, who have human hearts. I was safe with them, for they knew my nature to be like their own."

Fionn gave the enchanted woman his love, and took her as his wife, and she stayed at Almhuin. So great was his love for her that he gave up hunting and all the things he used to take pleasure in, and he gave his mind and heart to no other but herself.

◆

Venison Soup

Ker is one of the earliest names for the Great Mother as the Grain Goddess. Sometimes she is called the Deer Mother, and she is the consort of the stag god Kernunnos. Her image is preserved in Scottish and Irish faerie tales about women who could turn themselves into deer.

Marmite, a dark yeast extract commonly found in grocery shops, replaces the blood that was once used in this recipe.

2	pounds venison cut in cubes
8-10	cups water
1	onion, diced
8	medium potatoes, peeled and cubed
5	carrots, peeled and sliced
½	cup currants or raisins
1	stick celery, diced
¼	cup barley
1	teaspoon salt, or to taste
1	clove garlic, crushed
½	teaspoon pepper, or to taste
2	cups beef stock
1	teaspoon marmite
1	bay leaf
1	pound chopped, mixed vegetables (frozen package will do)

Sear venison until brown on all sides. Cover with water. Add all other ingredients with the exception of the frozen vegetables and cook until meat is heated through. Remove the bay leaf and add the frozen vegetables. Serve with fresh brown bread and herbal butter (page 142).

ASSOCIATED HOLIDAYS: SAMHAIN, HARVEST FESTIVALS,
YULE, WINTER FEASTS, ESBAT CELEBRATIONS

SERVES 4 TO 6

The swiftness of the deer is known

without loosing the hounds.

SCOTTISH PROVERB

◆

Cock-a-leekie

Chicken today and feathers tomorrow (Irish proverb).

1	(4-pound) chicken
12	cups water
6	leeks, washed, trimmed, and cut into 1-inch pieces
¾	cup uncooked rice
2	teaspoons salt, or to taste
1½	pounds pitted prunes
½	cup chopped fresh parsley

Wash the chicken thoroughly and put it in a large soup pot. Pour in the water and bring to a boil. Add the leeks, rice, and salt. Cover and simmer gently for 2 hours. Add the prunes and continue to simmer for another 40 minutes. Remove from the heat and lift out the chicken. When cool enough to handle, remove the skin and cut the meat into bite-sized pieces. Return the meat to the soup and adjust seasoning. Sprinkle with parsley before serving. Be sure each guest gets at least one prune in their bowl.

ASSOCIATED HOLIDAYS: SAMHAIN, YULE

SERVES 6

Game Soup

The spoon is precious while the soup is being sipped (Galician proverb).

4   cups beef stock (page 150)
1   medium onion, quartered
1   pheasant, partridge or other game bird carcass
    Forequarters of 1 rabbit or hare
1   large carrot, roughly chopped
4   bay leaves
    Juice of 1 lemon
    Salt and pepper to taste
½   cup port or dry sherry
    Croutons for garnish

Place the beef stock, game bird carcass, rabbit meat, carrot, onion, and bay leaves in a large soup pot. Bring to a boil, cover, and simmer for about 1 hour. Strain through a sieve, reserving the carrot, onion, and any pieces of meat. Purée the meat, carrot, onion, and stock in a blender. Return to a clean pot; add the lemon juice, salt, pepper, and port. Reheat and serve with croutons.

ASSOCIATED HOLIDAYS: SAMHAIN, HARVEST FESTIVALS,
YULE, WINTER FEASTS, ESBAT CELEBRATIONS

SERVES 4 TO 6

Sorrel Soup

She who has burnt herself once blows on her soup (Galician proverb).

2   sticks butter
2   large onions, thinly sliced
4   garlic cloves, peeled and chopped
10   cups sorrel leaves, tightly packed
4   cups chicken stock (page 149)
½   cup chopped parsley
1   teaspoon salt, or to taste
1   teaspoon pepper, or to taste
2   teaspoons nutmeg
     Pinch of cayenne pepper
1   cup clabbered cream (see note)
     Chives or hard-boiled eggs for garnish

Melt the butter in a saucepan. Add the onions and garlic, cover, and cook over medium heat until tender, about 15 minutes. Add the sorrel, cover and cook about 5 minutes. Add chicken stock, parsley, salt, pepper, nutmeg, and cayenne pepper. Bring to a boil. Reduce heat, cover, and simmer for 1 hour. Purée soup in a blender until smooth. Return soup to the pot. Heat and stir over low heat. Ladle into bowls and swirl in spoonfuls of sour cream. Garnish with chives or eggs.

Note: Clabbered or "curdled" cream, if unavailable in your local market, can be replaced with sour cream in this recipe.

ASSOCIATED HOLIDAYS: MIDSUMMER, BELTAINE

SERVES 4

It is good to be hungry when
there is something to eat.

SCOTTISH PROVERB

◆

Herb Strewers

It was once the custom for English kings to have a royal Herb Strewer. The last official one attended the coronation of George IV. She wore a white gown over which was a mantle of gold and scarlet, trimmed in black, and a crown of oak and laurel leaves. She was attended by six maidens dressed in white gowns and crowned in greenery. Each pair carried a basket between them from which they strewed fragrant herbs. When reading the description, it reminds me very much of tales of the Goddess of Sovereignty, who confirmed the rightful kingship of those that would rule.

◆

Garlic Pottage

This recipe comes from The Good Housewife, *1692:*

Take water and oatmeal, stir it together and when it is ready to boyle bruise as much garlick or onion as you please, to make it either strong or weak, put this bruised garlick into your boyling hot gruel, and brew it to and fro with your ladle that it may not boyl, for five or six minutes. Then take it off and let it stand a little, then add butter, salt, and bread and eat it as warm as your blood. Tis a brave, warm, cleansing gruel, nothing so strong and nauseous as that which is boyled for this way you do extract the strong, nauseous qualities behind, but on the contrary much boyling, or boyling according to custom, does destroy the good cleansing vertues and awakens the evil.

ASSOCIATED HOLIDAYS: SPRINGTIME MEALS,
AS A CLEANSER FOR THE BODY

Nettle Soup

One day, when Columba was visiting the graveyard in Iona, he saw an old woman cutting nettles.

"Why are you cutting nettles?" asked Columba.

"Dear abbot," she replied. "I have only one cow, and it has not yet borne a calf. So in the meantime I am living on soup made from nettles."

As he walked on, Columba decided that he too should eat only nettle soup. If this woman eats nettles in expectation of milk, cream, butter, and cheese, he thought, then I too must surely eat nettles in expectation of God's kingdom. So when he returned to the monastery, he ordered the monk who prepared food to give him nettle soup from then on.

The monk was anxious that such a meager diet would kill the beloved abbot. So he made a special stick, hollow in the middle, for stirring the soup. And as he stirred Columba's soup he secretly poured milk through the stick from a bladder he hid in his sleeve.

Far from becoming ill, Columba thrived on nettle soup, little knowing that it was laced with milk. Soon he was urging other monks to follow his example and, seeing how healthy Columba looked, many were eager to try his strange diet. The poor monk in the kitchen now had to make a huge cauldron of nettle soup, pouring milk secretly through his stick.

After a few days the monastery ran out of milk, and the monk had no choice but to confess his trick to Columba. For a moment Columba's face went red with anger, then it broke into uproarious laughter.

"It is God's joke against me," Columba said. "It was only pride that made me tell others of my diet—so I deserve to be tricked."

And he ordered that from then onwards all the monks on Iona should eat proper meals.

◆

Tender handed stroke a nettle

and it stings you for your pains.

Grasp it like a man of mettle

and it soft as silk remains.

AARON HILL, 1750

Nettle Soup

In Ireland there was once an annual feast on May 1 called Féile na Neantóg. *On that day the children would chase each other around with bundles of stinging nettles. If they wet the nettles beforehand it put extra "heat" in them.*

Older people believed that nettle stings helped to cure rheumatism. People would throw off their clothes and roll in a bed of nettles, or have a family member "whip" them with bundles. Nettles are still taken as a spring tonic in many rural places where people believe it will clear the blood and keep away "the pains" for the rest of the year. Boiled as spinach, they afford an excellent green food during the early spring, when green vegetables are scarce in the garden. They go especially well with poultry—and the birds themselves seem to love them.

Nettle is also invested with magical properties. Wearing a sachet around your neck will remove a curse.

> 3 tablespoons butter
> 3 cups potatoes, peeled and chopped
> 1 onion, chopped
> 2 medium-sized leeks, chopped
>   Salt and pepper to taste
> 5 cups chicken stock (page 149)
> 1 cup young nettles, washed and chopped
> 1 cup cream

Melt the butter in a soup pot. Toss the potatoes, onion, and leeks in the butter. Season with salt and pepper to taste and simmer, covered, for 10 minutes. Add the chicken stock. Bring to a rolling boil, reduce heat, and add the nettle leaves (young nettles can be handled without fear). Simmer just a few minutes. Add the cream. Purée in a blender until smooth and serve hot.

Associated Holiday: Beltaine

Serves 4

Vegetables

*It's no use boiling
your cabbage twice.*

IRISH PROVERB

Welsh Bubble and Squeak

In Ireland it was once the custom to carry a potato in your pocket as a means of curing rheumatism. As the potato blackened, it carried away "the pains."

Bubble and Squeak, which gets its name from the bubbling and squeaking that takes place while cooking, can be served as an entrée with soup or salad. It is a great way to use leftover vegetables and meat.

4	cups cooked potatoes, barely mashed
4	cups cabbage, chopped and blanched
1	onion
2	cloves of garlic, pressed
1	small bunch chives
1	cup cooked, diced ham
4	bacon slices, cooked; reserve drippings
	Pepper to taste
½	cup turnips, boiled and mashed (optional)

The potatoes should be only slightly mashed, leaving them somewhat lumpy. Mix all ingredients into the potatoes except the bacon drippings (some people add turnips or other ground vegetables to the mixture, but more often than not I was served bubble and squeak with only potatoes and cabbage). Heat the bacon drippings in a frying pan. Add the potato mixture and form a large, flat cake. Brown over medium heat. Invert over a plate and serve with stout or homemade ale.

ASSOCIATED HOLIDAYS: HARVEST FESTIVALS

SERVES 6

Beauty does not make the pot boil.

WELSH PROVERB

Red Cabbage

Cabbage has grown wild in the Celtic countries for centuries, and has long been used as a salad or condiment. It has also been taken as a digestive remedy, a joint tonic, and as a treatment for fevers and skin problems. Raw cabbage was eaten to prevent drunkenness, and is still believed by some to effectively treat migraines. To ensure a good relationship, it should be the first thing planted in the garden by a married couple.

- 1 onion, peeled and chopped
- 2 tablespoons butter or oil
- 1 small red cabbage
- 2 baking apples
- 1 tablespoon red currant jelly
- 2 tablespoons cider vinegar or gooseberry vinegar (see below)
  Salt and pepper to taste
  Dash allspice (optional)

Sauté the onion in the oil until soft but not brown. Shred the cabbage, peel and slice the apples, and add both to the onion. Stir in the remaining ingredients and bring the whole mixture to a boil. Stir until the jelly dissolves. Cover and simmer gently for about 45 minutes, until the cabbage is tender.

Gooseberry Vinegar

Gooseberry juice, if applied to warts and sties, will cause them to vanish (English folk belief).

- 1 quart fresh gooseberries
- 3 quarts boiled water, cooled
- 1 pound dark brown sugar

Bruise the berries with a mortar and pestle and add them to three quarts of water. Let stand, covered, for 24 hours. Strain through cheesecloth twice. Mix in brown sugar, stirring to dissolve it. Pour mixture into sterilized glass bottles and store in a cool, dark location. In 6 months it should be ready for use. Makes 3 quarts.

ASSOCIATED HOLIDAYS: LUGHNASADH, HARVEST FESTIVALS

SERVES 4 TO 6

Pease Pudding

If you happen to find a pod containing exactly 9 peas, hang it above your door. The next person to walk in will be your future mate (English folk belief).

Write on a piece of paper "Come in, dear one, and do not fear." Place this in an empty pea shell and lay it under the door. The name of the first one to come through the door will foretell the name of your future husband.

Eating marigold petals or brewing them in tea will promote clairvoyant dreams, improve psychic abilities, and allow you to see faeries (Irish folk belief).

Although traditional pease pudding does not list marigolds among the main ingredients, the petals can be added for extra color. You may serve pease pudding directly from the bowl in which it has been cooked, or invert it onto a serving platter. Leftovers can be cut into slices and fried in butter.

1 pound split peas
¼ cup marigold petals (optional)
½ stick butter
2 eggs
Salt and pepper to taste

Prepare split peas according to package directions. Drain the peas and purée them in a blender. In a medium mixing bowl blend the puréed peas, marigold petals, butter, eggs, salt, and pepper. Spoon the mixture into a buttered pudding bowl with a 3-cup capacity. Cover tightly with aluminum foil and secure it with a piece of string tied around the rim of the bowl. Place the bowl on a steamer rack and steam for 1 hour. If you do not have a steamer rack, you may place the bowl on an inverted dish in a pot containing several inches of water. Cover the pot and steam pudding over low to medium heat for 1 hour.

Pease Porridge hot,

pease porridge cold,

pease porridge in the pot,

nine days old.

Some like it hot,

some like it cold,

some like it in the pot

nine days old.

BRITISH NURSERY RHYME

ASSOCIATED HOLIDAYS: SAMHAIN, MABON, YULE

SERVES 4 TO 6

Champm

A beetle (referenced in the rhyme below) was a heavy wooden pestle used to mash large tubs full of potatoes in the days when they were the main food of the Irish. (This was usually considered to be a man's job.) A common Irish folk custom was to offer a bowl of champ to the faeries at Samhain. It would be left under hawthorn or whitethorn trees, which were also associated with the Goddess as Crone.

10	scallions, chopped
1½	cups milk
3½	cups hot mashed potatoes
4	tablespoons butter, melted
	Salt and pepper to taste

Cook the chopped scallions, including the green parts, in the milk. Drain and reserve the milk. Add the scallions to mashed potatoes. Beat together and add enough of the hot milk to make the dish creamy and smooth. Season to taste. Put into a deep warmed dish, make a well in the center, and pour the hot melted butter into it. The potato is dipped into the well of butter when serving.

Variations: You may wish to add chives or parsley to the milk while cooking the scallions, or omit the scallions altogether and add fresh peas, nettles, or leeks.

ASSOCIATED HOLIDAYS: SAMHAIN, ESBAT DINNERS

SERVES 4

There was an old woman who lived in a lamp

she had no room to beetle her champ.

She's up with her beetle and broke the lamp

and then she had room to beetle her champ.

IRISH NURSERY RHYME

Marigold Pudding

This is an old recipe I found in a seventeenth-century cookbook, where it was suggested the pudding be made "with flowers gathered at noon, or in the heat of the day," when they will strengthen the heart.

Marigolds are at their peak strength on Midsummer. Touching them to your bare feet will allow you to understand the speech of animals and birds, while placing them under your pillow will protect you from evil.

2	cups marigold petals
1	pint cream or new milk
1	pound beef suet
2	cups dried bread crumbs

Mix all ingredients together and pour into a pudding bag. Boil for 1 hour.

ASSOCIATED HOLIDAYS: MIDSUMMER, LUGHNASADH

SERVES 4

Buttered Leeks

Thyme wards off negativity. Add it to your vegetable dishes to promote a positive mental attitude.

Leeks are a native vegetable that have been grown in Britain for thousands of years. The eleventh-century Vision of Mac con Glinne *speaks of a forest full of leeks and onions as tall as trees. Leeks are particularly abundant in Wales and are used in many traditional Welsh recipes, such as the one given here. Leeks are associated with St. David of Wales, and should be eaten on his feast day.*

7	leeks
1	stick butter
5	teaspoons bread crumbs
	Juice and zest of 1 lemon
	Small sprigs of lemon thyme
	Salt and pepper to taste

Bring a medium pot of water to a boil. Cut away the tops and roots of the leeks and wash them in cold water. When the water is boiling, add the leeks and cook for 10 to 12 minutes. They are done when you can easily pierce them with a fork. Drain and set aside. In a separate pan, melt the butter and cook to a light brown color. Add the bread crumbs, lemon juice, zest, lemon thyme, salt and pepper. Fry until the bread crumbs are a golden brown color and pour over the leeks. Serve hot.

ASSOCIATED HOLIDAYS: ST. DAVID'S DAY, LUGHNASADH

SERVES 4

Peas with Onions and Cauliflower

It was believed that basil must be sown while spouting words of abuse, or else it would not flourish. The plant is said to be associated with death, but strangely, it is also a love charm. If exposed too long in the sun, according to several medieval herbals, "it will turn into wild thyme."

Planting and sowing should be attempted during a waxing moon, because the growth of the moon helps the young plants prosper. However beans and peas, whose vines grow counterclockwise, are usually planted during a waning moon.

- 4 cups fresh peas
- 2 medium yellow onions, sliced
- 1 sprig parsley, chopped
- 2 stalks fresh basil, chopped, or 1 tablespoon dried basil
- ¼ cup butter
- ¼ teaspoon salt, or to taste
- 8 small cauliflower florets
- ½ cup water
- 3 leaves green leaf lettuce

Put first 8 ingredients in a medium saucepan, covering with the lettuce leaves and a snug-fitting lid. Bring to a boil over medium heat and cook until peas are tender, about 15 minutes.

ASSOCIATED HOLIDAYS:
MIDSUMMER, LUGHNASADH

SERVES 4 TO 6

The Widow and the Wimblestone

The Wimblestone, which stands near Shipham, is said to conceal a great horde of gold, hidden away long ago by the faeries before they retired beneath the hills. An enchantment protects the stone, and anyone who dares to dig for the treasure is sure to encounter some terrible misfortune — or be swept away by the faeries, never to be seen in the mortal realms again.

Yet it must be tiring for a stone to remain standing for so long. Sometimes, it is said, the stone deserts its post as keeper of the gold for the pursuit of dancing—although nowadays these nights seem few and far between.

A young woman named Blathnet Davies was on her way back from hay-making on Midsummer's Eve when she saw a huge dark bulk rustling along the hedge near her garden. She was terrified and threw herself down in fear behind the rows of beans. Peeping through shaking fingers she saw the whole garden in bright moonlight and the Wimblestone hopping and skipping with cumbersome grace among the cabbage heads. In the place where the stone usually stood, a pile of bright stones glittered and shone. Blathnet's eyes widened with greed but then her fear again overcame her. She uttered a shriek and took to her heels and didn't stop running until she reached the safety of the local inn.

Of course her friends scoffed at her, most of them not daring to believe her tale, others calling her a fool for not filling her pockets when she had the chance. Blathnet thoughtfully sipped her pint of ale and said, "If you had been in my shoes, you would not say such things to me. If you had seen that great hulk of rock dancing in your cabbage patch, you would have run for your lives in terror."

Although the stone had returned to its rightful place, Blathnet's mother believed her daughter's story. "Strange magic is afoot," she whispered. "Midsummer magic—nothing good can come of it. I want that mischievous stone out of my garden!"

So the old widow woman harnessed her two strongest shire horses to the stone and spent all night vainly trying to topple it. The horses heaved until the sweat ran down their flanks—but to no avail. The widow even stepped into the yoke with the workhorses and pulled and tugged and strained until she too could hardly stand. All the time the stone budged not an inch.

"If I didn't know you, Blathnet," said her mother, mopping her face with a handkerchief, "I would not credit your story." And so the pair gave up and went back to their cottage. But as soon as they were out of sight, the Wimblestone creaked out of its position and started dancing through the garden. It trampled on the cauliflower and dug up the potatoes and beets. Then it skipped and stumped across the moors; it roamed and tripped along the hills; and it tumbled and rolled through the valleys until cockcrow. When the widow and her daughter awoke the next morning, they saw their garden was a shambles, and the Wimblestone back in its place.

Stoved Tatties

It may be surprising to learn that the potato, a staple crop in many Celtic lands, does in fact come from a family of poisonous plants that includes henbane and deadly nightshade. The foliage of the potato plant contains solanine, and can cause fatalities if taken internally. In some communities it was customary to give the name of a fertility goddess to the first potato harvested, and to divide it among the family. In Scotland potatoes are known as "tatties," and stoved tatties are so called because they are cooked on the stove.

When I was younger, we called these "salt-and-pepper potatoes," and ate them with hearty dollops of sour cream alongside pork chops and fried apples. Delicious!

> 5   potatoes, peeled and sliced thin
>   Butter or oil for frying
>   Salt and pepper to taste
>   Sour cream or herbal butter (optional)

Fry the potatoes in a heavy saucepan. Sprinkle with salt and pepper. Cover and cook over low heat for 30 minutes, or until the potatoes are soft. You may try serving these with sour cream or herbal butter (page 142).

ASSOCIATED HOLIDAYS: SAMHAIN, YULE

SERVES 4

It's easy to halve a potato

where there's love.

SCOTTISH PROVERB

Did you ever eat Colcannon

When 'twas made with thick'n'd cream

And the greens and scallions blended

Like the picture in a dream?

Did you ever scoop a hole on top

To hold the melting cake

Of clover-flavored butter

That your mother used to make?

Did you ever eat and eat, afraid

You'd let the ring go past,

And some old married sprissman

Would get it at the last?

God be with the happy times

When trouble we had not

And our mother made Colcannon

In the little three-legged pot.

Colcannon

Samhain has long been associated with divination spells. Today colcannon, like barm brack, is eaten at Hallowe'en and often has several charms added to it.

2–2⅓ pounds potatoes
1   cup cabbage, cooked
1   small onion, chopped, or scallions
  Butter
  Salt and pepper to taste
  Ring, coin, stick, pea, thimble
    (each wrapped in parchment, or waxed, paper)

Boil the potatoes; skin, drain, and mash. Chop up the cooked cabbage and mix in with the mashed potatoes. Chop the onion and sauté in butter until soft; mix into the potatoes and cabbage. Fold in the charms. The ring stands for marriage, the coin for wealth, the pea for poverty, the thimble for spinsterhood, and the stick for one who will travel far. Serve on hot plates with a well of butter in the center of each mound.

ASSOCIATED HOLIDAYS: SAMHAIN, ESBAT DINNERS

SERVES 4

Chestnuts and Brussels Sprouts

Although delicious with salt and pepper alone, chestnuts and brussels sprouts can be enhanced with herbs such as basil or dill, or with caraway seeds.

The name "Dill" is said to come from the Anglo-Saxon word dillan, *to lull, because a decoction was made from the seeds to soothe babies to sleep. Dill is often used in charms against harmful magic.*

Basil is also a magical herb, and if crushed between bricks it will turn into scorpions.

1	pound chestnuts, skinned
1½	pounds Brussels sprouts
	Salt and pepper to taste
	Pinch of ginger
¼	cup butter
	Basil, dill, and caraway seeds (optional)

For the best dish, choose the biggest chestnuts and the smallest sprouts. To skin the chestnuts, make a cut along the flat side of each nut and drop into a pan of salted water. Boil for 5 minutes, then remove a couple at a time, as they have to be peeled while hot. Remove outer shell and inner skin. Simmer skinned nuts in a pan of fresh, salted water for 15 minutes until tender. Drain and set aside. Cut a cross in the bottom of the stalk of each Brussels sprout. Soak in cold water for 10 minutes. Boil in a small amount of salted water for about 8 minutes; drain. Return the sprouts to the pan, add nuts, and season with salt and pepper. Stir in the ginger and butter just before serving.

Variations: If you enjoy herbs with your vegetables, try adding a dash of basil, dill, or caraway seeds to the Brussels sprouts when you add the salt and pepper.

ASSOCIATED HOLIDAYS: YULE, WINTER CELEBRATIONS, NAME DAYS/BIRTHDAYS

SERVES 6

Baked Onions

Throughout Ireland it is well-known that you must not leave cut-up onions or onion peels in the house; to do so is unlucky. Don't throw them away, however, for to do so you toss away prosperity. They should be burned, buried, or composted. In Wales, if you leave a cut onion on a saucer it will absorb harmful emotions of those around you. If left in a sick room, it will absorb the illness. In England, if you throw one at the bride as she leaves the church, she will never have cause to weep during her marriage.

1 large onion, peeled
  Water
  Salt and pepper to taste
  Herbal butter (page 142)

Put the onion in a baking dish with about 1 inch of water—no more. Bake onion at 275 degrees for 1½ to 2 hours or until it is soft when squeezed. Pull back the browned skin and cut off at the root. Eat with salt, pepper, and a little herbal butter.

ASSOCIATED HOLIDAYS: YULE, WINTER CELEBRATIONS

SERVES 1

For this is every cook's opinion,

No savory dish without an onion;

But lest your kissing should be spoiled

The onion must be thoroughly boiled.

Or else you may spare

your mistress a share,

The secret will never be known:

She cannot discover

The breath of her lover,

But think it as sweet as her own.

JONATHAN SWIFT

◆

Sweet Peas with Mint

Fresh mint will conjure friendly spirits to aid your magic spells. Make a brush of mint leaves, dip them in sea water (or salted water) and sprinkle the four corners of your home to drive out evil. The smell of the mint is also rather soothing.

In England and Wales the old name for mint was "Our Lady's Herb." In Italy it is called "Erbe Santa Maria," and in France, "Menthe de Notre Dame," names which honor the Virgin Mary, but which are probably even older than her. It is thought that there are at least thirty species of mint, with the most commonly used varieties including peppermint, field mint, and spearmint. All varieties have the property of preventing milk from curdling. An old folk belief says that you should never cut mint with an iron instrument, indicating the herb was once sacred to the faeries.

Mint is another plant that has a long history of medicinal as well as culinary uses. An infusion of the leaves can be used for nausea, travel sickness, flatulence, and migraines. Because I sometimes have problems drinking milk, I will soak a few leaves of mint in it first. A compress soaked in an infusion can be used to cool inflamed joints associated with rheumatism, while a steam created from boiling leaves in water can be inhaled to ease nasal congestion. It also makes an interesting accompaniment to vegetables, and is a great breath freshener.

- 1   pound fresh or frozen peas
- ¼   cup sweet cream butter
- 2   tablespoons chopped fresh garden mint
- 1   teaspoon sugar
-     Salt and pepper to taste
-     Green food coloring (optional)

If using frozen peas, cook according to package directions. For freshly shelled peas cook in boiling water for approximately 5 minutes. Drain and set aside. In another saucepan heat the butter until melted. Add the peas, mint, and sugar. Toss and heat gently for several minutes. Season to taste with salt and pepper and serve. A few drops of food coloring can be added to the peas while cooking to give it a gloriously green color.

ASSOCIATED HOLIDAYS: MIDSUMMER, LUGHNASADH, YULE,
WINTER CELEBRATIONS, ESBAT DINNERS

SERVES 4 TO 6

Mushrooms in Cream

Wild mushrooms, chanterelles, morels, hedgehogs, deceivers, and truffles can still be found in the woods of Celtic lands. There are many folktales and songs linking the Others with mushrooms, whose sudden appearance and rapid growth are surely a sign of magic. (If you look at a mushroom, however, it will cease to grow.) A circle of mushrooms growing in a grassy area is known as a faerie ring because the dancing feet of faeries created the mushrooms. Cattle are said to avoid faerie rings, and it is unwise to step into one or fall asleep inside it, as these circles are gateways to the faerie realm. The mushroom most associated with faeries is the red-and-white Fly Agaric, with hallucinogenic (and sometimes deadly) powers. While Viking warriors would eat this magical fungus to gain their fighting frenzy known as "Berserk," the Celts stayed away from it. They had a taboo on these red mushrooms, as they did many other red foods, considering them to belong to the Gods.

This recipe for mushrooms has to be one of the most widely traveled of Celtic recipes. Once, when I was trekking through Nepal, I stopped at a restaurant in Kathmandu run by an expatriate Irish-American. Among such surprises as huevos rancheros, *he had a number of typical British foods.*

If you have gathered the mushrooms yourself, be sure that you have properly identified them. Many species of mushrooms are poisonous.

1   pound mushrooms
2   tablespoons butter, melted
1   cup cream
    Fresh thyme and parsley (see note)
    Salt and pepper to taste

Clean but do not peel the mushrooms. Place them in a single layer in a buttered baking dish and dribble the butter over them. Bake at 400 degrees until soft (this should only take a minute or two). Pour cream over mushrooms and heat in the oven but do not allow to boil. Sprinkle with the chopped fresh herbs and the salt and pepper just before serving. Serve with bread to mop up the juices. A great accompaniment to grilled meats, particularly steak.

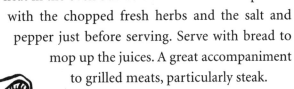

Note: Other herbs that go particularly well with mushrooms include coriander, tarragon, rosemary, oregano, and marjoram.

Associated Holidays: Beltaine, Midsummer, Lughnasadh, Yule

Serves 4

Beets with Cloves and Cinnamon

If you use beet juice to write your love letters, the object of your affection will find you irresistible (Irish belief).

1	pound small beets
	Salted water to cover
	Dash of cloves
	Dash of cinnamon
¼	cup butter
	Salt and pepper to taste

Wash the beets and cut off the stalks; do not remove the skins. Drop into a pan of boiling, salted water and cook until tender—about 45 minutes to 1 hour. If the skin comes off easily, they are done. Peel the beets and discard the cooking water. Return the beets to the saucepan and toss for a few minutes with the cloves, cinnamon, and butter. Season to taste with salt and pepper.

Variations: Beets are a versatile vegetable, and can be seasoned in a variety of ways. Instead of cloves and cinnamon, you can try parsley and chives. For a non-traditional variation, pineapples, orange slices, and brown sugar can be added for a sweeter dish—and one appropriate for sun celebrations.

ASSOCIATED HOLIDAYS: SAMHAIN, MABON, ESBAT DINNERS

SERVES 4

A farmer's work is never done.

IRISH PROVERB

Braised Spinach

Originally, the "wearing of the green" was not associated with St. Patrick's Day, but was used as a bit of sympathetic magic to encourage the arrival of springtime and the prosperity of the crops. Green was associated with the Otherworld, and faeries, sprites, and elves all are said to dress in green clothing. Robin Hood and his Merry Men—modern equivalents of the Green Man who attended the May Queen— were said to have dressed in green. Many captured mortals, such as True Thomas, wore green in the faerie realm.

Throughout much of British and Irish history, peasants used fennel to curb the pangs of hunger and to make aging food more palatable. In a seventeenth-century herbal we learn that "A serpent doth so hate the ashtree that she will not come night the shadow of it, but she delights in fennel so much, which she eats to clear her eyesight." Fennel was a versatile vegetable; the stalks were peeled and used in celery, and the leaves were used in salads. In magical terms, fennel may be used to weave protection spells, and should be hung over the doors and windows of your house on Midsummer's Eve to keep out unwanted spirits.

2   **pounds fresh spinach**
     Salted water for parboiling
3   **tablespoons olive oil**
¼   **teaspoon salt**
     Pinch each of ginger and allspice

Parboil the spinach in a large pot of water for about 4 minutes; drain, press out excess water with your hands, and chop. Put it in a saucepan or small casserole with oil and seasonings. Stir and leave to cook over very low heat for another 15 minutes, or put covered casserole dish in a slow oven for about 20 minutes.

Variations: Add parsley and fennel with a little chicken broth instead of the oil.

ASSOCIATED HOLIDAYS: LUGHNASADH, SAMHAIN, YULE

SERVES 4 TO 6

More grows on a tilled field

than is sown in it.

WELSH PROVERB

The Great Potato

Mairéad Ní Mhaonaigh lent herself out at the hiring fair in Donegal. Ciaran Byrne, her master, thought highly of her, and rich were his praises. But Mairéad had one problem, and that was that she was a terrible liar.

In harvest time, when they were digging potatoes, Ciaran dug up one the likes of which he had never seen. "Mairéad, my girl, did you ever see such a big potato on your father's farm?"

"I did," said Mairéad, brushing a strand of red hair from her eye. "And one that was bigger yet."

"Hmmph!" frowned Ciaran. "I don't believe you. You can't have seen a bigger one than this."

"There was one summer, back in '46, when the blight struck, and my father had a lot of rotten potatoes, all black and twisted," said Mairéad. "He threw them all into a compost heap, and the following summer a big potato stalk grew up out of the heap. It had plenty of manure in those potatoes, don't you see, and it grew as tall, aye taller, than the oak tree in the yard. I climbed to the top and could see the church spires in London Town, and I waved to the bellpuller in his tower. At harvest time father went to the compost pile, and he found that one giant potato grew from the plant. It took all six of my brothers to lift it, and it fed the village all winter long, although I must say come spring I was rather tired of it!"

"That was surely a big potato," said Ciaran, saying nothing more.

Yet sometime soon after that, Ciaran Byrne came into the cottage with a great cabbage head. "Mairéad! Come quick! Did you ever see a cabbage head bigger than this? Surely it will win me a prize at the fair!"

"Well," shrugged Mairéad, darning socks by the open window, "it's a fine cabbage, surely, and will no doubt win you some acclaim. But I would be lying if I said I never saw its like. In fact, I saw one that was much bigger."

"Did you, now?" said Ciaran, carefully placing the cabbage on the table.

"Aye, surely," nodded Mairéad. "There came a year when my mother had a very good crop of cabbage, on account of it having been blessed by the bishop himself. One rainy day the old speckled cow took shelter under one of the cabbage leaves. There was so much water trapped on that leaf that it rushed out in a stream, and swept our poor cow away. She drowned, you see, but she provided us with meat all the winter long. Although I must say that come spring I was rather tired of cabbage and beef."

"My, that was surely a big cabbage head, indeed," was all that Ciaran said.

A few days later he came into the cottage with a huge round of hard cheese. He hefted it up onto the table, and the wood creaked with the weight of it. "Did your mother ever make a round of cheese as great as this?" he said with pride.

Mairéad glanced up from where she was shelling peas. "She had, of course."

"Why don't you tell me about it."

"Well, one spring we had an awful lot of milk, and no place to store it. My mother dug a hole in the back field and poured the milk into it, with the hopes of making a cheese. I told her she was foolish, of course, for whoever heard of making cheese in that manner? But what did I know!

"We had a wolfhound at that time, and one day she disappeared, and we saw her no more. We thought that she had been stolen, and searched all over the village for her. I must say I was brokenhearted, for I was rather fond of that dear dog. At the end of summer my youngest brother, Teig, went to take a look at the cheese, and what should jump out but our dear wolfhound and a litter of pups! They had eaten their way out of the cheese, you see."

"That was a greater cheese than this," said Ciaran.

"It was, indeed. We shared it with our neighbors, and the people in the next parish, but we still had a great deal of cheese left over. That winter we ate it every day for supper—imagine that! But I must say I was rather tired of cheese come springtime."

Ciaran studied the girl for a moment. "Mairéad, listen to me now. There's a brother of mine to be hanged tomorrow."

"I did not know you had a brother. What did he do?" asked Mairéad.

"It does not matter, really. I think he was falsely accused. But what is important is that if there is anyone who can save his life, it's you. If you can, I'll give you a thousand pounds, and will release you from your contract."

"A thousand pounds! With that much money I'll be able to marry my sweetheart! He is, if you must know, the youngest son of the king of France, but he lost his inheritance while gambling on the racing tournaments in Dublin. I'll have a try," said Mairéad, "although I'm not sure what you expect me to do."

"Just be yourself, my girl, just be yourself," Ciaran laughed.

The next day Mairéad and Ciaran went to where his brother was to be hanged. There was a large crowd of people gathered to see the hanging, as there always is at such events. The noose was placed around the neck of the criminal, and the black-hooded hangman about to let him drop, when Mairéad suddenly shouted "Stop!"

All eyes turned to her, including those of the hangman. "What is it?" he demanded. "I hate being interrupted in my work."

"I have something to say to you all," Mairéad said, jumping up onto the gallows. "I've come to correct a grave error. A serious wrong! An innocent man is about to die, and there's one here in the crowd who ought to be hanged in his stead. I'm now going to tell you a story, and when I am done, the one who should be hanged will call me a liar."

"Very well," sighed the hangman. "Tell us your story, but be quick about it. There are those who have traveled far to see this man hanged, and I have itchy fingers."

Mairéad turned to face the crowd, and she said, "When my father died, the farm was divided between my five older brothers, my wee baby brother, and myself. A dozen acres were left to me in the will, along with instructions to tend it well. If not, I would have to give it to the local sisterhood for use by their dairy herd.

"I bought a strong plow horse, for my brothers left me none, and I plowed up the land. When I was done, I found that all the seed in Ireland had been purchased, and me left with none. My brothers had none to spare, for they had already planted it in their own furrows. There was no hope for it, but I'd have to go to Scotland. So one morning I got a blessing from the parish priest, saddled up my plow horse, and swam all the way to Aberdeen. Lucky for me my horse was a strong swimmer, descended as she was from the very same horses that pulled Mac Lir the sea god's chariot. I went ashore and bought a dozen sacks of grain at the market, although I think I paid too much for them. The Scots drive a hard bargain, as anyone can tell you. I tied the sacks of grain to the saddle of my horse, and sat on top of the load myself. And then we swam back to Donegal.

"Strong as my horse was, she was tired by that time, and who can blame her, poor thing? The teasing, taunting merfolk and selkies pulled on her mane and tail, trying to drag us below the waves.

"But we made it to shore, and when we did my horse sank to her knees on the solid ground. It looked as if she would never rise again, and I wept a moment, wondering how I would carry the grain back by myself. But there was a tree growing nearby. I broke off a branch of it and shoved it into the old horse to use as a new backbone. Up she jumped, good as new, and I was able to take the grain home.

"Well, I planted that grain, and when it was ready for harvesting, I went to take a look at the crop. I had no money to hire any help, my brothers were all busy, and it would take me a long time to reap it myself. I had about three or four sheaves cut with my reaping hook when a rabbit rose up at my feet. I threw the hook at her, already imagining a rabbit stew, and the handle of it stuck into her side. Down along the trench the rabbit ran, and I after her, trying to get back my hook. I loved that hook, and did not want another. I followed that beast up and down all the trenches until she ran out of the field at last. I was sorely angry at the loss of my hook and my dinner, but when I looked around me, wasn't the whole field of grain reaped by the rabbit herself? I carried it all into the barn and threshed it by myself. I had no money to hire a man to take it to the mill for grinding, and my brothers were all busy with their harvest, so I went in search of my old horse again. Round about supper-time I found her, with a fine sturdy tree growing out of her. The poor creature was rooted to the spot, terribly thirsty because the spring ran past the other side of the barn. I heard a sound above me, and I sprang upon the horse's back, and climbed the tree to the very top. Could you guess what I found there? A red salmon inside its nest, and plenty of water to quench my horse's thirst."

"You're a liar!" shouted an old fisherman who was in the crowd. "I've sailed the seas for seventy years, and that's one thing I'd swear a salmon never had— a nest!"

"Now, my friends," said Mairéad, "that's the man who should be hanged and not the other."

So they hanged the fisherman instead, and Mairéad, Ciaran, and his brother all went home.

A good farmer

is known by his crops.

Breton Proverb

Pan Haggerty

Plant your potatoes when you will, they won't come up until April (British folk belief).

You will need to use a firm-fleshed potato or risk them falling apart while cooking.

3 tablespoons bacon fat, butter, or lard
4 potatoes, peeled and sliced thin
2 onions, chopped fine
1 cup grated Lancashire, cheddar,
   or other sharp cheese
  Salt and pepper to taste
3 slices fried bacon, crumbled

Melt the bacon fat in a heavy oven-proof frying pan over low heat. Create layers of the potatoes, onions, and cheese, ending with a layer of potatoes on top. Season each layer with a little salt and pepper, if desired. Fry gently for about 30 minutes. Sprinkle with crumbled bacon and a little more of the grated cheese and transfer the pan to the broiler. Cook for about 5 minutes, or until the top is well browned and the cheese is bubbly. Serve straight from the frying pan.

ASSOCIATED HOLIDAYS: LUGHNASADH, SAMHAIN, YULE

SERVES 4 TO 6

Three sounds of increase:

the lowing of a cow in milk,

the din of a smithy,

the hiss of the plough.

WELSH TRIAD

Michaelmas Salad

Parsley should be planted by a pregnant woman to attract a good soul for the child in her womb. It's also taken to prevent miscarriages. Parsley should be raised in your own garden, and planted by the light of the rising moon at Ostara or Good Friday, depending on your traditions. If kept in the pocket, it will protect you from faerie mischief. It is bad luck to give away or to receive parsley as a gift. It is also bad luck to transplant it. It is said that parsley seed goes seven times to the devil and back before it germinates, and that is why it is so slow in coming up. To hurry it along, herbalist Thomas Hyll gave this advice:

To make the seedes appear more quickly steep them in vinegar and strew the bed with the ashes of beanwater with the best aqua vitae, and then cover the beds with a piece of woolen cloth, and the plants will begin to appear in an hour. You must take off the cloth so that they may shoot up the higher to the wonder of all beholders!

This salad is very good with smoked salmon and with any herring dishes. It is also delicious on its own or try with soda bread for a light lunch. Be careful how much mustard you use on the salad, for it is a fertility herb!

1½	pounds freshly boiled beets, chopped
1	bunch scallions, chopped
1	bunch fresh dill, chopped
2	tablespoons fresh parsley, chopped
2	hard-boiled eggs, chopped
1	carrot, thinly sliced
2	potatoes, boiled and diced
	Mustard
⅔	cup olive oil
1	clove garlic, minced
⅓	cup lemon juice

Put the first seven ingredients in a glass bowl. Dress with a vinaigrette made with the mustard, olive oil, garlic, and lemon juice. Toss well and serve at once.

ASSOCIATED HOLIDAYS:
MICHAELMAS, YULE,
ESBAT DINNERS

SERVES 4

Never bolt your door

with a boiled carrot.

IRISH PROVERB

Punchnep

The original jack o'lanterns were not pumpkins, but turnips. At Samhain all hearth fires were extinguished, and a new one kindled from the communal bonfire. Each family would cary home a coal in a hollowed turnip.

1	pound potatoes
1	pound turnips
1	stick butter, divided
1	small apple, peeled, boiled and mashed (optional)
¼	cup cream (optional)

This dish works best if you do not mash the vegetables and fruit together. Peel both the potatoes and turnips and boil them in separate pots until they are tender. Drain and mash them separately. (If desired, boil and mash an apple in a separate bowl for a dish with a slightly sweeter taste.) Divide the butter between the dishes and blend into the vegetables. Combine the mixtures and season to taste with salt and pepper. Beat thoroughly. If desired, make several holes in the purée with the end of a wooden spoon and pour the cream into the holes. Serve at once.

ASSOCIATED HOLIDAYS: LUGHNASADH, MABON, SAMHAIN

SERVES 4

Sunshine Mash

Place a few petals of marigolds in your pillow to promote good dreams of your future love.

½	pound carrots, peeled and sliced
1½	pounds parsnips, peeled and sliced
	Butter to taste
	Salt, pepper, and sugar to taste
	Chopped fresh parsley, marigolds, or other edible flowers for garnish

Bring a medium pot of water to a boil, and add a pinch of salt and sugar if desired. Add the carrots and cook until tender. Cook the parsnips in a separate pot of boiling, salted water until tender. Strain each, and mash or purée vegetables together. Add butter, salt, and pepper to taste and serve with a parsley or floral garnish.

ASSOCIATED HOLIDAYS: MIDSUMMER, LUGHNASADH, SUN FESTIVALS

SERVES 4

Seakale with Butter

Seakale, which grows on the rocky strands around the coasts of Ireland and Britain, is one of the most delicious of the wild vegetables. It need only be enhanced with a bit of butter and pepper to make an excellent side dish for seafood.

 1   pound seakale (see note)
     Sea salt and pepper to taste
 ½   cup butter, melted, or try
     with minted herbal butter (page 142)

Wash the seakale and trim into 3-inch pieces. Bring a medium saucepot to boil, and toss in a generous pinch of sea salt. Add the seakale, cover, and boil for about 15 minutes, or until tender. Drain and serve with additional sea salt, pepper, and melted butter.

Note: Seakale can sometimes be found in specialty food shops or growing along the coast of North America.

ASSOCIATED HOLIDAYS: BELTAINE, MIDSUMMER, ESBAT SUPPERS

SERVES 4

Fine words

butter no parsnips.

WELSH PROVERB

Green Beans and Almonds

There is a great deal of folklore surrounding beans. Because beans grow widdershins (anti-sunwise), they should be planted at night. But be careful not to fall asleep at the task, for sleeping in a beanfield will cause nightmares and unpleasant visions. Carrying a bean in your mouth is a charm against evil magic. Hold a bean under your tongue and spit it out at one you believe has cast an evil spell on you. He will no longer have any power.

The Scots believe that you should rub a dried bean on your warts or other skin lesions the night of the full moon. Then bury the bean. As the bean decays, so will your warts disappear.

The original Jack and the Beanstalk of British folklore was really the god Odin in his guise as Jalk the Giantkiller. Jalk was preserved in the Shrovetide carnival figure the King of the Bean. Likewise, the man who received a bean in his plum pudding in Scottish Twelfth Night festivities was known as the Bean King, he would be monarch of the festivities and all would do his bidding. Mary Queen of Scots added a Bean Queen to the celebration. In 1676, Henry Teanague wrote, "We had a great cake made, in which was put a bean for the King, a pease for the queen, a clove for the knave, a forked stick for the cockhold, and a rag for the slut."

1	**pound green beans**
2	**tablespoons slivered almonds**
2	**tablespoons herbal butter (page 142)**
	Juice of 1 lemon
	Fresh parsley garnish

Remove ends and strings on the beans and slice diagonally. Cook, covered, in a small amount of boiling salted water till crisp tender, about 3 to 5 minutes. Drain. Sauté almonds in butter until golden, stirring occasionally. Remove from heat and stir in lemon juice. Pour over the beans and serve with parsley for a garnish.

ASSOCIATED HOLIDAYS: YULE, TWELFTH NIGHT, WINTER CELEBRATIONS

SERVES 4

Sew peas and beans

in the wane of the moon,

who soweth them sooner,

soweth too soon.

ENGLISH RHYME

Watercress Salad

He saw three women dressed in battle clothes before him, and they said, "We are three sisters come from Tir na nÓg, the country of the ever-young, and we will help you. We will make druid armies for you from stalks of grass and from the tops of the watercress, and they will cry out to the strangers and strike them and take from them their strength" (from The Fionn Cycle*).*

1	**bunch watercress**
	Salt to taste
¼	**cup oil**
¼	**cup vinegar or lemon juice**

Clean and wash watercress, cut stems and drain thoroughly. Salt watercress. Mix with oil and vinegar, pour over watercress and serve.

ASSOCIATED HOLIDAY: MIDSUMMER

SERVES 4

The Three who are over me,

The Three who are below me,

The Three who are above me here,

The Three who are above me yonder;

The Three who are in the Earth,

The Three who are in the Air,

The Three who are in the Heavens,

The Three who are in the great pouring sea,

Bless and protect me from harm.

EARLY CELTIC PRAYER

Spinach Greens with Garlic

From King Arthur at Avalon: *We came to that green and fertile island which each year is blessed with two autumns, two springs, two summers, two gatherings of fruit. It is the land where pearls are found, where the flowers spring as you gather them, and where there are vast orchards. No tillage there, no coulter to tear the bosom of the earth. Without labor it affords wheat and grape. And there live nine sisters, whose will is the only law, and they rule over those who go from us to them. The eldest excels in the art of healing, and exceeds her sisters in beauty. She is called Morgana, and she knows the virtues of all the herbs of the meadow. She can change her form, and soar in the air like a bird. She can be where she pleases in a moment, and in a moment descend on our coasts from the clouds.*

2	pounds fresh spinach leaves
½	cup water
1	tablespoon butter
1	tablespoon flour
1	tablespoon sour cream
1	teaspoon crushed garlic
1	egg, beaten
	Salt and pepper to taste

Clean and wash the spinach leaves. Over very low heat, simmer spinach in the water for 10 minutes. Rinse in cold water, drain thoroughly, and chop in a blender. Set aside. Melt the butter and stir in the flour, making a smooth paste. Add the spinach, sour cream, garlic, egg, salt, and pepper. Toss well. Heat greens, stirring constantly, and serve.

ASSOCIATED HOLIDAYS: MIDSUMMER, LUGHNASADH

SERVES 4

Spring Pudding

Reminiscent of the virgin's cloak in medieval paintings, the leaves with scalloped edges are reputed to have given Lady's Mantle its name, although others claim the plant was sacred to the Goddess. Lady's Mantle became an important herb in the sixteenth century when alchemists would collect the magical dew that gathered in the leaves each morning. Like many herbs with "lady" or "mother" as part of their name, Lady's Mantle is a valuable gynecological herb, specifically for heavy menstrual bleeding. This pudding is still taken as a spring tonic.

1   pound young bistort leaves, nettle tops,
      dandelion leaves, and Lady's Mantle
¾   cup barley, washed
      Salt to taste
1   egg
1   tablespoon butter

Chop the greens and sprinkle the washed barley among them. Season with salt. Boil in a muslin bag for about 2 hours. Before serving, beat the mixture with the egg, butter, and salt. Form into cakes and fry in shallow fat.

ASSOCIATED HOLIDAYS: IMBOLG, BELTAINE,
SPRING FESTIVALS, ESBATS

SERVES 4 TO 6

Carry a bistort leaf over your stomach

if you wish to conceive.

ENGLISH FOLK BELIEF

◆

The Meadow Verse to Mistress Bridget

Come with the springtime forth, fair maid, and be
this year again the Meadows deity.
Yet ere ye enter, give us leave to set
upon your head this flowery coronet;
to make this neat distinction from the rest
You are the prime, the princess of the feast
to which with silver feet lead you the way
while sweet breath nymphs attend you on this day.
This is your hour; best you may commend
since you are here from the faerie land
full mirth wait on you, and such mirth shall
cherrish the cheek, but make none blush at all.

HERRICK, 1648

An Herbal Recipe to See Faeries

From a sixteenth-century herbal:

Take a pint of salad oil and put it into a glass vial that has been washed with rose water and marigold water. (The flower should be gathered while facing east.) Add to it the buds of hollyhock, the flowers of marigold, the flowers or tops of wild thyme, and the buds of young hazel. (The wild thyme should be gathered from the side of a hill where faeries are known to be.) Take the grass from a faerie hill, and add it to the oil in the glass vial. Let the mixture settle for three days in the sun, and then keep if for your own use.

How is it to be used? The manuscript does not say.

Flower Pudding

Cowslip flowers, if placed beneath your front step, will discourage unwelcome visitors and salesmen.

1	handful each cowslip flowers, gillyflowers, red and white rose petals (wild roses are the most flavorful)
1	tablespoon marigold petals
1	cup spinach leaves
1	slice white bread, shredded
	Sugar to taste
¼	cup scalded cream
1	pound blanched almonds, ground fine
2	tablespoons rosewater
½	cup dates
3	egg yolks
¼	cup golden raisins

Mince flowers and spinach leaves and place with the slice of bread in a baking dish. Sprinkle with sugar and pour scalded cream over. Add almonds, rosewater, dates, egg yolks, and raisins. Toss together and bake for 1 hour at 350 degrees.

ASSOCIATED HOLIDAY: MIDSUMMER

SERVES 4 TO 6

Eating a few almonds will keep you

from becoming intoxicated.

SCOTTISH FOLK BELIEF

———◆———

Nasturtium and Marigold Salad

Violets may be used to heal wounds and protect against malignant spirits. Pluck the first violet of spring and speak aloud your heart's desire, and your wish will come true.

Clover has long been associated with luck, and a four-leaf clover is all the more so. Keep one in your pocket as a protection against sorcery. Eat a few to enable you to see faeries and to keep your lover true.

Basil promotes clear thinking. Keep one on your desk to aid in creative work.

4	nasturtiums or other edible flowers
2	marigold blossoms' petals
8–12	red clover blossoms
4	sprigs fresh basil
4	sprigs fresh rosemary
4	leaves kale
4	red leaf lettuce leaves
4	green leaf lettuce leaves
8	dandelion leaves
12	violet leaves

Toss all ingredients together; top with the dressing of your choice.

ASSOCIATED HOLIDAYS: MIDSUMMER, LUGHNASADH, SUN FESTIVALS

SERVES 1 TO 2

Rosemary is one of the oldest incenses.

Burn it on your altar to dispel negativity.

TRADITIONAL

◆

Acorn Squash with Cinnamon and Honey

Acorns, whose resemblance gives this particular squash its name, can be used in a variety of magic spells. Place them on your window to prevent lightning from entering your home, or keep one in your pocket to protect you from storms while on the road. Carrying one will also protect you from illness and headaches, keep you young, and increase both fertility and sexual potency. Like many nuts, acorns can be used in money spells. Plant one in the dark of the moon to increase your profits in any business deals.

4   acorn squash
8   tablespoons honey, or to taste
8   tablespoons unsalted butter
8   teaspoons cinnamon
8   pinches of brown sugar

Halve each squash and remove seeds. Add 1 tablespoon honey, 1 tablespoon butter, 1 teaspoon cinnamon, and 1 pinch brown sugar to each half. Cover each with aluminum foil and place on a baking sheet. Bake at 350 degrees for 1½ hours.

ASSOCIATED HOLIDAYS:
SAMHAIN, MABON,
HARVEST FESTIVALS,
ESBAT SUPPERS

SERVES 8

There was a cauldron in the fort:

The calf of the three cows,

Thirty cows within its gullet,

That was its portion.

They used to go to that cauldron,

Delightful was the struggle,

Nor did they come away from it again

Until they left it full.

There was much gold and silver in it,

It was a goodly find.

I carried off this cauldron

with the daughter of the king.

THE TRAGIC DEATH OF CU ROI MAC DAIRI

Hedgerows

*In every hedge the hawthorn blooms
And the wild woodlarks chants his early song.*

TRADITIONAL

Hedgerows are a feature of the landscape not often found in America, with its wide, sweeping plains and vast stretches of farmland. But in Britain and Ireland they are a familiar landmark. Drive down any country road and you will see these living dividers crisscrossing the fields and marking boundaries. Many are only a few hundred years old, but some stretch back a thousand years and more into the past.

A hedgerow is not merely a living barrier. Up until our own century, they served as a source of fuel and food, providing many sorts of herbs for seasonings and medicine.

Originally a hedge was created from plants cut in the forests that once covered the land. Later, these would be replaced by living hedges raised from hawthorn and hazel seeds. Other trees would grow within it: elm, crabapple, oak. They formed a wall as impenetrable as any made of stone.

The herbs that grew within could be used for medicinal and magical purposes: agrimony would break hexes or cause one to sleep like the dead; comfrey was the traveller's herb, gathered by pilgrims to protect them on the road, and it also helped speed the healing of broken bones. Yarrow, which cleansed wounds and attracted love, was a familiar sight.

Hedgerows were a source of edible plants as well. Villagers could gather blueberries, crabapples, elder, mugwort, hazelnuts, raspberries, and wild cherries. Livestock could also graze on the hedgerow boundaries.

The wood from the trees that grew within the wall were fashioned into all sorts of household items, brooms, shovels, furniture, wagons, baskets, cooking utensils, ox yokes, barrels, and even coffins.

Nowadays, the Goddesses' bounty is quite ignored. People no longer gather wood to fuel their fires, but burn coal. Few know the secrets of the herbs, and buy their medicines from the apothecary. By and large people will go to the grocery to purchase gooseberry jam or raspberry conserve, rather than make it from the berries that grow along their yard. Nowadays the hedge is little more than a pretty border viewed as one drives by in a car.

As much as twenty-five percent of the hedges have been razed to make room for mechanized farms. Others have been sprayed with herbicides to cut back on the "undesired" growth.

Green Man Salad

The Green Man, also known as the Leaf Man, May King, or Jack in the Green, is an ancient image of the Goddesses' consort. Today he may be found decorating the pillars of old churches and cathedrals, where he peeks out from among stone carvings of branches and leaves.

5	cups green leaf lettuce
2	cups fresh dandelion greens
6–8	slices of bacon
2	tablespoons white vinegar
2	teaspoons sugar
	Salt to taste

Remove stems of greens and roughly chop leaves. Cut bacon into 1-inch square pieces and fry until crispy. Pour off the fat, reserving ½ cup. Add vinegar, sugar, and salt to the bacon and reserved fat and bring to a boil. Pour dressing over greens, toss and serve.

ASSOCIATED HOLIDAYS: BELTAINE,
MIDSUMMER, SPRING FESTIVALS

SERVES 4 TO 6

The man who is bad for hospitality

is good for directing you on the road.

IRISH PROVERB

Fish, Shellfish, and Seaweed

Soused Herring (or Mackerel)

The herbs and spices in this recipe have other uses as well:

Hanging a branch of dill over the crib of a child will protect him from being stolen by faeries. And, though many people find the taste unpleasant, chewing bay leaves will increase psychic powers and induce prophetic dreams. Burning the leaves in incense will cause the same.

To cure warts and other skin lesions, rub the afflicted area with an onion. Toss the remainder over your shoulder at a crossroads, and do not look back.

Cloves are a powerful love charm. Wear them in your hair or carry them in your pocket to attract a new lover.

8	herring or mackerel
	Sea salt and pepper to taste
2	bay leaves
1	large onion, sliced
6	whole cloves
1	teaspoon sugar
1¼	cups red wine vinegar
	Sour cream and chopped dill

Clean and gut the fish and remove the heads and tails. Pat dry. Lay them in a baking dish and rub a little sea salt into them. Add the bay leaves and onion, and sprinkle on the pepper, cloves, and sugar. Barely cover the fish with vinegar. Place in oven and cook at 325 degrees for 20 to 30 minutes. Leave to cool in the liquid. Remove and discard bay leaves. Serve chilled with sour cream and garnish with chopped dill.

Variation: Use tansy leaves instead of bay. Place a leaf inside of each fish.

ASSOCIATED HOLIDAYS: BELTAINE, LUGHNASADH

SERVES 4

Baked Cod and Bacon

Worship of the sun and moon was a common practice among Celtic tribes, judging by the abundance of solar and lunar motifs found in their art and literature. Up until this century, Manx fishermen who set foot on a ship still showed the proper respect for the deities, and were under a taboo that they could not refer to any of the heavenly bodies directly by name. Instead, the moon would be called the "Queen of the Night" or "The Shining Pearl" while the sun would be known as the "Glory of the Day" or "Heaven's Radiance."

- 1 medium onion, sliced
- 6 tablespoons butter, divided
- 1 pound potatoes, parboiled and sliced
  Sea salt and pepper to taste
- 4 cod steaks, or any white fish
- ½ pound smoked bacon
- 1¼ cups light cream
  Chopped fresh parsley

Preheat oven to 350 degrees. Sauté onion in 4 tablespoons of the butter until golden. Place some of the onions in the bottom of a baking dish and layer the sliced potato on top. Season to taste with salt and pepper. Put the cod steaks on top and cover with the bacon and remaining sautéed onions. Bake for 15 minutes. Pour in the cream and dot with remaining butter. Return to oven for another 40 minutes. Cover with parsley and serve.

ASSOCIATED HOLIDAYS: LUGHNASADH, ESBAT CELEBRATIONS

SERVES 4

Son of the Waves

Many hundreds and hundreds of years ago, on a Saturday afternoon it was, a fisherman from Bantry was fishing in the deep waters of the Atlantic. Donagh O'Donovan his name was, and there was nothing he liked better than the solitude he found out at sea, with the sun shining down on his head and the wind at his back.

The day was right fair, and fish were plentiful. Toward sundown Donagh felt a great tug on his line. Why, it's quite a large fish, judging by the strength of it! he thought. It'll bring me enough money for a pint or two at O'Malley's, and leave me with some coins to jingle in my pocket! He struggled to haul the fish onto the deck, and when he had it on board, his eyes nearly popped from their sockets. He had caught a real, live boy! His hair was as red as the flesh of a salmon, and his eyes as green as mist over the ocean. Gills opened and shut uselessly on the sides of his neck.

Donagh was very proud of his catch. Who wouldn't be? "The money I'll make showing such a marvel!" he exclaimed. "People will pay good silver to see such a sight!" The boy ran and hid behind a pile of nets, and stayed there until the fisherman pulled into the harbor.

Donagh took him home. "Maura!" he called. "Come look at what I caught today!" His wife, wiping her hands on her apron, came out to the yard to see what her husband was shouting about. But as soon as he set the boy down on the ground, the boy raced into the cottage and hid under the bed. No one could get him to come out, neither with coaxing nor with offers of food.

Even Donagh's eldest son, when he threatened the sea child with a pitchfork, couldn't get him out. Of course Donagh and Maura couldn't sleep with the boy under the bed, but there the boy stayed through the long night and into the following day. They again tried to get the child to eat a morsel of food or take a sip of water, but it was no use.

"There's nothing to do but call on Father William," said Maura. "He'll be able to help."

And so Donagh

went into the village to talk to the priest, and tell him all that happened. Father William considered a moment, and said, "You must take him out on the waters with you tomorrow, as close as you can remember to the spot where you found him. Toss him back into the sea again."

"But Father," protested Donagh, "I found him, I should get to keep him."

"Like belongs with like," the priest said sternly. "Return him to the sea." And so the fisherman took him in the boat the next day and rowed toward the spot where he had caught him. All at once the boy let out a laugh of pure delight. He ran past Donagh with nary a glance and jumped, head first, into the waves. Down, down, down he dived, like a great sea bird, and was seen no more. In the whole time he had been with Donagh, he had never said a word.

Celtic Fisherman's Prayer

Pray White Lady lead us,
Pray White Lady speed us,
From all evil defend us,
Fish for our pains do send us.
Well to fish and well to haul,
And what you please to pay us all.
A fine night to cast our nets,
And safely to the land return.
Pray Lady, hear our prayer.

Tweed Kettle

The worldwide symbol for the Mother Goddess is the pointed oval sign of the yoni, known as the vesica piscuis, Vessel of Fish. This symbol was so well known that early Christian leaders were unable to rid themselves of it, and so adopted it as a symbol for Christ as the Fisher of Men. Still, it took a long time for the transition to take place, and there are many medieval paintings that show the Christ child inside the vesica piscuis.

2–3	pounds salmon
	Sea salt and pepper to taste
3	cups white wine
2	teaspoons chopped chives
½	stick butter, softened
1	tablespoon parsley
	Zest of 1 lemon

Simmer the salmon for 5 minutes in a pan of boiling water. Drain and remove the skin and bones. Cut the salmon flesh into stew-sized pieces and season with salt and pepper. Place the fish in the pan. Pour in wine, sprinkle with chives and simmer, uncovered, for 5 minutes. Remove the fish pieces and place them on a serving platter. Cover to keep warm. Turn up the heat to reduce the cooking liquid to approximately 1 cup. Stir in the butter and pour the mixture over the salmon. Garnish with parsley and lemon zest to serve.

ASSOCIATED HOLIDAYS: IMBOLG, OSTARA, BELTAINE, MIDSUMMER

SERVES 4

I see the moon and the moon sees me,

Lady bless the sailors on the sea.

CELTIC PRAYER

◆

The Ocean's Powerful Sway

Most early Celtic villages (like many major cities today) were located close to rivers or along the coastline. The reason for this is a simple one: the sea provided an abundance of food—seaweed, crustaceans, and fish—throughout most of the year. The earliest gods and goddesses rose from this watery abode to help and hinder the lives of humans, and many legends link our own beginnings with the sea. The sea was thus worshipped, prayed to, feared, and sacrificed to.

◆

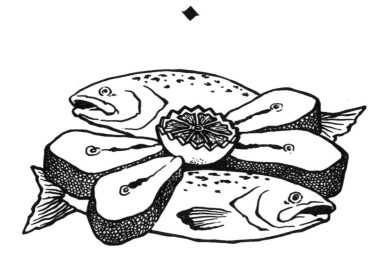

Water Magic

If you are ever out walking and feel yourself pursued by danger, or know that evil is watching over you, try to cross over running water either by crossing a bridge or wading through a stream, or even by stepping over water running in a gutter or a ditch. Moving water is part of the wild magic, neutral in nature, and cancels out spells both good and evil.

Streams are sacred to the Goddess, and are considered to be the veins of her body. By dipping an object into the water, a stream may be used to cleanse, to remove negativity, and to promote healing. There is a cheese festival in Frome, England, where cheeses are dipped into the local stream for good luck. If you choose to bless your food in such a manner, be sure to leave a bit behind as an offering to the Goddess and to the local faeries.

◆

Baked Salmon

Salmon is mentioned frequently in early Celtic literature. The most famous salmon of all was named Fionntán, and it was he that gave the gift of knowledge to the young Irish hero, Fionn Mac Cumhaill. According to the legend, there grew over Fionntán's pool a tree whose branches held the hazelnuts of wisdom. The nuts dropped into the well, and Fionntán ate these nuts. Anyone who was able to catch and eat him would gain this knowledge for himself. A druid by the name of Finnégeas sat beside the pool for seven years with the hopes of catching this miraculous fish, and finally succeeded. The druid gave it to his pupil Fionn to cook for him. The young man prepared a fire made of applewood, and carefully cooked the fish. The fish cooked too quickly, however, and a blister rose to the surface, which Fionn burst with his thumb. He burned his thumb and sucked it to relieve the pain. Inadvertently, he became the first to taste the salmon and so gathered the gift of knowledge through inspiration for himself. By sucking his thumb, Fionn was able to come up with ingenious solutions to the problems he faced.

It is not known if Fionn cooked his fish with sorrel, but today it is a common method. Dried sorrel leaves, if made into sachets for your dresser, will protect the owner from disease—especially heart ailments. Burned as an incense, it drives away snakes. Shamrock, also known as wood sorrel, is sacred to leprechauns and will attract them to your home if planted in the garden.

 1   (5-pound) whole fresh salmon
     Fresh parsley
 ½   cup butter
     Sea salt and pepper to taste
 1   tablespoon lemon juice
     Watercress or sorrel leaves for garnish

Clean and de-scale the salmon; trim fins, leave or remove the head and tail. Stuff parsley into the gullet. Butter a large piece of baking parchment or aluminum foil and form a loose wrap around the fish. Seal both ends. Before closing the top, dot fish with the rest of the butter, season, and sprinkle with the lemon juice. Leave a small vent for the steam to escape. Place the salmon in a baking pan and bake at 350 degrees for about 1¼ hours. When done, remove the skin, place on a platter, and garnish with the watercress or sorrel leaves. May be served hot or cold.

ASSOCIATED HOLIDAYS: IMBOLG, OSTARA, MIDSUMMER,
LUGHNASADH, ESBAT DINNERS

SERVES 4

Dublin Lawyer

Better is a small fish than an empty dish (Irish proverb).

  1 (2-pound) fresh lobster
½ cup butter
½ cup Irish Whiskey, warmed
½ cup cream
    Salt and pepper to taste

For the best flavor, the lobster should be killed just before cooking by plunging a sharp knife into the cross on the back of the head. Before cooking, remove the meat from tail, claws, and head of the lobster, retaining shells. Cut into chunks and heat in butter over medium heat for a few minutes until cooked. Season to taste. Pour in the Irish Whiskey and set fire to it. When the flame is out, mix the cream with the pan juices and heat, but do not boil. Adjust seasoning and serve in the half shells.

ASSOCIATED HOLIDAY: LUGHNASADH

SERVES 1

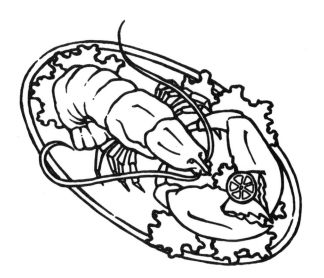

*There are finer fish in the sea
than have ever been caught.*

IRISH PROVERB

Fried Herring in Oatmeal

Herring was a staple food of the Celts for centuries, and is today a popular breakfast dish.

6 herring fillets
3 tablespoons flour
2 eggs, beaten
8 tablespoons oatmeal
4 tablespoons butter, divided
2 lemons, cut in rounds
   Sprigs of fresh parsley
   Brown bread for serving

Wash and thoroughly dry the herring fillets. Dip each fillet into the flour, then into the egg, and lastly into the oatmeal, making sure that the fish is completely coated in each. Press the oatmeal well onto the surface of the fish so that it adheres. Melt half of the butter in a large frying pan and heat it until it just begins to foam. Put in the fish and cook on one side, over a medium flame, until the oatmeal is evenly browned—about 5 minutes. Turn the fish fillets over to cook on the other side. You may need to add more butter. Serve with sprigs of fresh parsley, rounds of lemon, and hearty slices of fresh brown bread. It is also good with a mustard sauce.

ASSOCIATED HOLIDAYS: LUGHNASADH, MABON

SERVES 3

Seven herrings are a meal

for a salmon.

GALICIAN PROVERB

◆

Sea Salt

One of the few substances known to the early Celts that could preserve food was sea salt. It was, like honey, a symbol of rebirth. The custom of putting a plate of salt upon a corpse or a vial within the coffin is still practiced in parts of rural Britain. Salt was also seen as a substitute for blood in certain rituals, as it came from the Mother's sea womb. Altars that once may have been blessed by the blood of animals may instead be sprinkled with salt. There arose a fear that spilling salt was like spilling blood. Although the action has lost much of its significance, we throw a pinch of spilled salt over our shoulder as a way of putting the curse of spilled blood behind us.

Salt and pepper were perhaps first combined in a protection spell for the home. Scattered about the perimeter of the yard, it will block evil spirits and prevent your neighbors' ill wishes and malicious gossip.

◆

She Sells Sea Shells

Sea shells are one of the most powerful tools for performing sea-related magic. Conch shells may be blown to invite the gods and goddesses to your ceremony or feast, or they may be placed on your altar as a symbol of the element of water. Smooth round shells symbolize female deities (scallop shells have long been associated with Bridgit) while twisting, spiraled shells stand for the male aspect of deity.

◆

Ginger and Rosemary Pike

Ginger added to a magical potion will speed the results. My aunt buries a piece of ginger with a statue of St. Joseph (upside down and facing away from the house) whenever she sells a house. It hasn't failed yet!

Rosemary is one of the oldest incenses, burned to clean a workspace of negative thoughts and emotions prior to working any magic. I keep a pot in my kitchen where I can inhale its distinctive fragrance. It always seems to clear my head. A friend of mine swears that the aroma of rosemary keeps her young.

1 or 2	whole pike, cleaned and split
	Sea salt and pepper to taste
½	cup red wine
2	teaspoons cider vinegar
¼	teaspoon ginger
¼	teaspoon rosemary

Season the pike to taste and grill under a broiler for 5 minutes on each side. In a small pot, combine the wine, vinegar, ginger, and rosemary. Simmer over low heat for about 10 minutes. When the fish is done, transfer it to a serving platter and pour the sauce over it.

ASSOCIATED HOLIDAYS: MIDSUMMER, LUGHNASADH

SERVES 2

Why it is I cannot tell,

but this I know full well:

with wind in the east

fish bite not the least.

SCOTTISH SAYING

Fried Whitefish with Roses and Almonds

The sauce for this dish is enhanced with saffron, an expensive herb that should be reserved for special dinners and important magic spells. Drunk in a tea, saffron will bring about happiness and dispel ill thought. In Ireland women would wash sheets with saffron water to strengthen the body and spirit of a person as they slept.

Roses have a long association with the Goddess, and should be placed on the altar whenever possible. If grown in gardens they will attract faeries. Almost every part of the rose can be used in love spells and enchantments. Rose petals added to potions and recipes will bring about dreams of your own true love. According to English folk belief, roses grow better when stolen.

2	pounds whitefish fillets, cleaned
	Flour for dredging fish
	Butter for frying

Sauce:

3	tablespoons ground almonds, divided
2	tablespoons cornstarch
3	tablespoons cold water
2	teaspoons brown sugar
	Small pinch saffron
1	cup red rose petals
1	cup milk
¼	teaspoon each cinnamon and nutmeg
½	teaspoon salt
¼	teaspoon ginger

Dredge fish in flour and fry in butter over medium heat until tender—about 4 minutes per side. Remove to a serving platter and keep warm. The sauce should be made at the last minute, as the roses do not keep well. Dissolve cornstarch in 2 tablespoons cold water. Add brown sugar, 2 tablespoons of the ground almonds, and the saffron. Bring to a boil and stir until thick. Set aside. Grind rose petals with remaining almonds with a mortar and pestle (or use a blender), adding a bit of the cooked sauce to make a smooth paste. Blend in cinnamon and nutmeg. Stir this paste into the sauce base and reheat to the boiling point. Season with salt and ginger and pour over the fried fish.

ASSOCIATED HOLIDAYS: BELTAINE, MIDSUMMER, LUGHNASADH, ESBAT DINNERS

SERVES 4

Mushroom and Scallop Pie

Christian pilgrims once wore a scallop shell to show that they had visited the shrine of St. James of Compostela in Spain. This shrine had been taken over from the Goddess Bridgit, whose yonic symbol was also the scallop shell.

8	scallops
1	cup milk
½	teaspoon sea salt or to taste
¼	teaspoon pepper or to taste
2	tablespoons butter, divided
1	tablespoon flour
¼	pound mushrooms
5	tablespoons cooking sherry
3	cups cold mashed potatoes
1	tablespoon parsley

Cut the scallops in half; simmer in milk with salt and pepper for 15 minutes. Strain; reserve the milk. Melt 1 tablespoon butter in a saucepan; add flour and mix well. Gradually stir in reserved milk until smooth. Add mushrooms, sherry, and scallops. Pour into a baking dish; cover top with mashed potatoes. Dot with remaining butter and bake at 350 degrees for ½ hour. Garnish with parsley.

ASSOCIATED HOLIDAY: IMBOLG

SERVES 6

*It is not a fish until
it is on the bank.*

SCOTTISH PROVERB

The Changeling

There was a woman in the upland of Benbecula who bore a fine big child. But the midwife was in a hurry, and she forgot to baptize the child, and the handmaidens were sleepy and they neglected to burn the old leather shoes. And the outcome of all that was that the faeries came down and lifted the child with them high on their shoulders, and out they went by way of the hen hold, leaving an ancient changeling in the child's place.

The child that was left was thriving neither by day nor yet by night, for all that he was eating and drinking and putting away without stop or stay, without rest or pause. The poor woman knew not what to say or do. Every last woman in the village would come to the house, and if they were not many they were not few, and they would say to the poor mother, "Is not your child small? Is not your child wan? Is not your child green? Is not your child sallow? What a sorrow!" The same dismal tone of disaster came from every last one of them, like the scream of the seagulls at the skate. The poor mother was vexed to distraction with them, without relief or hope, and she did not know how to make reply.

Finally, she went to the wise woman of the village, and told her about the child, every word, every turn, how he was eating and drinking without stop or stay, without rest or pause, and for all that and despite it had neither thriving nor growth on his head nor his legs, on his form nor his frame. How that when she would go to the well the milk-pitcher would be drained; when she would go to the cattlefold the cake would be eaten; when she would go to the moor the butter basket would be made away with; and not a living creature on the bare flat of the floor save the child in the cradle could be seen.

The kindly old woman listened mildly, mannerly, to the woman's words, and she said to her, "It is an ancient changeling you have, my poor dear. The midwife has been forgetful and the handmaids neglectful, and the faeries have come and lifted the child away with them, and have left an ancient changeling in his place."

"But what can I do?" wailed the poor mother.

"Go home, and do not let it be known that you have spoken with me. Go to the strand and bring home a good supply of shellfish of every sort, and after parboiling them, scatter the shells on the bare flat of the floor around the hearthstone. Leave the changeling in the cradle, and go out as if you were going to the well for a pail of water. Don't go very far, but keep an eye and an ear behind the door to see what you shall see and hear. The sprite will reveal himself, and after that, go to the shellfish strand, and place the changeling stretched out at the water's edge, and put a slumber-croon in his ear and sing him to sleep. When the first wave of the rising tide strikes him the changeling will wail, but take no mind of this and do not let on that you heard. When you reach home you'll find your own baby back in the cradle."

The woman went home, and she did as the old woman asked, and she left nothing forgotten. She went to the strand and brought home the fill of a big creel of shellfish of every sort. She parboiled them and spread the shells on the bare flat of the floor around the hearth as the old woman bade. Then she said, "My darling baby, I'm going to the well. I'll be back shortly."

The changeling smiled, and closed his two little eyes in sleep. The mother went out with a pitcher in her hand, and she closed the door behind her. But instead of going to the well she put eye and ear to the peg-hole in the door to see what she should see or hear.

Instantly the changeling leapt from his cradle, and where did he land but among the shells on the floor!

"Ov! Ov! Ov! My feet cut and injured with the shells!" yelped the changeling in spite of himself. "Ov! I have been living since I was born and never before in the creation have I seen such shells—never never have I seen them! Shells here and shells yonder, shells up and shells down, everywhere I put my foot!"

The changeling looked at the shells, he gazed to and fro, up and down, here and yonder, and he began to sing:

> Brown crab, cockle, oyster,
>
> Mussel, bruiteag, limpet,
>
> Bearded mussel, miasag, scallop—
>
> Alas my reaving, my heels!
>
> Lobster, squid, green crab,
>
> Red crab, seashore flea,
>
> Cowrie, maighdeag, little limpet
>
> Alas my wounding, my heels!

> Whelk, whorl, barnacle
>
> have pained me to my bones,
>
> And the crafty sea urchin—
>
> so many a prickle in my heels!
>
> Slender sand-eel and razor fish,
>
> Hose-fish, black-snout, limpet...

But the changeling had got no opportunity to put a finish to the croon of the shells when he heard the noise of the woman's footsteps as she pretended to come home with a pitcher of water. He quickly ate the food and scrambled back to his cradle, and he closed his eyes as if he had been asleep all along.

"Did you see, my darling, who ate the butter and who devoured the bannock and who drank my milk today?" demanded the mother when she came into the croft.

"I saw nothing, mama, I was fast asleep in the cradle and didn't wake up at all," said the changeling.

"Hmmm, strange it is," said the mother. "But no matter. The height of the spring tide is today. We shall go to the strand of shellfish and see if I can get a boiling for the hens, and you shall get pullets' eggs for me."

The woman placed the faerie changeling in the small creel and put the sling over her head. She lifted him high on her shoulders and departed for the strand of shellfish with a step light and jaunty, and the faerie changeling in the small creel on her back. She laid the pigmy sprite quietly and gently down at the water's edge by the shallow ripples, and said to him, "Sleep, my pretty treasure, sleep my little man, and I will sing to you while I work."

The tiny elf closed his eyes and the woman sang:

> Sleep by the wave's side
>
> Sleep now, my love,
>
> Sleep by the wave's side,
>
> Till I cease from the shellfish gathering.
>
> Goats' milk I'd give to you,
>
> And sheeps' milk I'd give to you
>
> And milk of mares I'd give to you,
>
> my love, if you were my son.

Beer and wort I'd give to you

and the white barley of the plains,

and wine of the chalice I'd give to you,

my love, if you were my own.

The plucks and sguithim I'd give to you,

And the lapwings' yellow eggs,

And the autumn carrot I'd give to you,

my love, if you were my son.

Sweet maize I'd give to you

earthnut, lard, and whiting,

and the spring tansy I'd give to you,

my love, if you were my own.

Milk and feast-fare I'd give to you,

Cheese, and crowdie and mild whisky,

And kail dressed with butter I'd give to you,

my love, if you were my son.

Rough meal porridge I'd give to you,

And honey and foaming milk,

And goodly sowens I'd give to you,

my love, if you were my own.

The first thing the trickster knew on awaking was the first wave of the ris-ing tide driving in below and above him at the margin of the waves. The changeling uttered the wail of death at the pitch of his voice, and he made a lightning leap to his feet upon the bare flat of the strand. The woman did not let on that she had seen or heard him, nor so much as raised her head, but kept on singing her slumber-croon and gathered shellfish. But in the twin-kling of an eye the changeling's screechings were like the seagulls at herring frys. The faeries lifted him up and spirited him away to the faerie hill.

The woman ran swiftly home, and the foot that was hindmost was the foot that was foremost as she sped down the path. The poor woman found her own frail little child there before her in the cradle. A cleric was found, and the child was baptized, and neither faerie nor elf nor pigmy sprite ever came to trouble them again.

Oyster Soufflé

In Ireland and the British Isles, oysters are in season from September until March. The best way to eat them is raw, just like our earliest ancestors did. Oysters were once held sacred by the Celts, or rather the pearls they contained were. The Cauldron of Regeneration is said to have been lined with pearls, and the Goddess, when she appeared in the guise of the moon, was sometimes called the Pearl of the Sea. In fact, pearls were believed to have been created from moonlight and water, and so should only be worn at night. Many people today still believe in the aphrodisiac qualities of oysters, so do eat them sparingly.

1	dozen shelled oysters, reserve the liquid
	Juice of ½ lemon
½	cup fresh white bread crumbs
½	cup cream
2	eggs, separated
	Mace, salt, and pepper to taste

Drain the oyster liquid and add it to the lemon juice, then heat and pour over bread crumbs. Chop the oysters and add to the crumbs; mix in the cream. Beat the egg yolks and add to this mixture, then season to taste. Beat the egg whites until stiff and fold into mixture. Butter individual cups and pour in the soufflé mixture. Leave one inch of space from the top to allow for rising. Cover with buttered waxed paper and steam for forty minutes in a pan filled with boiling water. Turn out carefully and serve hot.

ASSOCIATED HOLIDAYS: ESBAT DINNERS, BELTAINE

SERVES 2

The oyster is a gentle thing,
it will not come unless you sing.

MANX SAYING

Gooseberry Mackerel

At one time in Scotland, when the necessary preparations had been made and the mackerel boat was ready for pushing off, the crew would form a little group on the deck, throw down their caps in their midst, and join in an invocation, such as the Celtic fisherman's prayer on the following page.

Fennel may be hung near windows or above the door to ward off evil. Place the seeds in keyholes to keep unwanted ghosts from entering your home.

A nutmeg strung around a baby's neck will absorb the pain of teething (Irish folk belief).

4	cleaned and filleted mackerels or herring
1	tablespoon butter, softened
	Salt and pepper to taste

Stuffing:

4	heaping tablespoons breadcrumbs
1	tablespoon chopped parsley
2	egg yolks
	Grated peel of 1 lemon
	Pinch of nutmeg
	Salt and pepper to taste

Sauce:

½	pound gooseberries
2	tablespoons sugar
1	tablespoon butter
2	tablespoons chopped fennel

Mix all the stuffing ingredients together and place on each filleted mackerel. Fold over and secure with toothpicks. Rub a little softened butter over fillets and broil or grill gently on both sides until fish is tender and flaky. (Herrings can be prepared in the same fashion.)

Cook the gooseberries in ½ cup water with all other ingredients. Do not let them overcook, but heat just until they burst open. Serve hot with fish.

ASSOCIATED HOLIDAYS: MIDSUMMER, LUGHNASADH, MABON

SERVES 4

The Island of Paradise

The early Celts noticed that the sun, moon, and stars all travelled to the west to die out and to be reborn so they could rise again. Therefore, they believed that far beyond the western rim of the ocean there is a magical land where humans go after death to await rebirth. This land went by many names, among them the Isles of the Blest, Tir na nÓg (Isle of the Ever-Young), and Avalon— where King Arthur himself is said to await Britain's greatest hour of need.

◆

Celtic Fisherman's Prayer

Watch, barrel, watch,
Mackerel for to catch.
How shall they be?
Like blossoms on a tree.
We'll catch some by their noses,
We'll catch some by their fins,
Lady send us quickly out
and give us a fair wind in!
Please, dear Lady,
may we have a good haul!

Stewed Eels

The Korrigans are water spirits who live in underground caves, but spend their time near springs and rivers found near standing stones. They are beautiful maidens with long golden hair and clear blue eyes that sparkle like sunlight on the water. The Korrigans are shapeshifters, and they can take on the appearance of spiders, snakes, or eels. The springs they inhabit are infused with healing qualities, and there are many holy wells in Britain and Ireland said to contain a sacred eel. Each Imbolg, the Korrigans dance in honor of poetry and wisdom, and all who drink from their wells that night will have the gift of divine inspiration.

2   pounds eels
1   pint white sauce (below)
    Parsley

Skin and clean the eels, then cut into 3-inch pieces. Place in a pot, cover with cold water, and bring to a boil. Simmer for 5 minutes and then drain. Add white sauce. Stew for 45 minutes, add the chopped parsley, and serve.

White Sauce

1   tablespoon butter
    Pinch salt
¼   cup flour
2   cups milk

Combine all ingredients over medium heat, stirring until thickened.

ASSOCIATED HOLIDAYS: IMBOLG, BELTAINE, MIDSUMMER

SERVES 4

*It's late to be mending nets
when the eels are in the river.*

IRISH PROVERB

Fried Eels with Butter Sauce

Legends of mermaids inhabiting the waters of Ireland and Britain abound, but some folklorists believe that they were not really water maidens, but giant eels. As late as the nineteenth century, British law claimed that all mermaids found within the territory were property of the Crown.

2	tablespoons flour
½	teaspoon sea salt
⅛	teaspoon pepper
2	pounds eel, cleaned, skinned, and cut into 2-inch pieces
1½	sticks butter, divided
	Juice and zest of 1 lemon
1	dozen small sprigs of parsley
	Butter for frying

Sieve together the flour with the salt and pepper. Dredge the pieces of eel in the seasoned flour. Fry the eel pieces in half of the butter until they are golden brown. Remove to a serving platter and keep warm. Melt the remaining butter, mix it with the lemon juice and zest, and add the parsley. Fry the parsley until soft, and pour the sauce over the eel. Serve hot with fresh brown bread and sloke (page 248).

ASSOCIATED HOLIDAYS: IMBOLG, BELTAINE, MIDSUMMER

Oh Sabrina fair, listen where thou art sitting

under the glassy, cool, translucent wave

in twisted braids of lilies

knitting the loose train

of thy amber dropping hair.

JOHN MILTON

Sloke

While in Egypt one year, I met a Welsh gentleman named Rob who was searching out connections between Celtic and Egyptian mythology. He was a virtual font of information on folklore customs, and told me that to attract money I should keep a piece of dried seaweed in my pocket, or place a small piece in a jar of whiskey and set it in a sunny spot. Seaweed was once more popular than it is now, but can still be found in markets throughout Britain and Ireland, and along the North American coasts.

Sloke, also known as sea spinach, is a type of seaweed found all around the coast of Ireland. Don't replace it with spinach, but other seaweed is okay. It is traditionally served as a vegetable alongside fish. It is also an aphrodisiac, so be careful who you serve it to!

2 pounds sloke
1 tablespoon butter
Juice of ½ lemon
1 tablespoon cream

Wash the sloke to remove all traces of sand and cut away any fibrous stems. Cut into small pieces. Cover with water in a large pot and bring to a boil. Reduce heat and simmer for about an hour. Pound the sloke in a mortar and pestle until it is somewhat liquefied (don't use a blender). Boil slowly for another hour. Drain thoroughly and mix in the butter, lemon juice, and cream.

ASSOCIATED HOLIDAY: MIDSUMMER

SERVES 2

Carrageen Winkles

Dried carrageen is available at many Irish import shops and specialty groceries.

- ½ cup dried carrageen moss
- 2½ cups water
- 2½ cups milk or cream, or a combination of both
- 2½ cups cooked and shelled shellfish (Cockles, winkles, et cetera)
- Salt and pepper to taste

Cook the carrageen in the water for 30 minutes. Most of it will disintegrate but you can rub any larger pieces through a sieve. Add milk or cream; simmer for 10 minutes. Add the flesh of the shellfish and the seasoning and bring just to the boiling point. Eat it at once as a delicious fish soup with lots of brown soda bread.

ASSOCIATED HOLIDAYS: IMBOLG, OSTARA

SERVES 2

Easterly winds and rain,
bring cockles here from Spain.

IRISH PROVERB

Salmon and Raisin Pie

On my first trip to Ireland I was surprised to learn that palm trees sometimes grow along the southern coast. Dates are eaten to promote fertility in women and sexual prowess in men.

1	pound cooked salmon, cut into bite-sized pieces
	Juice of one lemon
1	cup figs, chopped
1	cup white wine
½	cup dates, pitted and chopped
	Pinch of ginger
	Dash of pepper
¼	teaspoon ground cloves
¼	teaspoon cinnamon
¼	teaspoon salt, or to taste
¼	cup sultanas or golden raisins
¼	cup currants
1	unbaked 9-inch pie shell and top crust
2	tablespoons almonds, chopped

Pastry Glaze:

¼	cup ground almonds
⅛	teaspoon saffron
2	tablespoons milk

Drizzle lemon juice over salmon pieces. Simmer chopped figs in wine over low heat for about 10 minutes; remove figs with a slotted spoon and set in mixing bowl. Simmer dates in same pot of wine; remove dates with a slotted spoon and set aside in a separate bowl. Add ginger, pepper, cloves, cinnamon, and salt to the figs. Toss to mix thoroughly. Add sultanas and currants and toss again. Line the pie shell with the fig mixture, spreading evenly. Scatter chopped almonds evenly. Spread a layer of salmon, a layer of dates, and another layer of salmon on top of the pie. Place the top piece of pastry over the pie and crimp the edges to seal. Slice a cross into the top to allow steam to escape. Combine ground almonds, saffron, and milk and brush onto the top of the pie with a pastry brush. Bake for 30 to 45 minutes at 375 degrees, or until the crust is a golden brown. Serve immediately.

ASSOCIATED HOLIDAYS: LUGHNASADH, MABON, YULE

SERVES 4 TO 6

Scrying Mirror

Lakes are sometimes known as The Virgin's Mirror, in honor of the Triple Goddess in her youthful aspect. A good way of scrying is to sit on the water's edge. Breathe deeply and calmly to clear the mind, relax the eyes, and gaze at the water's surface. If you have a particular question in mind, think of it now, and wait until the answer makes itself known. Be aware of false answers— those your heart wishes to make true. If you have no specific question in mind, simply listen to the water and the wind, and see what images, symbols, and emotions they evoke. Although this is possible to do at any time—at night when all is still or during the day when the sunlight dances on the water's surface—the night of the full moon is the most auspicious time, as the Goddess is in the full of her power. If you cannot be near a lake, sometimes capturing the moon's image in a bowl of water and gazing on that works well, too.

◆

An Ancient Sacrifice

A villager was returning from Dolgellau to Llanegryn across the mountain one evening just past dusk when he heard a deep, booming voice calling out over the waters of Lake Gwernen, "The hour is come but not the man. The hour is come but not the man."

As he stood in bewilderment, he saw running down to the water's edge a wild-looking man wearing not a stitch of clothing. The man rushed pell mell into the waters, and disappeared beneath their surface.

It is well known that sacrifices were once made to the spirit of this lake. Is it possible the lake still demands them?

Hakka Muggies

Fish stomachs (muggies) can be obtained from a fishmonger or seafood counter, or you may catch your own fish.

1   fish stomach (muggie)
1   cod liver
    Salt and pepper to taste
    Oatmeal
    Fresh bread for serving

Carefully wash the muggie and tie the small end with string. Break up or slice the cod liver, season well with salt and pepper, and fill the muggie with alternate layers of liver and oatmeal until the stomach is ⅔ full. Close, leaving enough room for the oatmeal to swell, and tie tightly with string. Plunge into boiling salted water and boil gently for 30 minutes. Remove from water and serve with fresh bread.

Associated Holidays: Lughnasadh, Mabon

Serves 2

Stewed Dulse

This reddish brown seaweed is found all along the coasts of Ireland, Britain, and North America, and is also known as dillisk, dilís, or dillesk. If you are not lucky enough to live near the sea, many fish markets carry it or you can sometimes find it at grocery/import shops. It is still served each August at the Lammas Fair in Bally-castle, originally held in honor of the sun god Lugh.

Dulse is an aphrodisiac. A pinch of dried dulse added to any drink is a powerful love charm.

I've never had anyone tell me specific measurements, and it works well to use your own personal taste in deciding what amounts to use.

> **Dulse**
> **Butter**
> **Milk**
> **Salt and pepper**

Cut the dulse from the rocks at low tide. Spread out on the grass, a shingle, or on a tin roof to dry in the sun. Wash well to remove any sand and place in a saucepan with milk, butter, salt and pepper, and stew for 3 to 4 hours until tender. Serve with oat cakes.

Variation: Dulse can be eaten raw or added to stews or fish soups. It can also be mixed into champ instead of the traditional scallions, and eaten with bread and butter in the form of sandwiches.

ASSOCIATED HOLIDAYS: LUGHNASADH, SUN FESTIVALS

The Ninth Wave

If you have the opportunity to stand near the shore of the ocean, observe the waves. The ninth wave in a series should be larger than the others, and is the wave that carries the strongest magic.

◆

The Wonderful Tune

Maurice Connor was the king, and that's no small word, of all the pipers in Munster. He could play jig and planxty without end, and Ollistrum's March, and the Eagle's Whistle, and the Hen's Concert, and odd tunes of every sort and kind. But he knew one far more surprising than the rest, which had in it the power to set everything dead or alive to dancing.

In what way he learned it is beyond my knowledge, for he was mighty cautious about telling how he came by so wonderful a tune. At the very first note of that tune the brogues began shaking upon the feet of all who heard it—old or young, it mattered not—just as if their brogues had the ague. Then the feet began going, going, going from under them, and at last up and away with them, dancing like mad, whisking here, there, and everywhere, like a straw in the storm—there was no halting while the music lasted.

'Twas really then beyond all belief or telling the dancing. Maurice himself could not keep quiet; staggering now on one leg, now on the other, and rolling about like a ship in a cross sea, trying to humor the tune. There was his mother, too, moving her old bones as light as the youngest girl of them all. But her dancing, no, nor the dancing of all the rest, is worthy the speaking about to the work that was going on down upon the strand. Every inch of it covered with all manner of fish jumping and plunging about to the music, and every moment more and more would tumble in, out of the water, charmed by the wonderful tune. Crabs of monstrous size spun round and round on one claw with the nimbleness of a dancing master; and twirled and tossed their other claws about like limbs that did not belong to them. It was a sight surprising to behold. But perhaps you may have heard of Father Florence Conry, a Franciscan friar, and a great poet; belg an dans, as they used to call him—a wallet of poems. If you have not, he was as pleasant a man as one would wish to drink with of a hot summer's day; and he had rhymed out all about the dancing fishes so neatly, that it would be a thousand pities not to give you his verses; so here's my hand at an upset of them into English:

> The big seals in motion
> Like waves of the ocean
> or gouty feet prancing,
> Came heading the gay fish,
> Crabs, lobsters, and cray-fish,

Determined on dancing.
The sweet sound they followed,
The gasping cod swallow'd;
'Twas wonderful, really!
And turbot and flounder,
'Mid fish that were rounder,
Just caper'd as gaily.
John-dories came tripping;
Dull hake by their skipping
To frisk it seemed given;
Bright mackerel went springing,
Like small rainbows winging
Their flight up to heaven.
The whiting and haddock
Left salt water paddock
This dance to be put in.
Where skates with flat faces
Edged out some odd places;
But soles kept their footing.
Sprats and herrings in powers
Of silvery showers
All number out-numbered
And great ling so lengthy
Were there in such plenty
The shore was encumbered.
The scallop and oyster
Their two shells did roister,
Like castanets fitting;
While limpets moved clearly,
And rocks very nearly
With laughter were splitting.

Never was such an hullabaloo in this world, before or since. 'Twas as if heaven and earth were coming together, and all out of Maurice Connor's wonderful tune!

In the height of all these doing, what should there be dancing among the outlandish set of fishes but a beautiful young woman—as beautiful as the dawn of the day! She had a cocked hat upon her head; from under it her long green hair, just the color of the sea, fell down behind her, without hindrance to her dancing. Her teeth were like rows of pearl; her lips for all the world looked like red coral; and she had an elegant gown, as white as the foam of the wave, with little rows of purple and red sea-weeds settled out upon it; for you never yet saw a lady, under the water or over the water, who had not a good notion of dressing herself out.

Up she danced at last to Maurice, who was flinging his feet from under him as fast as hops—for nothing in this world could keep still while that tune of his was going—and says she to him, chanting it out with a voice as sweet as clover honey—

> I'm a lady of honor
> who lives in the sea.
> Come down, Maurice Connor,
> and be married to me.
> Silver plates and gold dishes
> you shall have, and shall be
> the king of the fishes,
> when you're married to me.

Drink was strong in Maurice's head, and out he chanted in return for her great civility. It is not every lady, may be, that would be after making such an offer to a blind piper. Therefore 'twas only right to him to give her as good as she gave herself. So says Maurice,

> I'm obliged to you madam:
> off a gold dish or plate,
> if a king, and I had 'em,
> I could dine in great state.

With your own father's daughter

I'd be sure to agree;

but to drink the salt water

wouldn't do so with me.

The lady looked at him quite amazed, and swinging her head from side to side like a great scholar, "Well," says she, "Maurice, if you're not a poet, where is poetry to be found?"

In this way they kept at it, framing high compliments, one answering the other, and their feet going with the music as fast as their tongues. All the fish kept dancing, too. Maurice heard the clatter and was afraid to stop playing lest it might be displeasing to the fish, and not knowing what so many of them may take it into their heads to do to him if they got vexed.

Well, the lady with the green hair kept on coaxing of Maurice with soft speeches, till at last she overpersuaded him to promise to marry her, and be king over the fishes, great and small. Maurice was well fitted to be their king, if they wanted one that could make them dance; and he surely would drink, barring salt water, with any fish of them all.

When Maurice's mother saw him, with that unnatural green-haired lady as his guide, and he and she dancing down together so lovingly to the water's edge, through the thick of the fishes, she called out after him to stop and come back. "Oh, then," says she, "as if I was not widow enough before, there he is going away from me to be married to that scaly woman. And who knows but 'tis a grandmother I may be to a hake or a cod—Lady help and pity me, but 'tis a mighty unnatural thing! And may be 'tis boiling and eating my grandchild I'll be, with a bit of salt butter, and I not knowing it! Oh Maurice, Maurice, if there's any love or nature left in you, come back to your own old mother, who reared you like a decent man!" Then the old mother began to cry and ullagoane so finely that it would do anyone good to have heard her.

Maurice was not long getting to the rim of the water; there he kept playing and dancing on as if nothing was the matter, and a great thundering wave coming in towards him ready to swallow him up alive. But as he could not see it, he did not fear it. His mother it was who saw it plainly through the big tears that were rolling down her cheeks; and though she saw it, and her heart was aching as much as every mother's heart ached for a son, she kept dancing,

dancing all the time for the bare life of her. Certain it was she could not help it, for Maurice never stopped playing that wonderful tune of his.

He only turned the bothered ear to the sound of his mother's voice, fearing it might put him out in his steps, and all the answer he made back was, "Whisht with you, Mother, sure I'm going to be king over the fishes down in the sea, and for a token of luck, and a sign that I'm alive and well, I'll send you in every twelvemonth on this day a piece of burned wood to Trafraska." Maurice had not the power to say a word more, for the strange lady with the green hair, seeing the wave curling over twice as high as their heads, burst upon the strand, with a rush and a roar that might be heard as far as Cape Clear.

That day twelvemonth the piece of burned wood came ashore in Trafraska. It was a queer thing for Maurice to think of sending all the way from the bottom of the sea. A gown or a pair of shoes would have been something like present for his poor mother; but he had said it and he kept his word. The bit of burned wood regularly came ashore on the appointed day for as good, ay, and better than a hundred years. The day is now forgotten, and maybe that is the reason people say how Maurice Connor had stopped sending the luck-token to his mother. Poor woman, she did not live to get as much as one of them; for what through the loss of Maurice, and the fear of eating her own grandchildren, she died in three weeks after the dance. Some say it was the fatigue that killed her, but whichever it was, Mrs. Connor was decently buried with her own people.

Seafaring people have often heard, off the coast of Kerry, on a still night, the sound of music coming up from the water; and some, who have good ears, could plainly distinguish Maurice Connor's voice singing these words to his pipes:

Beautiful shore with the spreading strand,

Crystal water, and diamond sand;

Never would I have parted from thee

but for the sake of my fair lady.

Holy Wells

> Wishing well,
>
> wishing well
>
> Make my wish come true
>
> I will throw in a bent pin
>
> to make my dream come true.

Water is the essential fluid that nurtures and nourishes all life, second only to air in its importance. It is the element of purification, the subconscious mind, love, and emotion. Water sustains us and heals us, and many are the old tales that speak of quests in search of "The Fountain of Youth" or "The Water of Life."

But water is more than a healing fluid, for the Celts—and many ancient civilizations—saw it as the source of life itself, the birth waters of a primordial female goddess whose womb symbols are well, font, and cauldron. The Goddess' energy flows from the depths of her earth-body womb out through springs in the earth. The waters flow in rivers back to the great oceans, from which it evaporates and returns to us as rain.

Because natural springs, fountains, ponds, and wells are considered water-passages to the womb of the Goddess, the veneration of them was a significant part of early Celtic society. Many votive items—swords, shields, jewelry, helmets, and even human skulls—have been found in every major waterway.

Some of the most mystical forms of water are the gypsy streams that appear mysteriously, as if from nowhere. They can rise at any time, after a heavy rainstorm or even during droughts, and they may flow for a month or two before disappearing. Sometimes they leave virtually no trace, as their presence is not tied to old river beds, and they sometimes flow through meadows. The early inhabitants of Britain believed that such a source of unlimited, pure water was a gift of the Goddess. If you are lucky enough to discover such a gift, bottle the water for use in later rituals.

Throughout Britain the underground womb was associated with Hel, the Goddess of regeneration, whose name gave rise to the words "healing" and "holy." Many wells were named after her; others were named after the Goddess Bridgit. The new Christian religion could not stamp out the veneration of wells, and so adapted them. Many of Hel's sacred wells and springs were renamed "Helen's Well," after Emperor Constantine's mother, and those dedicated to Bridgit were converted to serve the Christian saint.

People still visit these holy wells to receive the benefits of their healing waters at auspicious times of the year—Imbolg, Beltaine, Midsummer, Lughnasadh, and Samhain if they are of the pagan tradition, on saints' days if they follow the Christian god. The ritual might involve decorating the well with flowers and greenery or drinking the waters.

Early on Beltaine morning is the best time to collect the healing waters from sacred wells. The devotee should always walk deosil three times the well, which is sunways, not speaking a word the entire time. He or she may drink the water, or bathe in it, or use it to wash an area affected by disease. An offering should be made, a bit of pretty cloth attached to a nearby tree will do, for it will flutter in the wind like a prayer flag, carrying mantras and prayers to the God/Goddess.

One of the most famous modern-day well-dressing customs takes place in the English villages of Tissington and Buxton each Ascension Day. Each well is decorated with large framed panels consisting of elaborate pictures of biblical stories. The surface of each panel is spread with smooth clay, dampened with salt water, and decorated with an assortment of pressed leaves, flower petals, moss, bark, berries, fir cones, and bits of stone. Different subjects are chosen every year, and the damp clay keeps the pictures fresh for several days. In Buxton the entire village is decorated with flags, flowers, and greenery, and after the wells are blessed by the local vicar, a festival is held and a Queen is chosen. It is a perfect blending of the old May Day rites and modern Christian beliefs.

◆

Baked Trout

The fish is a symbol of life, and the Celts believed that eating fish would attract new life to a woman's womb. The Irish hero Tuan, for example, was eaten by the Queen of Ireland while he was in the form of a fish; he was reconceived and later born again.

2	tablespoons chopped fresh parsley
½	cup butter
4	trout, cleaned
	Sea salt and pepper to taste
½	bottle dry white wine
	Juice of 1 lemon

Mix the chopped parsley in the butter and divide into five parts. Rub salt and pepper into each trout and place them in a baking dish. Put one pat of butter on each fish, and set aside remaining butter. Pour in the wine, cover, and cook at 350 degrees for 20 minutes. Add the juice of one lemon and the rest of the butter cut into small pieces. Cover and cook again for another 10 minutes.

ASSOCIATED HOLIDAYS: IMBOLG, OSTARA, BELTAINE, MIDSUMMER

SERVES 4

Magic Waters

Young girls who visit Gulval Well in Fosses Moor, Cornwall, may speak the following words:

> Water, water, tell me truly,
>
> Is the man I love duly
>
> On the earth or under sod,
>
> Sick or well—in the name of God.

If the party be living and healthy, the still water of the well will instantly boil up as a pot; if sick, foul and puddled waters; if the party be dead, it will neither bubble, boil up, nor alter its color or motion.

◆

Meat and Wild Game

*Tethered sheep
will not thrive.*

IRISH PROVERB

◆

Braised Beef

From The Tale of Macc Da Thó's Pig: *Each cauldron contained beef and salted pork, and as each man passed by he thrust the flesh-fork into the cauldron, and what he brought up is what he ate. If he brought up nothing on the first try, he got no second chance.*

1 cup red wine
2 tablespoons tomato paste
2 teaspoons fresh basil
1 teaspoon fresh marjoram
3 garlic cloves, crushed
1 teaspoon salt, or to taste
1 cup ½-inch pieces rutabaga
3 pounds beef shanks, cut in cubes
1 leek, cut in 1-inch cubes
1 potato, cut in cubes
3 carrots, cleaned and sliced
2 tablespoons flour
2 tablespoons water
1 tablespoon grated lemon zest
1 garlic clove
¼ cup fresh parsley

Combine wine, tomato paste, basil, marjoram, garlic, and salt in slow cooker—either a crock pot or over an open fire pit. Add rutabaga and top with beef, leek, potato, and carrots. Cook, covered, on low heat for 9 hours, or on high for 4½ hours, or until you can flake the beef apart with a fork. Place beef and vegetables in serving dish. Pour cooking liquid into small pot and skim off any excess fat. Beat together the flour and water in small bowl until smooth. Beat in a little of the cooking liquid. Add flour mixture to pot. Cook over medium heat, stirring, until mixture bubbles and thickens, about 3–5 minutes. Spoon sauce over meat and vegetables. Toss together lemon zest, garlic, and parsley. Sprinkle over beef and serve.

ASSOCIATED HOLIDAYS: YULE, NEW YEAR'S EVE, WINTER FESTIVALS, NAME DAYS/BIRTHDAYS, ESBAT SUPPERS

SERVES 4

Bookmaker's Sandwich

This hearty sandwich is often taken to race meetings, sporting events, or while out hunting.

1   (1½ to 2-pound) sirloin steak
1   long loaf crusty Vienna bread
   Butter
   Mustard
   Salt and pepper to taste

Slice the loaf lengthwise and butter it. Grill the steak according to taste, but do not overcook it. Trim off any fat and put the steak on one half of the loaf. Season to taste and spread with mustard, if desired. Put the top on and press down. Wrap in waxed paper or foil and put a light weight on top. The juice from the meat should absorb into the bread and keep it moist. When cold, cut into slices and put back into wrapper.

ASSOCIATED HOLIDAYS: SUMMER DAYS, SAMHAIN

SERVES 1

The best horse doesn't always

win the race.

IRISH PROVERB

———◆———

Sacred Bulls

In Celtic mythology, the bull is a symbol of strength and virility. The most famous bull story is, of course, the *Táin Bó Cuailgne*, when Queen Maeve and her husband Ailill of Connacht invade Ulster to steal the great Brown Bull of Cuailnge. The *Book of the Dun Cow* describes a bull feast where the flesh and blood of a bull was used in the divination of a new king:

A white bull was killed, and one man ate his sufficiency of the flesh and of the broth; and he slept after having partaken of that meal, and a charm of truth was pronounced upon him by four druids. There in a dream was shown to him the form of the man who should be made king, his appearance and manner, and the sort of work that he was engaged in. Out of his sleep the man uttered a cry and he described to the druids the thing he saw, and named a young man strong and noble.

With the Goddess typically portrayed as a white cow, it only stands to reason that nearly every god of the ancient world was sooner or later incarnate as a bull. The cult of the bull was so widespread that images appear from Britain to India, from Scandinavia to Greece. When representing the Goddess' consort, bulls were used as sacrifice.

Remnants of bull worship remain in the Twelfth Night games of Britain. A large cake with a hole in the middle was placed on the bull's horn. If the bull tossed his head and threw the cake behind him, the cake would belong to the mistress of the house. If the cake were thrown in front, it would belong to the farm hands. If the bull didn't cooperate, he would be tickled. Afterwards, cider would be drunk and a wassailing performed in the orchards, with each person drinking to the health of their master.

Sometimes a cake would be placed on a heifer's horn, then the verse would be altered, perhaps like the following one from Scotland:

> Here's to the health of the heifer,
>
> and to the white teat
>
> here's wishing the mistress a house full of meat
>
> with curds, milk, and butter, fresh every day,
>
> and grant the young men keep out of her way!

◆

Corned Beef and Cabbage

Once a traditional food for Easter, this is now linked with St. Patrick's Day in the minds of Americans. The cabbage should have as much dark green leaf as possible for flavor as well as tradition.

3 pounds corned beef brisket
1 whole onion, peeled
4 whole cloves
1–2 bay leaves
6–8 peppercorns
   Shredded cabbage

Place brisket in a saucepan and cover with cold water. Stick cloves into the onion; add to saucepan with bay leaves and peppercorns. Bring to a boil, cover, and simmer until meat is tender—about 2 hours. Cook cabbage in the meat stock just until tender and serve with the beef. Many families serve this with a mustard sauce.

ASSOCIATED HOLIDAYS: IMBOLG, OSTARA, BELTAINE, ST. PATRICK'S DAY

SERVES 4

*The taste of the clover makes
a thief of the cow.*

IRISH PROVERB

Pan-Fried Steak with Irish Whiskey

This is a favorite Sunday dish when watching Gaelic football matches on TV.

1 (8 to 12-ounce) sirloin steak, room temperature
   Black pepper to taste
1 tablespoon butter or lard
1 teaspoon olive oil
¼ cup Irish Whiskey
1 cup heavy cream
   Salt to taste

Season steak with pepper. Add butter and oil to a hot pan. When butter is foaming, add steak so the fat maintains the heat and seals the meat quickly. Reduce heat and cook to taste (3 to 4 minutes rare, 4 to 5 minutes medium, 5 to 6 minutes well done), turning steak only once. Remove steak to warm plate. Pour off fat from pan; discard. Add whiskey and cream to pan, stir until thickened. Season to taste and pour over steak.

ASSOCIATED HOLIDAYS: SAMHAIN, MABON,
HARVEST FESTIVALS, NAME DAYS/BIRTHDAYS

SERVES 1

The Farmer and the Faerie

Over the cattle I will not watch
Over the cattle I will not be
Over the cattle I will not watch,
For my joy is in the faerie hill.
Though I have ceased from the cattle herding,
A little trouble is on my mind,
That my courtly lover will go from me,
With my green-clad child to the faerie hill.

◆

Meat Pies with Butter Sauce

"The Dagda put up his cooking oven, and this is the way it was. The axle and the wheel were of wood, and the body war iron, and there were twice nine wheels in its axle, that it might turn the faster; and it was as quick as the quickness of a stream in turning, and there were three times nine spits from it, and three times nine pots. And it used to lie down with the cinders and to rise to the height of the roof with its flames" (translated by Lady Gregory in Gods and Fighting Men).

4	eggs, beaten
2½	cup water
1½	cups mashed potatoes
3	cups flour
2	pounds ground round steak
½	pound ground kidney suet
2	slices of bread, softened in milk and squeezed dry
½	cup water
	Salt, pepper, thyme to taste
1	medium onion, chopped fine
1	stick of butter

Mix together eggs, water, and mashed potatoes. Add enough flour to make a smooth dough. Roll out dough and cut into 3-inch rounds. With your hands, mix the beef, suet, bread, water, and spices until sticky, but firm. Place 1 tablespoon of the mixture in the center of each pastry round; fold over and pinch to seal. Bring 4 quarts of water to a boil on the stove and drop the meat pies in. Cook until they swell and float, about 12 to 15 minutes. Remove with a slotted spoon to the platter. Sauté onions in the butter and pour over the meat pies.

ASSOCIATED HOLIDAYS: SAMHAIN, MABON, HARVEST SUPPERS,
YULE, ESBAT SUPPERS

SERVES 8

Traditional Spiced Beef

The long list of ingredients—and the ten days' preparation time—may seem like too much of an effort, but spiced beef made in the traditional Celtic manner is well worth it. Try serving it instead of roast goose or ham at your next Yule celebration, or for the winter Esbats when the family is together. Spiced beef can be served hot or cold, but I think cold is best, sliced thin and served with fresh homemade bread.

1	(4-pound) tip beef roast
¾	cup salt
¾	cup brown sugar
1	teaspoon saltpeter
1	quart cold water
1	tablespoon black pepper
2	bay leaves, crushed
1	tablespoon juniper berries
2	teaspoons ground cloves
1	teaspoon ground nutmeg
1	teaspoon ground mace
1	tablespoon allspice
1½	teaspoons ground ginger
1	teaspoon chopped fresh thyme
1	small onion, chopped fine
1	cup Guinness or other stout

Place beef in a large saucepan. Add the salt, brown sugar, saltpeter, and water; bring to a boil for 15 minutes. Cool and transfer meat and liquid to a suitable container. Refrigerate for 5 days, turning meat each day. Remove meat from liquid and drain, discarding liquid. Mix together spices, thyme, bay leaves, berries, and onion; rub the mixture into the meat and refrigerate 4 more days, turning and rubbing meat daily. To cook the beef, place meat in a saucepan and cover with water. Cover pan tightly and bring to a boil; reduce heat and let simmer 3½ hours. During the last hour, add the Guinness to the cooking liquid. When the meat is done, allow to cool in liquid. Drain, wrap in foil, and refrigerate. It will keep about a week.

ASSOCIATED HOLIDAYS: YULE, NEW YEAR'S EVE,
NAME DAYS/BIRTHDAYS

SERVES 6

Highland Cow Song

It is said that highland cows differentiate between the aires sung to them, giving their milk freely with some songs and withholding it with others. Occasionally a cow will withhold her milk till her own favorite song is sung to her.

> Give the milk, my treasure!
>
> Give the milk
>
> and you'll get a reward:
>
> Bannock of quern,
>
> sap of ale-wort,
>
> wine of chalice,
>
> honey and the wealth of the milk,
>
> my treasure!
>
> Give the milk, my treasure!
>
> Give the milk,
>
> and you'll get a reward:
>
> Grasses of the plain,
>
> milk of the fields,
>
> ale of the malt,
>
> music of the lyre,
>
> my treasure!

◆

Scotch Collops with Cream

If you have gathered the mushrooms yourself, be sure they are properly identified. Many varieties of mushrooms are poisonous. Several grocery stores now have access to wild mushrooms so, unless you are an experienced mushroom hunter, this may be a safer bet.

- ½ stick butter
- 1 tablespoon oil
- 4 medium onions, chopped
- 6 (6-ounce) slices rump roast
  Salt and pepper to taste
- 3 cups wild mushrooms, sliced
- 2 tablespoons cream

Sauté the onion in butter and oil until golden brown. Remove from heat and set aside. In the same pan, brown the steaks on both sides for 2 minutes each. Place on top of the onions in a warmed serving dish. Season with salt and pepper. Sauté the mushrooms and cream in the frying pan for 3 minutes, seasoning with a bit of salt and pepper if desired. Scatter them over the steak and serve.

Holidays: Midsummer, Lughnasadh, Samhain

Serves 6

When the moon is at the full
mushrooms you may freely pull;
but when the moon is on the wane
wait 'ere you think to pluck again.

Scottish Belief

The Cow That Ate the Piper

It was late November, the harvest was in and there was no work left for the hired hands. So after paying them their wages, the farmer sent three of his workers home. "Come on back in the spring," he said. "I'll need help with the planting then. There'll be no need for you to go to the Hiring Fair." The men packed their sacks and set out on the long walk back to their homes in Donegal, each with a freshly roasted potato in his pocket.

Later that evening, with the food gone and the north wind picking up strength, a rain began to fall.

"Just what we need," grumbled Branduff, the eldest. The three men were soon soaked through to their skin, but there was nowhere for them to take shelter, not a village or farm or even an old shack could be found. They hastened their pace, they joked and laughed about the foolish farmer and his wife, and they told silly stories to one another; and after a while they came upon a piper. He was in worse shape than any of them, for his clothes hung on him in rags and he had no shoes. Obviously he was not a very good piper.

"Hello, boys!" He grinned and waved despite the pouring rain. "You won't mind if I travel with you a ways, will you?"

"Not at all." The men couldn't help smiling back. "The more the merrier, they say."

The wind howled more fiercely than ever, and the rain turned to snow. "If we don't keep moving, we're dead," the piper said grimly.

"Then why don't you tell us a story?" suggested Macauly, the next eldest of the field hands.

"It seems to be the night for it," the piper agreed. "It's few enough people who would brave the late hours to travel on the open roads. There's no telling what we might run into."

"W-w-what do you mean by that?" trembled Nevan, the youngest.

At first it appeared that the piper was not going to answer, for he had such a faraway cast to his face. When he looked up his eyes held a wicked gleam, and when he did speak his voice was as chill as the northern wind blowing down their necks. "Oh, nighttime is for the creatures of the dark, my boy, not for men such as we. Back during the famines two children, a boy and a girl, were abandoned by their parents who were themselves starving and had no food to share with extra mouths. Left alone, they wandered the ravaged countryside. They might have gone on until they succumbed to starvation like so many others, had they not come upon a small cottage. It was a well-kept place, decorated with intricate carvings that spoke of an older, darker time. From the chimney drifted the fragrant smell of smoke, and cooking smoke meant food. The children knocked at the door, too hungry to be ashamed of begging.

"The door opened with a rush and a pair of long, greenish arms jerked them inside. The thing that held them fast was manlike but was not a man. It was huge and hairy, and shuffled its way across the room, huge claws tearing into the dirt floor as it walked. It locked the door behind them and put the key in its pocket. The children were trapped!

"But at least the ghoul fed them. Day after day the ghoul spoon-fed them porridge and roasted potatoes, and every third day they were given meat. They had never eaten so well! Each day the ghoul would poke their stomachs and cruelly pinch their flesh. 'Not quite yet, not quite,' it would mumble to itself in a gravely voice. 'Not yet, but soon.'

"At last the day came when the ghoul was satisfied. It dragged each of the kids to the big, blazing oven and said, 'I like my meat plump and tender, and well-cooked.' He grabbed the girl by the . . .'"

"Arrrrrrgggghhhhh!" the piper was suddenly interrupted.

"Come on, Nevan," said Branduff, the eldest. "The story isn't that scary. My mother told me more frightening stories when I was misbehaving."

"N-n-n-n-no. I-I m-mean look!" said the trembling young man.

The men all looked to where Nevan's shaking finger was pointing, and they saw a dead man lying right in the road. He was wearing a brand spankin' new pair of brown leather boots.

"Lord God!" the piper whistled. "Will you look at those shoes!"

The men looked down at the shiny leather, then at the piper's bare feet.

"They're no use to him anymore, are they? And me with my feet turning blue!"

The three hired workers stared at him silently.

"I'll take them off of him then. If you protest, dear Sir," he addressed the corpse, "please, you only need say so. No? Well then, I'll help myself." He got down in the muddy lane and tugged at the dead man's feet. But try as he might, he could not remove them, only loosen the laces.

"Holy Mother!" grumbled the piper. "They're frozen fast to his feet!"

"Well, that's it then!" laughed Macauly nervously. "Let's be on our way! I'm near about frozen through myself!"

"Now wait a minute..." said the piper thoughtfully.

"Say now," said Branduff, "we're all of us decent men, here."

"Lend me your pocket knife," said the piper.

"What?" the hired men asked in unison.

"I said lend me your pocket knife, someone. Let's see if I can't cut them off."

And so with Nevan's knife the piper cut off the dead man's feet, clean through the ankles. He wrapped them in a bit of rag and placed them into his sack. "Now to find a place to thaw them out!" he laughed out loud, although no one shared the humor.

Just around midnight, they came to a farm house. "Thank the gods," they all breathed in relief.

It was apparently a wealthy farm they stumbled into. The woman who answered the door was dressed in a red skirt of finely spun wool, heavily decorated with swirling embroidery. The room they were admitted to had been freshly whitewashed and a blazing turf fire lit the room from the stone fireplace. On it hung a steaming pot of stew. The tables and chairs were carved with the same fancy designs as on the lady's clothes, and on the table were the remains of a great feast. In the far corner were tied three cows. Cows, as anyone will say, are the greatest wealth a man could own next to his horse and his land, and were thus well treated.

"Welcome!" The maid smiled. "I was just cleaning up what's left of our little celebration. It was the master's birthday today. You can eat your fill, and sleep in here. But stay away from that old brown cow, she's the devil incarnate, and would eat the clothes off your hides if given even half the chance." Then she closed the door behind them and went upstairs to her own bed.

The three workmen, warm, dry and well fed, settled down by the glowing peat embers and were soon sleeping heavily. The piper, however, had a little work to do. He opened up his backpack and pulled out the feet, shoes and all. After heating them over the fire for a few moments, he was able to pull the shoes free.

"So here we go!" he whispered. He slipped his own dirty feet into the shoes and wiggled his toes. "A perfect fit!" He stood and danced a little jig, laughing silently all the while. With hardly a thought, he tossed the dead man's feet into the corner with the three cows. Then he stole some of the farmer's clothes that had been hanging by the fire, for he was a thief as well as a piper, and repacked his pipes. Silently he slipped out of the farmhouse. The snow had stopped.

At dawn the maid was the first to arise and she sleepily stumbled down the stairs, yawning all the while. "Blasted creature!" she cursed at the brown cow when she spied her laundry. "You've eaten the master's clothes, you have! Won't he be fit to be tied!"

Then she roused the group of sleepers. She wanted to put them to work helping her with breakfast. "Up, up you blaggards! Up I say!" The three hired men stretched, yawned, and opened their eyes.

"Say!" said the girl. "Last night there were four of you men. Where is the other? You know, the scurvy-looking fellow with the pipes."

The men looked around in confusion. "I haven't a clue," said Branduff.

"Nor I," said Macauly. "I didn't know we were to keep track of him."

"He was here when we went to sleep last night," said Nevan helpfully.

At that moment the girl caught sight of the feet at the far end of the room where the cows were tied. "By the cloak of Bridgit!" she shouted. "The cow has eaten him!"

"What?!?" they all yelled.

The girl ran toward the stairs yelling, "The cow! That devil of a cow! That wicked brown cow! She's eaten him. She's eaten the piper!"

"What's that? What's that you say?" the farmer nearly tumbled down the stairs, still dressed in his nightshirt and fumbling for his glasses.

"That cursed brown cow has eaten the piper!" the girl wailed. "What are we to do?"

The farmer scratched his head and looked from the three hired hands to the pair of feet and back again. "I was told there were four of you," he said.

"There were last night," said Nevan.

"And our good friend the piper has been eaten by your cow!" said Branduff, quick to recognize a good opportunity when he saw it.

The farmer glanced nervously up the stairs to see if anyone else had been woken by the racket. "No one need hear about this, you know."

"But our friend was eaten."

"Hush, hush!" The farmer waved his hands. Then he went to his chest against the wall, withdrew a key to unlock it, and pulled out a sack of coins. These he handed to Branduff. "This is for your trouble, now be off with you all!"

As soon as they had packed their sacks and had eaten a hearty breakfast, the men were ready to get started on their journey. Each carried a dinner for later in the day. They left the farm behind them and continued down the path that would take them back to Donegal.

It wasn't more than an hour down the twisting path before they met a man in shiny new shoes and brand new clothes, playing on a set of pipes. He was so respectable-looking that they did not at first recognize him.

"What's that tune that you're playing?" called out Macauly.

"The tune?" the man asked with a wicked glint to his eye. "Why, I think I'll call it 'The Cow That Ate the Piper.'"

Chicken with Almond Rice

We have always thrown rice at newly wed couples coming out of the church, but do you know that this is to increase their fertility? Take care when you do so, however, as the Irish have a folk belief that says throwing wild rice in the sky will encourage rain.

1	cup uncooked rice
1	chicken, cut in pieces
½	cup ground, blanched almonds
1	tablespoon butter or lard
1	teaspoon sugar, or to taste
¼	teaspoon ginger
1	teaspoon salt, or to taste
⅛	teaspoon cardamom
3	tablespoons slivered almonds, lightly browned in butter

Rinse rice in water; drain. Cover with cold water and leave to soak. In another pan, cover the chicken pieces with salted water and let simmer over low heat for 1 hour. Skim off the fat and measure 3 cups of the broth into a separate saucepan. Add the ground almonds to the liquid and let steep about 10 to 15 minutes. Drain the rice and cook it in the broth until tender. Remove the skin and bones from the chicken and cut into bite-sized pieces. Add chicken to the rice mixture along with the butter or lard, sugar, ginger, salt, and cardamom. Cover and cook over low heat for about 15 minutes, or until meat is thoroughly heated. To serve, garnish with the slivered almonds.

ASSOCIATED HOLIDAYS: LUGHNASADH, SAMHAIN, MABON, YULE, NEW YEAR'S EVE

SERVES 4

Honey Glazed Chicken

Rubbing an apple on your shirt (over your heart) before taking a bite does more than polish it—it drives out any demons hiding inside. Demons can be very small, such as the demon of gluttony who sat on the belly of a king in the medieval Irish story The Vision of MacConglinne.

1   (4-pound) roasting chicken
    Salt and pepper to taste
1   large apple, peeled, cored, and quartered
1   large onion, sliced
    Pinch of cloves, cinnamon
4   tablespoons butter, melted
4   tablespoons honey, divided

Season the chicken inside and out with salt and pepper to taste. Toss the apple and onion with the cloves and cinnamon, fill cavity of chicken and sew or tie shut. Brush the chicken with melted butter and place it in a roasting pan. Brush 2 tablespoons of honey on top. Cook for about 1½ hours at 325 degrees, basting frequently. Halfway through the cooking, brush on the remaining honey. Serve hot.

ASSOCIATED HOLIDAYS: IMBOLG, OSTARA, BELTAINE, LUGHNASADH

SERVES 4

A rambling bee

brings home the honey.

SCOTTISH PROVERB

———◆———

Capon in Wine Sauce

When the Danaans came to Ireland, they brought three great treasures with them. The first treasure was the Lia Fail, or Stone of Destiny, on which the High Kings stood when they were crowned, and which would roar in confirmation of the rightful monarch. The second treasure of the Danaans was the invincible sword of Lugh of the Long Arm. The third treasure was the Cauldron of the Dagda, a vessel with the ability to feed a host of warriors without ever being emptied—a container that would come in handy during the holidays at my house!

1   capon, cut in pieces
    Butter for frying

2   cups chicken stock (page 149)

1   cup white wine

¼   teaspoon each cinnamon and mace
    Pinch of ground cloves

¼   teaspoon salt, or to taste
    Pinch of pepper

2   teaspoons vinegar

¼   cup white breadcrumbs

In a large saucepan, brown the capon pieces in butter. Add the broth, wine, and spices. Simmer for 30 minutes. Take a little of the broth and combine with the breadcrumbs and vinegar to form a paste. Return this to the pot and stir until thickened. Serve hot with slices of fresh bread.

ASSOCIATED HOLIDAYS: LUGHNASADH,
MABON, HARVEST DINNERS, YULE

SERVES 2 TO 4

Boiled Pigeons

Pigeons were one of the few forms of fresh meat to be had in the dark of winter, and pigeon dishes played a major role in midwinter feasts. They were not only valued for their meat, but for their eggs. A single pair of pigeons could produce upwards of twenty chicks a year.

From The Queen's Closet, *published in 1655, we find the following recipe:*

"To boyle pigeons: Stuffe the pigeons with parsley, and butter, and put them into an earthen pot, and put some sweet butter to them and let them to boyle, take parsley, thyme, and rosemary, chop them and put them to them; take some sweet butter and put it withall some spinages, take a little gross pepper and salt and season it withall, then take the yelk of an egge and strain it with verjuice, and put to them, lay sippets in the dish and serve it."

Partridges in Orange Sauce

On the first day of Christmas / my true love gave to me / a partridge in a pear tree (Traditional).

- 2 roasted partridges, pigeons, or other small game birds
- 2 oranges, sliced but not peeled
- 1 cup white wine
  Juice and zest of ½ lemon
- ¼ teaspoon ginger
- ¼ teaspoon salt, or to taste

In a medium pot, combine orange slices, wine, lemon juice and zest, ginger and salt. Cook over medium heat for about 15 minutes. Cut up the roasted birds and arrange in a stove-proof casserole dish. Pour the sauce over and cover. Simmer until meat is heated through.

ASSOCIATED HOLIDAYS: BELTAINE, MABON, YULE, ESBAT SUPPERS

SERVES 2

Roast Pheasant

The hen is generally tastier than the better-looking cock. The bird should be hung to age—an old test was to hang it by the tail and, when it fell to the cellar floor, it was ready for the pot.

1	stick butter, divided
3	tablespoons flour, divided
1	brace pheasants (2 pheasants)
1	teaspoon sage
4–6	slices bacon
1	medium onion, chopped fine
½	cup wild mushrooms, sliced
1	cup port
1	cup chicken stock (page 149)
	Salt and pepper to taste

Melt ½ stick of butter in a roasting pan. Dredge the pheasants in 2 tablespoons of the flour and gently brown them over medium heat for 2 or 3 minutes. Combine half of the remaining butter with the sage and rub inside each pheasant. Place the pheasants breast up in the roasting pan and cover with the bacon slices. Roast the birds for 35 minutes at 400 degrees and baste frequently to ensure they will not dry out. Transfer the pheasants to a serving dish. Leave just enough of the fat in the pan to brown the onion. Add the mushrooms to the onion and toss for a few minutes. Add the remaining tablespoon of flour and gradually pour in the port and the chicken stock. Bring the mixture to a boil and simmer for 10 minutes. Remove any scum from the surface, season to taste with salt and pepper, and serve on the side as a gravy. Roasted potatoes make an excellent side dish.

ASSOCIATED HOLIDAYS: SAMHAIN, MABON, YULE,
NAME DAYS/BIRTHDAYS

SERVES 4

A flying bird is anyone's shot.

BRETON PROVERB

◆

Wild Duck with Spiced Oranges

The oranges should be prepared about two months in advance to age properly, although I've successfully used them after two weeks. These oranges are so delicious that I often make extra just for snacking!

Because orange juice is a symbol of the sun, and belongs to the element of fire, it can be used in Sabbat rituals in place of wine.

Oranges:

8	large thin-skinned oranges
2½	cups white wine vinegar
6½	cups sugar
2	cinnamon sticks
¼	teaspoon ground cloves
6	blades of mace

Duck:

2	wild ducks
¼	cup butter
1¼	cups port, warmed
	Juice of 1 orange
	Salt and pepper to taste
1	bunch watercress

Slice oranges into ¼-inch slices. Place them in a large pot and cover with water. Simmer until the orange peel is tender, then remove from heat. Put the vinegar, sugar, and spices in another pot and boil together for about 15 minutes. Drain the oranges and keep the liquid. Put half the oranges in the syrup mixture, making sure it completely covers the slices. Simmer for 30 to 40 minutes, until the fruit turns clear. Lift out and place in a dish to cool. Repeat the procedure with the remaining oranges. If too much of the syrup has boiled down, add some of the orange cooking liquid.

Turn everything into a glass or porcelain bowl (non-metal!) and leave overnight. If the syrup is too thin, remove the oranges and boil the liquid in a saucepan until slightly reduced. If the syrup is thick enough, just bring the fruit and liquid to a boil again and pour into clean, sterilized jars. If you do not have enough syrup to completely cover the oranges, use the same proportions as above to make more syrup. Seal the jars and store in a cool, dark place.

Preheat oven to 400 degrees. Rub the birds with butter and roast for 30 minutes. (Wild ducks are significantly smaller than domestic ducks. If you use domestic ducks, follow the package directions for cooking times.) Add the warmed port and put back in the oven for 10 minutes. Remove the birds from the pan to a serving platter and keep warm. Add the orange juice to the pan and cook over high heat until the liquid is reduced. Pour the juices over the birds and decorate with sprigs of watercress. Serve on a bed of heated, spiced oranges.

Associated Holidays: Beltaine, Mabon, Yule, Name Days/Birthdays, Esbat Suppers

Serves 4

*I*t's natural for ducks to go barefoot.

Irish Proverb

Turkey Breast with Cherry Sauce

To learn what age you will live to be, walk deosil around a cherry tree nine times, and then shake the tree. The number of cherries that fall to the ground will indicate the age you will be when you are to die. A word of advice: Make sure the cherries are ripe and shake the tree hard!

1	turkey breast, roasted
1	pound fresh liver sausage
4	tablespoons butter, melted
1	pound cherries, pitted
3	tablespoons brown sugar
3	tablespoons water
½	teaspoon basil
⅛	teaspoon cinnamon

Cut turkey breast into four equal slices. Spread the liver sausage over each slice and place in a casserole dish. It is okay if they touch, but do not overlap. Drizzle butter over each slice and heat in warm oven. Place cherries in a saucepan with the remaining ingredients. Simmer until fruit is pulpy and then run through a grinder. Pour sauce over the slices and return to the oven for 5 minutes. Serve immediately.

ASSOCIATED HOLIDAYS: YULE, NEW YEAR'S EVE

SERVES 2

Basil should be one of the traditional gifts to give a
new homeowner, as it signifies good luck. The others
are salt for prosperity, so you'll never be poor;
bread for food, so you'll never be hungry; and a broom,
to sweep all of your troubles away.

TRADITIONAL FOLK BELIEF

Geese

We all grew up hearing the story of the goose that laid the golden egg, but we have long since lost track of its significance. Originally the goose was the Egyptian Goddess Hathor, who took the form of a goose to give birth to the sun. I have a wonderful papyrus of this event hanging in my living room.

Caesar, when writing of the early Celtic tribes, said they considered geese to be sacred and would not eat them because of their connection with the life-giving sun egg. Up to the Middle Ages a goose could not be killed at midwinter, when the sun was about to be reborn. To do so could throw us into a never-ending winter.

In later years, geese were associated with prosperity. They were tended by women, and there was a tradition of giving away geese to the poor.

In 1284, Edward I of England granted a charter to the burgesses of Nottingham to hold a twelve-day festival and fair. All manner of things were sold at the Goose Fair, as it soon came to be known: sheep, cattle, pigs, horses and, of course, geese for the Michaelmas supper. The Goose Fair has been celebrated for over seven centuries.

◆

Christmas is coming

the goose is getting fat,

please do put a penny

in the old man's hat.

If you haven't got a penny

a ha'penny will do.

If you haven't got a ha'penny

God bless you!

TRADITIONAL CAROL

Michaelmas Goose with Sage and Onion Stuffing

"If you eat goose on Michaelmas Day (September 29), you'll never want money all year round," says an old proverb. You should select *"green geese,"* those fed on pasture. Late September geese are less fatty than Christmas geese. The goose should be served with sage and onion stuffing and plum sauce or applesauce on the side.

The wild barnacle goose was thought to come not from eggs, but from either a giant seaworm or shellfish, which grow from waterlogged wood in the sea. Gerald of Wales, in his History and Topography of Ireland, *wrote, "In some parts of Ireland bishops and religious men eat them without sin during a fasting time, regarding them as not being flesh, since they were not born of flesh."* Right up to this century it was a common belief that the wild barnacle goose was a fish, not fowl or flesh, and so could be eaten on days of abstinence.

Stuffing:

¼	cup butter
2	large onions, chopped fine
1	apple, peeled, cored, and chopped
½	pound ground pork
1	teaspoon dried sage
½	teaspoon thyme
2	cups fresh breadcrumbs
1	egg
¼	cup slivered almonds (optional)
1	cup milk or chicken stock
	Salt and pepper to taste
	Giblets from goose

Goose:

1	(10-pound) goose with giblets
2	tablespoons butter
1½	tablespoons flour
	Salt and pepper to taste
½	cup white wine
2	cups chicken stock (page 149)

Stuffing: Melt the butter in a frying pan and sauté the onions until soft. Mix all other ingredients together in a bowl, add the onions, and season generously with salt and pepper.

Goose: Remove fat from inside the goose, stuff it and sew it. Place on a rack in a roasting pan and prick skin in several places with a fork. Rub with butter and half a tablespoon of the flour, then sprinkle with salt and pepper. Pour the wine into the pan and roast the goose for 1 hour, basting every 15 minutes. After an hour, skim ¾ of the fat that has accumulated. Prick skin again and return to the oven for another 1 to 1½ hours. Mix pan juices with flour and stock to make gravy.

ASSOCIATED HOLIDAYS: MICHAELMAS DAY, SAMHAIN, MABON, YULE

SERVES 6

The Goose and the Four-Leaf Clover

Once there was a great harvest festival held in Fishguard. 'Twas a good many years ago, I should think, for my grandmother was but a wee girl then. All of the villagers were gathered at the seaside as they did every year. Whoever else was there my grandmother never said, but she remembered a traveling tinker, and the matter was that he had a goose walking down the street with him. And this goose was dragging a great log, which was tied to his leg. At least all the people of Fishguard thought it was a log, and everyone was running after the goose as it went down the street. The growing crowd tossed bright shilling coins to the tinker who had taught the goose such a marvelous feat.

Many of them called out, "Did you ever see such a marvel? That wee goose dragging that great oak log? And he's able to pull it down every road, and it tied to his leg?"

"All that he's pulling is a bundle of onions," said my grandmother. She had walked all the way to Fishguard from the village of Eglwyswrw with a sack of cabbages to sell at the fair.

The tinker heard what she had said. Quick as a flash he approached her. "How much for your cabbage?" he asked.

"One pound," she demanded, seeing a good bargain.

"Done," said the tinker, producing a note.

"No, I wish hard currency," said my grandmother, never a fool. As soon as the tinker took the load of cabbages from my grandmother, she followed after the goose. And she would later swear that the goose was dragging a log behind it. "I don't know how I ever thought it was a bundle of onions," she said.

What I'm guessing happened is that my grandmother unknowingly carried a four-leaf clover with her, tied up in the bundle of cabbage. That's why she saw a sight different from all the others, and that must be why the tinker was willing to pay three, aye, four times the worth of her cabbages. The four-leafed clover has that kind of power.

◆

Pigs

Easal of the Golden Pillars owned seven magical pigs. Although they were killed every night, they were found alive again the next day, and there was no disease or sickness on any person that ate their share of them (from The Sons of Tuireann*).*

Pigs have a special place in Celtic legend, and are considered to be magical animals with certain powers of enchantment. Besides the pigs owned by Easal, there is the tale of King Arthur trying to capture the boar of March ap Meirchion; of Culhwch stealing a comb from the head of a magic boar Twrch Trwyth; of the pigs of Pryderi, which were stolen by Gwydion; and of the pigskin of Tuis, which cured all wounds and sickness and which could turn water into wine. The Welsh saints Kentigern, Brynach, and Dyfrig all founded monasteries on the spot chosen by a magical white sow.

A white sow was one of the most popular animal forms of the Goddess, whether she be known as Demeter, Freya, Marici, or Cerridwen. Cerridwen is the Celtic name for the Triple Goddess, particularly in her crone aspect as the corpse-eating sow. Her followers lived throughout Britain and Ireland, and parts of France and Spain. Harvest dances in Galicia, a region of Spain, were called pig dances, and celebrated the Goddess as the creator—and devourer—of life.

If the Goddess appeared as a sow, it would stand to reason that her consort would appear as a boar. The boar representing the God was sacrificed at Yule, usually with an apple in its mouth. The apple was the Goddess' most sacred fruit, and contained the gift of immortality itself, as seen in the northern legend of Iduna's magic apples, and the Christian legend of the apples of paradise.

◆

Boiled Limerick Ham

Parsley did not always serve as a decorative garnish. It was placed on the side of dishes to absorb any disease or poisons the food might contain.

- 1 (10-pound) cured ham
- 1 large onion, peeled and chopped
- 1 laurel leaf
- ½ cup white vinegar
- 1 quart cider
- ½ cup sugar
- 1 bunch parsley
- 1 clove garlic
- 4 tablespoons bread crumbs
- 3½ tablespoons brown sugar
- Whole cloves

Cover ham with water and let soak 24 hours in the refrigerator. Place ham in a large pot; add onions, laurel leaf, vinegar, cider, sugar, parsley, garlic, and enough cold water to cover ham completely. Bring to a boil, reduce heat and let simmer 30 minutes for each pound of meat. Remove from heat and let stand ½ hour before removing from the pot. Peel skin from ham and cut off excess fat. Combine bread crumbs and brown sugar and press mixture into ham. Generously decorate surface of ham with cloves and place in oven to glaze. Let stand ½ hour before carving.

ASSOCIATED HOLIDAYS: SAMHAIN, MABON, YULE, ESBAT SUPPERS

SERVES 6 TO 8

Never give cherries to a pig

or advice to a fool.

IRISH PROVERB

Pork Ciste

It is not the big sow that eats the most (Welsh proverb).

    5   boneless pork chops
    2   pork kidneys
    1   large onion
    1   carrot
    1   potato, peeled
        Pinch each thyme, oregano, rosemary,
           parsley, salt and pepper; or to taste

Pastry:
    ½   pound flour
    ¼   pound grated suet
    1   teaspoon baking powder
        Salt to taste
    ⅔   cup milk

Slice the kidneys, carrot, onion, and potato; place in a large pot along with the pork chops. Sprinkle with herbs. Add enough water to cover and cook over low heat for about half an hour. Combine the flour, suet, baking powder, salt, and enough milk to make a soft dough. Roll out onto a floured board. Cut to fit the inside of the pot and place the dough directly on top of the meat. Cover with a lid; a large pot is necessary to allow the dough room to rise. Continue to cook for an hour and a half over low heat. Serve.

ASSOCIATED HOLIDAYS: SAMHAIN, MABON,
HARVEST SUPPERS, YULE, ESBATS

SERVES 4

Dried bay leaves, when combined in an

incense with sandalwood and lavender,

will remove any hex placed on you.

WELSH BELIEF

◆

Cruibíns (Pig's Trotters)

"I have a seven-year old boar that since it was a piglet has eaten nothing but gruel and meal and fresh milk in spring; curds and sweet milk in summer; nuts and wheat in autumn; and meat and broth in winter. I have a lordly cow that is also seven years old, and, since it was a calf, it has eaten nothing but heather and twigs and fresh milk and herbs and meadow grass and corn. I have one hundred wheat cakes cooked in honey; twenty-five bushels of wheat were brought for these cakes, so that each bushel made just four cakes. That is what the champion's portion is like at my house" (from Bricriu's Feast*).

Cruibíns (also spelled Crubeens), cured pig's feet, are one of the oldest dishes still served in pubs. There are numerous ways to serve them. They may be served cold with a vinaigrette dressing, or hot. To serve hot, coat them with bread crumbs, season with nutmeg and cinnamon, and brown in a broiler. They are especially good if washed down with a pint of ale or lager.

4	cruibíns (cured pig's feet)
	Cheesecloth and string
1	cup white wine
	Water
1	bay leaf
1	teaspoon white wine vinegar
1	carrot, chopped
1	onion, chopped
1	stalk celery, chopped
3–4	cranberries for garnish

Tie the cruibíns in pairs, using a cheesecloth to bind them together. Put the cruibíns in a saucepan with the remaining ingredients and cover with water. Bring to a boil; reduce heat and simmer, covered, for about 4 or 5 hours until tender. More water can be added if necessary.

ASSOCIATED HOLIDAYS: SAMHAIN, MABON, YULE;
DINNER AT YOUR FAVORITE PUB

SERVES 1

Sul of the Hot Springs

Sul is the goddess of springs, whose sacred waters always run hot. Prince Bladud discovered these springs in 863 B.C.E., and built a shrine to Sul near Aquae Sulis, where the popular modern-day spa town of Bath, England, is located. The waters were once believed to hold powerful healing magic, and many claim this is still true. It is believed that Sul is another aspect of Bridgit, the goddess of healing.

Bladud was the eldest son of Lud Hudibras, the eighth king of Britain, and was greatly beloved by the people for his kindness, intelligence, and honesty. So it is no surprise that the entire court was devastated when the dreaded white spot of leprosy appeared on his hand. At first his father tried to hide Bladud away in a secret room at the palace, but the news leaked out. Terrified of an epidemic, King Lud's subjects begged for Bladud to be sent away. It was with heavy hearts that his parents agreed. They could not even kiss him good-bye for fear of infection, but as his weeping mother said her farewells she tossed a fine, intricately carved ring to him.

"Keep this with you always, my son," she said. "If the gods see it in their hearts to restore your health, come back to me, and I will know you by this ring."

Bladud took the ring and threaded it on a fine gold chain around his neck. He tucked it in his shirt and wore it over his heart. And then he wandered away, his life in ruins. He slept on the rough ground and lived on berries and nuts, keeping well away from the sight of men in the dense oak forests that covered the west of Britain.

At last hunger drove him to look for work, and he camouflaged his sores with mud. An old farmer took pity on the boy and gave him the lowliest job of all, as a swineherd, driving the herd from pasture to pasture. The herd of pigs flourished and grew fat on acorns and truffles until, to Bladud's horror, they caught his dreaded disease and became as scaly and leprous as himself.

Bladud dared not go back to the farmer's cottage, but drove the pigs ever further into the woods. At a spot where the River Avon ran shallow he saw on the far bank a rich bed of acorns. The pigs plunged and snorted to be allowed across, so Bladud drove them through the river and set up camp among the trees.

The next day, as he led the pigs out of their pens, they were seized with mass hysteria and, maddened by the pain of their disease, they rushed along the forest paths and down into the valley. Bladud followed as fast as he could but only found them hours later, rolling and snorting in a warm swamp thick with rotting leaves and smooth bubbling mud. Bladud washed them down and for once they didn't roll or scratch the bleeding sores on their sides. He examined them carefully, hardly daring to believe his eyes. Their scaly patches were beginning to fade and they already looked healthier.

Each day he let them wallow in the mud to their heart's delight, and within a few weeks they were cured. He tried the same treatment on himself and at last he too walked from the warm springs without a mark on him. He reached for the ring his mother gave him years before, then drove the pigs back to the farm. Somehow he convinced the old man that his story was true, and the two set off for the court of Lud Hudibras.

A feast was in progress and the retainers, seeing a filthy old man and his ragged boy, wouldn't let them in. Bladud begged a servant to drop the ring into the queen's goblet. She drained the cup in the final toast, and caught her breath as she saw the exquisite band of bright gold. She let out a shout and cried, "My son! My child! Bladud is here! He is here! I must see him!" Bladud was ushered in and given a place of honor as his parents wept for joy.

In later years, when Bladud came to the throne, he set up his court around the hot swamp that had cured his leprosy. Here he built his capital, which he called Caer Badon, and dedicated the springs to the Goddess Sul.

Ham with Cream

What can you expect from a pig but a grunt? (Irish proverb)

    1   cup dark brown sugar
   3½   tablespoons mustard powder
    1   pound cooked ham, thickly sliced
    1   cup heavy cream
    1   bunch watercress

Mix the brown sugar and mustard in a small bowl. Place the ham in a small casserole dish and sprinkle about a tablespoon of the mustard and sugar mixture over each slice. Put any remaining mustard and sugar over the top slice and pour in the cream. Cover and bake for 35 minutes at 300 degrees. Garnish with watercress and serve.

HOLIDAYS: IMBOLG, OSTARA, BELTAINE, SAMHAIN

SERVES 2

Pork Tart

From The Voyage of Malduin: *"Under the trees went red beasts, like fiery swine, and they kicked the trees with their legs. When the apples fell, the beasts consumed them. These swine came out at morning only, when a multitude of birds left the island, and swam out at sea until night, when they ate the apples."*

   1½   pounds ground pork
    ½   cup chopped dates or apple
    ¼   cup grated Parmesan cheese
    4   eggs, beaten
        Pinch each of salt, pepper, nutmeg, ginger, cardamom,
        and saffron, or to taste
        Zest of one lemon
    1   (9-inch) pastry shell, uncooked

Mix together pork, dates, Parmesan, eggs, seasonings, and lemon zest. Spoon mixture into a pastry shell and bake for 45 minutes at 375 degrees, or until meat is cooked through. The tart may be served either hot or cold.

ASSOCIATED HOLIDAYS: SAMHAIN, MABON

SERVES 4

Garlic Pork with Chestnuts

Wrap a dollar bill around a chestnut and place it in your purse to attract money (English belief).

1	pound chestnuts
1½	pounds boneless pork loin, cut into cubes
½	stick butter
½	teaspoon sage
	Pinch of thyme
2	cloves garlic, pressed
1	cup sherry
¾	cup hot water
	Salt and pepper to taste
	Parsley for garnish

Skin chestnuts by making a cut along the flat side of each one and dropping them into a pan of boiling, salted water. Boil for about 5 minutes. Chestnuts must be peeled while hot, so only take out a couple at a time. Remove both the outer shells and inner skins. In a fresh pan of water, simmer the peeled chestnuts for about 15 minutes until they are tender (be careful to not overcook them, or they will fall apart). Gently brown the pork loin in the butter. Transfer to a casserole dish and add the chestnuts, along with the remaining ingredients. Cover and cook in the oven for 2 hours at 300 degrees, stirring occasionally. Garnish with parsley and serve.

ASSOCIATED HOLIDAYS: SAMHAIN, YULE, NEW YEAR'S EVE, WINTER CELEBRATIONS

SERVES 2

Now thrice welcome Christmas

Which brings us good cheere

Minced pies and plum porridge

Good ale and strong beer

With pig, goose and capon

the best that shall be.

TRADITIONAL

Skinless Pork Sausage

In earlier times pigs were kept near the house, and sometimes even in the cottage itself, for they were valuable possessions. The killing of a pig was an important social event, and neighbors would travel from miles around for the occasion. Each would bring a fistful of salt for the curing, and would get a share of the pork for their efforts.

When I stayed with the O'Brien family in Dalkey, just south of Dublin, we would eat sausage and apples for breakfast—a meal that would last the morning.

1   pound ground pork
    Generous pinches of fresh parsley, chives,
        thyme, marjoram, and sage
1   cup soft breadcrumbs
1   clove garlic, pressed
    Salt and pepper
1   egg, beaten
    Oil for frying

Combine all ingredients thoroughly. Fry a teaspoonful of the mixture to check the seasonings and adjust accordingly. Divide into 12 equal portions and fry in a little oil until golden brown and cooked through. Serve with applesauce.

ASSOCIATED HOLIDAYS: OSTARA, SAMHAIN

Today I was changed into a black boar,

and I was glad.

I was king of the boar herds,

and I sang a song about it

THE BOOK OF THE DUN COW

◆

Roast Venison

Carry garlic to sea to prevent a shipwreck (Sailor's belief).

1	5-pound venison roast

Marinade:

1	teaspoon Worcestershire sauce
3	cloves garlic, crushed
1	small onion, chopped
½	teaspoon parsley
½	cup red wine
½	cup orange juice

Sauce:

4	tablespoons port
1	pound red currant jelly
1	stick cinnamon
	Zest of 2 oranges

Marinate the venison roast in the marinade sauce overnight. Place everything in a roasting pan and add enough water to half-cover roast. Cook at 350 degrees until tender, roughly 10 minutes per pound. Baste continuously. Serve with currant sauce, made by combining port, red currant jelly, cinnamon and the orange zest.

ASSOCIATED HOLIDAYS: SAMHAIN, MABON, HARVEST SUPPERS,
NAME DAYS/BIRTHDAYS, YULE

SERVES 4 TO 6

The older the buck,
the harder the horn.

SCOTTISH PROVERB

Venison Balls with Sour Cream

From The Fionn Cycle: *"When they were hunting on the edge of a little wood, they saw a strange beast coming toward them with the quickness of the wind, and a red woman on its track. Narrow feet the beast had, and a head like the head of a boar, and long horns on it; but the rest of it was like a deer, and there was a shining moon on each of its sides."*

2	pounds venison, ground
4	large potatoes, boiled and mashed
2	medium onions, grated
	Salt and pepper to taste
1	egg, beaten
½	stick of butter
1	tablespoon oil
1¾	cups sour cream, divided

Mix together venison, potatoes, onions, salt, pepper, and egg. Shape mixture into balls and fry in the butter and oil until browned. Add half of the sour cream and simmer for 20 minutes. Add the rest of the sour cream and bring to a boil. Serve immediately.

ASSOCIATED HOLIDAYS: HARVEST SUPPERS, ESBAT CELEBRATIONS, YULE

SERVES 4 TO 6

Red Deer

From The Queen's Closet Opened, *1655:*

"Take a buttock of red deer or beefe, cut it the long waies with the grain, beat it well with a rowling pin, then broyl it upon the coals, a little after it is cold, draw it through with lard, then lay in some white wine vinegar, pepper, salt, cloves, mace, and bay leaves, then let it lye three or four days, then bake it in rye past, and when it is cold fill it up with butter, after a fortnight it will be eaten."

ASSOCIATED HOLIDAYS: SAMHAIN, MABON

St. Patrick's Breastplate

This poem is also known as *The Deer's Cry* and was quite popular in the seventh century. According to legend, St. Patrick was on his way to the High King's seat at Tara, where he was to confront the pagan religion. Assasins were in wait for Patrick and his companions, but as the saint chanted this hymn, it seemed to the hidden men that a herd of deer was walking by.

> I arise today through the strength of Heaven:
>
> the rays of the sun,
>
> the radiance of the moon,
>
> the splendor of fire,
>
> the speed of lightning,
>
> the swiftness of the wind,
>
> the depth of the sea,
>
> the stability of the earth,
>
> the firmness of rock.
>
> I arise today through the power of God:
>
> God's might to comfort me,
>
> God's wisdom to guide me,
>
> God's eye to look before me,
>
> God's ear to hear me,
>
> God's word to speak for me,
>
> God's hand to lead me,
>
> God's way to lie before me,
>
> God's shield to protect me,
>
> God's Heavenly Host to save me
>
>> from the snares of the devil,
>>
>> from temptations to sin,
>>
>> from all who wish me ill,
>>
>> from near and afar,
>>
>> alone and with others.

May Christ shield me today
    against poison and fire,
    against drowning and wounding,
    so that I may fulfill my mission
    and bear fruit in abundance.
Christ behind and before me,
Christ beneath me and above me,
Christ with me and in me,
Christ around and about me,
Christ on my right and on my left,
Christ when I lie down at night,
Christ when I rise in the morning,
Christ in the heart of every man who thinks of me,
Christ in the mouth of everyone that speaks of me,
Christ in every eye that sees me,
Christ in every ear that hears me.

I arise today through the might of the trinity,
    through faith in the threeness,
    through trust in the oneness,
    of the maker of heaven and the maker of earth.

◆

Shepherd's Pie

The best shepherd's pies still seem to be found in country pubs, where the lamb is raised locally. There are literally hundreds of ways to cook the pie; here is but one.

2	medium onions, chopped fine
2	cloves garlic, pressed
3	tablespoons butter
1½	pounds ground lamb
1	(6-ounce) can tomato paste
1	cup chicken stock (page 149)
1	heaped tablespoon flour
½	cup white wine
½	cup water
	Pinch of parsley, thyme
	Salt and pepper to taste
½	teaspoon tarragon
3	large potatoes, peeled
1	stick butter
¾	cup milk
½	cup cooked corn
½	cup carrots, chopped fine
2	tablespoons Parmesan cheese (optional)

Sauté the onion and garlic in the butter over low heat until soft. Turn up the heat and add the lamb, stirring until it is well browned. Drain off any fat and add the tomato paste, chicken broth, and flour. Cook, stirring, for about a minute before adding the wine and water. Add parsley, thyme, salt, pepper and tarragon. Simmer gently for 15 minutes. Boil and mash the potatoes. Add the butter and milk, and season with salt and pepper. Put the lamb mixture in a large greased baking dish. Spoon the corn and carrots over the lamb and spread the mashed potatoes on top so that the meat and vegetables are completely covered. Sprinkle cheese over the potatoes and bake for 30 minutes at 350 degrees. Place under the broiler for a few minutes to brown the top and serve.

ASSOCIATED HOLIDAYS: SAMHAIN, MABON, HARVEST SUPPERS, YULE, ESBAT SUPPERS

SERVES 2

Haggis

O ne often yearns

for the land of Burns,

the only snag is

the haggis.

The above phrase, obviously penned by an Englishman, shows the ridicule this tra-
ditional Scottish dish often faces. At my first Burns Night Dinner, I was told that a
haggis is a small, scruffy, hairy animal that runs backwards through hedges. The
ingredients of haggis are unlikely to get your mouth watering, but once you've got-
ten over any prejudice you may have towards tucking in to chopped lungs, heart,
and liver mixed with oatmeal and boiled in a sheep's stomach, it can taste surpris-
ingly good. Haggis should be served with potatoes and a large glass of whiskey.
Although the dish is eaten at any time of the year, it's central to the celebration of
January 25 in honor of Scotland's national poet, Robert Burns. Scots unite all
around the world on Burns Night to revel in their Scottishness. A piper announces
the arrival of the haggis, and Burns' poem Address to a Haggis *is recited to the*
"Great Chieftain o' the pudding race" before the stomach is lanced with a dirk
(dagger) to reveal the steaming offal within. This recipe is from a friend, Carol
Robenhurst.

1	sheep's paunch (stomach bag)
	Heart, lungs, and liver of a sheep
1	teaspoon salt
	Black pepper, nutmeg, and ground mace to taste
2	medium onions, chopped
1½	cups toasted oatmeal
4	cups beef suet
1½	cups beef stock (page 150)

This recipe is not for the faint of heart. Wash the paunch in cold water.
Turn it inside out and scrape clean. Boil heart, liver, and lungs until tender,
hanging the windpipe out over the edge of the pan so it drains into a bowl.

Chop meat fine and grind liver. Spread out and add salt, pepper, mace,
nutmeg, onions, suet, and oatmeal. Mix well with stock and fill paunch.
Leave room for oatmeal to swell. Sew it up with a tressing needle and

course thread. Prick all over with needle and put into boiling water for 3 hours. Remove from pan and place on a hot plate. Remove thread and slit bag and serve steaming hot with mashed potatoes or mashed turnips.

ASSOCIATED HOLIDAYS: YULE, NEW YEAR'S EVE, BURNS' NIGHT DINNERS, ESBAT SUPPERS

A Shepherd's Count

A relic of an ancient counting system, based on five, can still be heard in Yorkshire and Cumberland. Shepherds have used this system for perhaps a thousand years: "Yan, tan, tethera, pethera, pimp, sethera, lethera, hovera, covera, dik, yan-a-dik, tan-a-dik, thethera-dik, pethera-dik, bumfit. Yan-a-bumfit, tan-a-bumfit, tethera-bumfit, pethera-bumfit, figgit." If I've figured right, that will give you one hundred sheep.

A similar version was recorded in the Appalachians shortly before World War I. I don't know if it is still used, but the origin is obvious: "Een, teen, tuther, futher, fipps, suther, luther, uther, duther, dix, een dix, teen dix, thuther dix, futher dix, bumpit, anny bumpit, tanny bumpit, tuther bumpit, futher bumpit, gigit." Again, you have one hundred. I rather like these methods of counting, and it's delightful to hear the shepherds when they count aloud to one another.

♦

Idle dogs worry sheep.

WELSH PROVERB

——◆——

Poacher's Pie

There was a common folk belief that rabbits sucked the milk from sleeping cattle, and that witches, who would keep rabbits as familiars, would even take the form of a rabbit to steal their neighbor's milk. Like other much maligned animals, the rabbit was sacred to the Goddess. Celts imagined they saw a rabbit in the moon, and this moon-hare would lay eggs for children to eat—the origin of the Easter Bunny.

1	bay leaf
6–10	bacon slices
1	pound wild mushrooms, sliced
2	leeks, chopped into 1 inch pieces
1	rabbit, cut into small portions
	Salt and pepper to taste
3	tablespoons parsley, chopped
3	potatoes, peeled and sliced
1	tablespoon red wine vinegar

Place the bay leaf on the bottom of a large ovenproof dish that has a cover. Place half of the bacon over the bay leaf and cover with half the mushrooms and half the leeks. Place the rabbit pieces on top of the vegetables and cover with the remaining mushrooms and leeks. Season with salt and pepper and sprinkle on half of the chopped parsley. Place the potatoes over the top so that everything else is completely covered. Add a little more salt and pepper and the remaining parsley. Place the rest of the bacon slices on top and pour the vinegar over them. Put a tight lid on the pot and cook for approximately 2 hours at 325 degrees. Try not to check the pie too often, as the lid will seal in the natural juices.

ASSOCIATED HOLIDAYS: OSTARA, SAMHAIN, MABON

SERVES 2 TO 4

The Song of Amergin

I am a stag of seven tines

I am a flood across the plain

I am a wind on a deep lake

I am a tear the sun lets fall

I am a hawk above the cliff

I am a thorn beneath the nail

I am a wonder among flowers

I am a wizard

who but I sets the cool head aflame with smoke?

I am a spear that roars for blood

I am a salmon in a pool,

I am a lure from paradise,

I am a hill where poets walk

I am a boar ruthless and red

I am a breaker threatening doom

I am a tide that drags to death

I am an infant

who but I peeps from the unhewn dolmen arch?

I am the womb of every holt

I am the blaze of every hill

I am the queen of every hive

I am the shield for every head

I am the tomb of every hope.

◆

Desserts

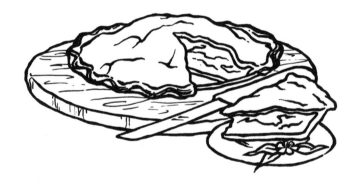

Don't expect a cherry tree

from an acorn.

IRISH PROVERB

First Foot, Lucky Foot

On New Year's Eve, in churches throughout Scotland and Northern England, a Midnight Watch is held, and the bells are pealed on the stroke of twelve. Ships, in port and at sea, and fire engines at the station will sound their sirens, and wherever people are gathered, toasts are drunk and good wishes exchanged. The traditional New Year's Eve song, with words by Scottish poet Robert Burns, are sung in nearly every Scottish village and city, and nearly every other city around the world, "Should auld acquaintance be forgot . . . ."

And it is in Scotland that the custom of first-footing is still observed. A dark-haired man must be the first person to step across the threshhold after the stroke of midnight, and he should bring gifts of bread, salt, coins, and whiskey for the family. Oftentimes coal is carried by the first-footer as a token of good luck. Under no circumstances should a fair-haired individual, a child, or a woman be the first through the door. Red-haired men and women are considered the most unlucky. The first-footer should not be a doctor or a lawyer, a clergyman or a priest. He should not wear or carry any sharp tools, not even a pocket knife.

No one should speak until the coal is placed by the fire and the first-footer has poured a glass of whiskey to the head of the household. If this guest is mistreated in any way, he could walk around the fire widdershins and leave a curse of ill luck for the following year. At the end of the ceremony, someone will often open the front door to allow the new spirit to take up residence.

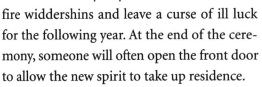

◆

Shortbread

While we always seem to have shortbread in our house, traditionally it is eaten during the season of the winter solstice. It is a custom in Scotland and Northern England to offer shortbread to the "first-footers," those who are first to enter your house after midnight on New Year's Day.

1¾	cups flour
4	tablespoons sugar
	Pinch of salt, or to taste
1	stick of butter
1	teaspoon farina (cream of wheat)
1	egg yolk, beaten
2	tablespoons milk
	Vanilla sugar (see note)

Sift together the flour, sugar, and salt. Cut the butter into cubes and rub in with your fingers until mixture is crumbly. Make a well in the center of the bowl and pour in the egg yolk and milk. Work into a smooth dough. Transfer the dough to an 8-inch cake pan and spread it evenly out to the sides. Crimp the edges with a fork and mark into slices. Prick with a fork. Chill in the refrigerator for 30 minutes. Heat the oven to 400 degrees and bake the shortbread for 5 minutes. Turn down the heat to 300 degrees and bake for an additional 30 minutes. The shortbread should be a pale golden color. Remove from the oven and cut it into slices while it is still warm. Do not attempt to remove from pan until it has cooled. Sprinkle with vanilla sugar before serving.

Variation: Replace ¼ cup of the flour with ground almonds for a wonderfully nutty flavor. Other old cookbooks recommend lemon peel and caraway seeds.

Note: A vanilla bean placed in a bowl of sugar will distribute love in the home. The vanilla-scented sugar can then be used in recipes as a sweetener.

ASSOCIATED HOLIDAYS: MIDWINTER, WINTER SOLSTICE, NEW YEAR

Apple Cinnamon Cake

In A.D. 77 Pliny wrote, "Cinnamon is said to grow in marshes under the protection of a terrible kind of bat . . . a tale no doubt invented by the natives to raise the price." Nowadays cinnamon is much easier to come by and, when paired with apples, as in the recipe below, makes for a spectacular dessert.

Cinnamon can be used in spells to attract love or increase sexual prowess. It increases clairvoyant abilities and can be used in protective spells.

Originally this cake would have been baked in a pot beside the hearth, but for practicality you can use your oven.

2	eggs
1	plus ½ cup sugar
⅓	cup cream
1	stick butter, softened
	Pinch of salt
1	apple, peeled, cored, and grated
1½	cups flour
1½	teaspoons baking powder
1½	teaspoons freshly ground cinnamon
4	medium-sized cooking apples, peeled, cored, and sliced

Beat the eggs with 1 cup of the sugar. Combine cream, butter, and salt in a small saucepan. Heat until near boiling. Remove and immediately pour onto the egg mixture. Fold in the grated apple, flour, baking powder, and cinnamon. Pour the batter into a greased 9 by 9-inch baking pan. Arrange the apple slices on top and sprinkle with the remaining sugar. Bake for about 20 minutes at 400 degrees, or until cake is firm to the touch. Serve warm.

ASSOCIATED HOLIDAYS: LUGHNASADH, MABON, SAMHAIN, HARVEST FESTIVALS, ESBAT SUPPERS

SERVES 4 TO 6

Don't throw apples into an orchard

or carry turf to a bog.

IRISH PROVERB

◆

Midwinter Suns

Nowadays it is possible to buy oranges in winter, and I serve this dish for our family Christmas gathering. The round orange sphere and citrusy smell are reminders that the warm and pleasant days of summer are not too far off.

7	large oranges
6	tablespoons sugar
9	egg yolks
3	tablespoons port
1½	sticks butter
1	plus ½ cup heavy cream
	Crystallized flowers (page 322) for decoration
	Whipped cream for decoration

Hold the orange so that the stalk is facing down. Use a sharp knife to cut off the top, about ⅓ of the way down. With a small spoon, scoop out all the flesh, but be careful not to break the shell. Repeat this procedure with all but one of the oranges. The top portions of each orange can be discarded.

Grate the peel from the remaining orange and set aside. Squeeze all the juice from this orange into a bowl. Place the fruit you scooped out from the other shells into a sieve and press all the juice into the same bowl. Discard the orange pulp.

Mix the orange juice with the sugar and egg yolks in a double boiler over very low heat. Beat with a wire whisk until the mixture thickens. Remove the top bowl of the double boiler that contains the mixture and cool it in a sink of cold water while you continue to stir. Add the port. If you do not have a double boiler, you may improvise by placing a bowl over a pot of boiling water. When cool, remove the bowl from the cold water. Cut the butter into 1-inch cubes and mash it into the fruit mixture a little at a time. Add the orange peel and set aside. Whip 1 cup of the cream and fold it into the fruit mixture. Pour the fruit into the six orange shells and refrigerate for several hours. Whip the remainder of the cream and give each orange a hearty dollop. Place a crystallized flower on top of each orange and serve.

ASSOCIATED HOLIDAYS: MIDSUMMER, LUGHNASADH,
SUN FESTIVALS, MIDWINTER

SERVES 6

Winds of Fate (Scottish Divination)

The one who is born when the wind is from the west,
He shall obtain clothing, food he shall obtain;
He shall obtain from his lord, I say,
No more than food and clothing.
The one who is born when the wind is from the north,
He shall win victory, but shall endure defeat.
He shall be wounded, another shall he wound,
Before he journeys to his eternal rest.
The one who is born when the wind is from the south,
He shall get honey, fruit he shall get,
In his house shall entertain
Bishops and fine musicians.
Laden with gold is the wind from the east,
The best wind of all the four that blow;
The one who is born when that wind blows
Wants he shall never taste in all his life.
Whenever the wind does not blow
Over the grass of the plain or mountain heather,
Whosoever is then born,
Whether boy or girl, a fool shall be.

◆

Marmalade Cake

Cherries aid in creative endeavors. Place a branch of cherry blossoms in your home to generate positive energy (Celtic belief).

The list of ingredients makes this an expensive cake, so it's best saved for special occasions.

¾	cup sultanas or golden raisins
½	cup raisins
½	cup currants
⅓	cup candied orange and lemon peel
¼	cup glacé cherries, chopped fine
2	tablespoons thick cut marmalade
½	cup ground almonds
2	sticks butter
⅔	cup sugar
⅓	cup brown sugar
	Grated zest of 1 orange and 1 lemon
4	eggs, beaten
2¼	cups flour
1	teaspoon baking powder
1	tablespoon port
¼	cup blanched almonds

Mix the sultanas, raisins, currants, peel, cherries, marmalade, and ground almonds together and set aside. Cream the butter and sugars in a separate bowl until light and fluffy; add the orange and lemon zest. Gradually add the beaten eggs to the mixture. Sift together the flour and baking powder and fold into the mixture. Add the port and all the fruit. Pour the batter into a heavily greased 8 by 8 by 3-inch cake pan; arrange the almonds on the top in circles. Bake for 2 to 2½ hours at 300 degrees, or until knife comes clean. Allow the cake to cool for 15 minutes and then turn it onto a wire rack and cool fully before serving.

ASSOCIATED HOLIDAYS: ESBAT DINNERS, NAME DAYS/BIRTHDAYS, YULE

Seedy Cake

Caraway is said to render a witch invisible when mixed with a number of other secret ingredients.

When baked into cakes, breads, and cookies it is an aphrodisiac, so be careful who you serve this to!

    1   cup butter
    1   cup sugar
    4   eggs
    1½ cups flour
    1   tablespoon ground almonds
    1   teaspoon caraway seeds
    2   tablespoons milk
    2   tablespoons Kirsch liqueur
        Confectioners' sugar
        Caraway seeds for sprinkling

Cream butter and sugar together, beat in eggs one at a time, adding a little flour each time to prevent curdling. Fold in the rest of the flour, ground almonds, and caraway seeds. Stir in the milk and Kirsch. Bake in a round 8-inch pan lined with waxed paper and greased for 1½ hours at 350 degrees. Leave to cool in pan for several minutes before turning out on rack. Dredge the top of the cake with confectioners' sugar and sprinkle on additional caraway seeds. This cake keeps well in an airtight container.

ASSOCIATED HOLIDAYS: ESBAT DINNERS

When the weirlings shriek at night

Sow the seeds with the morning light.

But 'ware when the cuckoo swells its throat,

Harvest flies from the mooncall's throat.

SCOTTISH SONG

◆

Lemon Curd

Lemon curd is easy to make and delicious on a slice of freshly buttered bread, or when spread on apple potato cake (page 317).

4 tablespoons unsalted butter

½ cup sugar

½ cup fresh lemon juice

4 egg yolks

1 tablespoon grated lemon peel

In a small saucepan, combine butter, sugar, lemon juice, and egg yolks. Over low heat, stir with a wooden spoon, being careful not to let the mixture boil or the yolks to curdle. Cook until mixture coats back of a spoon. Pour into a small bowl and stir in lemon peel. Allow to cool. Store in a Tupperware or other airtight container. It will last for several days in the refrigerator.

ASSOCIATED HOLIDAYS: LUGHNASADH, SUN FESTIVALS

Yellowman

"Did you ever treat your Mary Anne / to Dulse and Yellowman / At the Ould Lammas Fair / At Ballycastle, o?"

The Lammas Fair has been held in Ballycastle, Co. Antrim, for the last 350 years. Dulse (page 253), a dish made from seaweed, and yellowman are still the traditional foods sold at the fair.

1 stick butter

1 pound brown sugar

1 pound light corn syrup

2 teaspoons vinegar

1 teaspoon baking soda

Combine butter, sugar, syrup, and vinegar in a medium-sized saucepan. Boil, without stirring, until a drop hardens in cold water. Remove from heat and stir in the soda, which will foam up. Pour onto a greased board. When cool to the touch, turn edges to center and pull until pale yellow in color. Pour into greased pie tin and let cool. Break into chunks and store in an airtight tin.

ASSOCIATED HOLIDAYS: LUGHNASADH, SUN FESTIVALS

Lammas Cookies

These sunny cookies are eaten at feasts honoring the sun god Lugh.

1   cup butter, softened
1   cup sugar
3   eggs
2   cups flour
¼   cup Irish Whiskey
¼   cup candied lemon peel, chopped
¼   cup sultanas or golden raisins
¼   cup almonds, chopped

Preheat oven to 375 degrees. Cream together butter and sugar. Beat in eggs, one at a time, until blended. Add flour and Irish Whiskey and beat until smooth. Add fruit and nuts and mix well. Drop dough from a table-spoon onto a greased cookie sheet and bake for 6 to 8 minutes at 375 degrees. Remove from sheet while cookies are still warm.

ASSOCIATED HOLIDAYS: LUGHNASADH, SUN FESTIVALS

MAKES 5 DOZEN

Apple Potato Cake

In many parts of Britain and Ireland it was the custom to give gifts of apples or oranges studded with cloves or nutmeg and topped with a sprig of mistletoe. It was often mounted on a tripod of twigs. It was called a callenig, or apple gift, and was carried by carolers at New Year to bring luck to one and all.

- ¼ cup butter
- 6–8 ounces flour
- ½ teaspoon salt
- ½ teaspoon baking powder
- 3 cups freshly mashed potatoes, made with milk
- 2 large cooking apples
- 1 teaspoon cinnamon
  Sugar to taste
- ½ teaspoon ground cloves
- 2 tablespoons butter

For Potato Cakes: Cut butter into flour until crumbly. Add salt and baking powder; mix well. Mix in potatoes. Knead for a few minutes. Divide dough into 2 balls. Roll each ball into a circle ½ inch thick. Peel and core apples and slice thinly. Layer apple slices on one of the circles of dough. Sprinkle with sugar, cinnamon, and ground cloves; dot with butter. Cover with other circle and pinch edges to seal. On a greased griddle or frying pan, cook slowly over low heat for 15 to 20 minutes, turning once. Serve with cream, custard, or lemon curd and hot tea.

Variation: For Simple Potato Cakes, roll out the potato dough onto a lightly floured board with a flour-coated rolling pin. Cut into rounds and cook on a dry griddle or skillet until brown on both sides.

ASSOCIATED HOLIDAYS: LUGHNASADH, MABON, ESBAT DINNERS

Don't wait for apples,

gather your own windfalls.

IRISH PROVERB

Apples in Red Wine

This recipe combines apples and wine, two festival foods traditionally associated with Samhain and Mabon. The long simmering time burns out most of the alcohol, so it is okay to serve this dessert to children.

6	large Granny Smith apples
½	bottle red wine
2	cloves
½	cup sugar
1	stick cinnamon
½	teaspoon vanilla
1	tablespoon cornstarch
	Whipped cream

Peel, core, and segment the apples. (Toss the apple peels over your shoulder before composting—the letters they may form will indicate the initials of the next guest to your home.) In a saucepan, bring the wine, cloves, sugar, cinnamon, and vanilla to a boil. Add apples, reduce heat, and let simmer for about an hour, until fruit is almost transparent. Remove the apples and blend the cornstarch into the sauce. Cook the syrup for a few minutes until thickened. Pour it over the apples and serve or chill it in the refrigerator for later use. Top with whipped cream or vanilla ice cream. This dessert will keep for several days in the refrigerator, and can be reheated.

Variation: Try pears in place of the apples.

Associated Holidays: Lughnasadh, Mabon, Samhain, Harvest Festivals

Serves 6

When the apple is ripe it will fall.

Manx Proverb

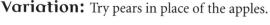

Rice Custard

I love the smell of rice custard baking in the oven. The aroma of vanilla and cinnamon always reminds me of cold winter days when I would come home from school to find this warm dish waiting for me.

> 1 cup uncooked rice
> 2 cups whole milk
> ½ cup sugar
> ¾ teaspoon vanilla extract
> ⅛ teaspoon salt
> Dash of cinnamon or nutmeg
> Brown sugar and cream

Soak rice in water overnight. Drain and place in a pie dish. Preheat oven to 350 degrees. Combine milk and sugar in a saucepan; heat to near boiling, stirring until sugar has dissolved. Remove from heat, add vanilla and salt; pour over rice. Sprinkle with cinnamon or nutmeg. Bake for about 1 hour 30 minutes or until a light crust forms on surface. Serve warm with brown sugar and cream.

Associated Holidays: Imbolg, Ostara, Beltaine, Yule

Serves 4

Flower Pudding

From the recipe book of John Nott, Cook to the Duke of Bolton, 1723:

"Mince cowslip flowers, clove, gillyflowers, rose petals and spinach of each a handful, take a slice of manchet (white bread) and scald it with cream. Add a pound of blanch'd almonds pounded small with rose water, a quarter pound of dates, sliced and cut small, the yolks of three eggs, a handful of currants, and sweeten all with sugar. When boiled pour rosewater over and scrape on sugar."

Candied Rose Petals

The rose is an ancient symbol of the Goddess. Throughout the Orient it was called the "Flower of the Goddess," while in the West the white rose was a sign of the Virgin and the red rose represented the Goddess in her full sexual maturity. Christians adopted these symbols as representations of Mary, who is often addressed as the "Mystic Rose" or "Queen of the Rose Garden." Before the change of the calendar pushed May 1 up by several days, roses were common in Beltaine garlands to honor the Goddess. Folklore and faerie tales contain other surviving images of the Goddess. The legend of Sleeping Beauty, or "Briar Rose" as she is called in the British version of the tale, tells the story of a beautiful virgin trapped in a castle surrounded by thorny rose bushes.

1 cup rose petals
1 cup sugar
¾ cup water
  Confectioners' sugar

Although cultivated roses can be used, wild roses have the best flavor. Select choice blossoms and petals; wash gently, then spread on paper towels to dry. Trim away the ends, as these tend to be bitter. Combine sugar and water in a saucepan; boil until you can spin a thread when mixture is dropped into ice water (230 degrees to 234 degrees F on a candy thermometer). Pour syrup into a bowl on a bed of cracked ice. When syrup begins to crystallize, hold blossoms with tweezers and dip one at a time into syrup. Place petals on waxed paper to dry. As they harden, dust with confectioners' sugar. Store in an airtight container.

ASSOCIATED HOLIDAYS: BELTAINE, MIDSUMMER

SERVES 4

All night by the rose, the rose,

all night by the rose I lay,

dare I not steal the rose

and yet I bore the flower away.

MEDIEVAL BALLAD

Candied Blossoms

Candied violets, borage, roses, geraniums, violas, and other edible flowers put pretty finishing touches on custards, cakes, ice creams, sherbets, parfaits, and other light desserts. Or you can simply serve them in a bowl or little baskets as candy.

> 3 cups blossoms
>
> 3 cups sugar
>
> 2 cups water

Wash the blossoms quickly and remove the stems. Pat dry with paper towels.

Combine sugar and water, bring to a boil, and cook to the soft ball stage (about 275 degrees on a candy thermometer). Pour half of the syrup into a shallow pan and let both quantities cool. Position the flowers on a rack inside the pan so that they float on the syrup. Cover the top of the pan with a damp cloth and let it sit in a cool place for several hours. Then cover the flowers with the remaining cooled syrup. Let them stand at least twelve hours in a cool place with a cloth over the pan to keep dust out.

Remove the rack and place it where the flowers can drain and dry. When the flowers are completely dried, store them in an airtight container between layers of waxed paper to prevent them from sticking together.

ASSOCIATED HOLIDAYS: BELTAINE, MIDSUMMER

Beauty without virtue is like

a rose without scent.

WELSH PROVERB

———◆———

Fruits and Preserved Flowers

From The Whole Body of Cookery Dissected, *1675:*

"Take a large dish, cover it with another of the same bigness, and lay the uppermost all over with almond paste; inlaid with white, red, green, blue or white marmalad in the figures of banks of flowers. Then take branches of candy'd flowers and stick them upright in the paste in as handsome orders as you can, then erect little bushes covered with paste, and upon them fasten preserved apples, aprichochs, currants, gooseberries, peaches, plums, etc, and for leaves you may make use either of colored paste, parchment, or horn. This will be very proper in winter."

Crystallized Leaves and Blossoms

Sugar-coated herb petals and leaves make exquisite garnishes for desserts or can be eaten as candy.

Pick roses, violets, johnny-jump-ups, or attractive leaves of borage, sage, mint, or other sweet foliage. Wash the petals or leaves quickly, and gently pat them dry with a paper towel. Separate the individual flower petals, and if you're using roses, cut away the bitter white and yellow tips of the petals.

Beat egg whites until foamy, and brush them on each side of the leaves or petals with a pastry brush or your fingers, but do not dip them into the egg white. Surfaces should be moist but not dripping. Shake or dust fine granulated white sugar on both sides. Place them gently on a tray, and let them dry in the refrigerator for several days.

ASSOCIATED HOLIDAYS: BELTAINE, MIDSUMMER

Love is a flower which
at marriage bears fruit.

SCOTTISH PROVERB

Irish Tea Brack

Eat apricots to sweeten your temper and appearance. Carry the stone in your pocket to attract love (Scottish belief).

2	pounds fruit: raisins, sultanas, currants, candied peel, et cetera
2½	cups brown sugar
2	cups strong black tea, hot
2	cups Irish Whiskey or Scotch
3	cups flour
3	eggs, beaten
1	tablespoon baking powder
2	teaspoons apple pie spice

Place fruit and sugar in a bowl. Pour hot tea and whiskey over them. Stir to dissolve sugar and soak overnight. Add flour, eggs, baking powder, and spices to the fruit mixture. Mix well and pour into 9 by 5-inch greased bread pan. Bake one hour at 350 degrees. Allow to cool in the pan slightly before turning out to cool on wire racks. This type of brack can be given a sticky glaze, such as honey or sugar, or served with fresh butter. Brush on the glaze 10 minutes before the end of baking.

ASSOCIATED HOLIDAYS: NAME DAYS/BIRTHDAYS, ESBAT SUPPERS, YULE

Chranachan (Toasted Almond Pudding)

Traditionally, a feast would start with soup and end with nuts, so chranachan pudding is a good dessert choice. People have long held nuts in awe, for they seemed to pack powerful magic in a very small space; we still frequently hear the phrase, "Mighty oaks from little acorns grow." It was a common custom to distribute almonds as a fertility charm and a blessing for marriage. Even today you will find bundles of candy-coated almonds at wedding banquets. People rarely eat them, but keep the almonds around for luck. In this recipe, almonds are paired with another food with fertility associations—raspberries. Raspberry tea is still taken to prepare the body for childbirth.

⅔	cup uncooked oatmeal
⅓	cup slivered almonds
1¼	cups whipping cream
	Honey
5	tablespoons Irish Whiskey
	Juice of one lemon
	Strawberries or raspberries to garnish

On a baking sheet, toast the oatmeal and almonds at 300 degrees for 5 to 10 minutes, stirring frequently. Whip the cream, being careful not to overbeat it unless you want to end up with butter. Stir in honey and whiskey. Gently fold in almonds and oatmeal. Stir in lemon juice. Divide into individual long-stemmed glasses. Serve at room temperature or chill, garnish with berries.

ASSOCIATED HOLIDAYS: SAMHAIN, YULE

SERVES 6

From soup to nuts.

SCOTTISH SAYING

Porter Cake

This recipe is a happy combination of cake and ale, and can be used in Esbat gatherings. Porter is a type of dark beer that's not easily come by anymore, but Guinness or any other black stout can be substituted in its place. The cake tastes wonderful fresh out of the oven, but it's best when allowed to age for a week. Store in an airtight container.

- 4 cups flour
- ½ teaspoon baking soda
- Pinch of salt
- 1 teaspoon mixed spice
- ½ teaspoon nutmeg
- Grated zest of 1 lemon
- 2 sticks butter
- 1 cup dark brown sugar
- 1¼ cups porter or stout
- 6 cups dried or candied fruit (raisins, currants, crystallized cherries, apricots, candied peel, et cetera)
- 3 eggs

Sieve together flour, baking soda, and spices. Add the lemon zest and set aside. In a saucepan, melt the butter and sugar into the porter. Add the fruit and let simmer for 10 minutes. Allow mixture to cool, then add the dry ingredients. Beat the eggs and mix in with a wooden spoon. Pour into a greased 9-inch cake pan and bake on middle rack of 350-degree oven for about 2 hours. A toothpick skewer will come out clean when the cake is ready.

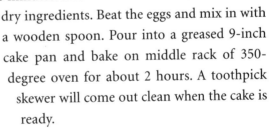

ASSOCIATED HOLIDAYS: NAME DAYS/BIRTHDAYS, ESBAT SUPPERS, YULE

Christmas Plum Pudding

For this recipe you will need a pudding mold, an earthenware basin found in most kitchen stores or antique markets (although with an antique there is the risk of lead in the glaze). If you cannot locate one, a Pyrex bowl may be substituted instead.

3	carrots, chopped
2	pounds candied fruit, chopped
1	pound seedless raisins
1	pound currants
½	cup chopped almonds
	Grated rind of 1 lemon
	Grated rind of 1 orange
7	cups dry bread crumbs
2	cups flour
1	cup sugar
1	teaspoon salt
1	teaspoon cinnamon
1	teaspoon cloves
1	teaspoon nutmeg
3	eggs, beaten
¼	cup dark molasses
1	cup milk
1	pound beef suet, ground

Brandy Butter:

6	tablespoons butter
4	tablespoons brandy, or to taste
¾	cup powdered sugar

Mix carrots, candied fruit, raisins, currants, almonds, and grated rinds. In another bowl, mix crumbs, flour, sugar, salt, cinnamon, cloves, and nutmeg; add eggs, molasses, milk, and suet. Add fruit mixture and combine thoroughly. For luck, everyone in the family must stir the pudding and make a wish. Cover with a cloth, leave mixture out overnight, and stir again in the morning. Pack into a greased 2½-quart mold, filling ⅔ full. Cover with lid or foil. Place on a rack set in a large kettle; pour boiling water halfway up sides of mold. Simmer, covered, for 4 hours. Cool on rack 10 minutes. Recover with new foil or waxed paper tied around with string. Store in a cool, dark place until ready to serve. On Christmas Day, steam pudding for an additional hour or so. Splash a little whiskey or poitín over the top of the pudding and set alight at the table. Serve on heated plates with brandy butter on the side.

For brandy butter (on the day you will serve the pudding): Cream the butter and sugar until light and fluffy. Beat in brandy a little at a time.

ASSOCIATED HOLIDAYS: YULE,
NEW YEAR'S EVE

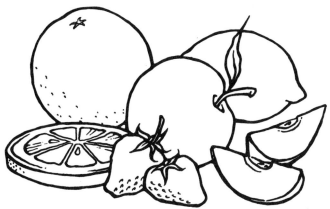

Flour of Ireland, fruit of Spain,
Met together in a shower of rain;
Put in a bag, tied up with a string,
If you tell me this riddle I'll give you a ring.

———◆———

Funeral Cake

In Ireland she is called the Bean-sidhe *(banshee), a ghostly lady in white whose shriek brings death to those that hear it. In Brittany she is the* Bandrhude, *or Bane Druid, a faerie woman whose sobbing proclaims the death of an individual. And in Wales she is known as the* Gwrach y rhibyn, *a Death Hag who sometimes took the form of a crow. All of these characters represent the Goddess in her Crone aspect, when she calls her children home. Yet death was not something to be feared but rather celebrated, for the Goddess restores life to her followers in her cauldron of regeneration.*

Therefore wakes, while primarily a time to mourn the dead, were also important social occasions; there's an old proverb that says "Many a match was made at a wake." Friends and relatives gathered in the house to pay their last respects, and the corpse was laid out in the best room in the house—sometimes the kitchen. Oftentimes a pinch of salt was placed in the coffin, salt being a symbol for eternal life and resurrection. It was important to feed the guests, and certain foods were always served: cold meats and cakes with stout, whiskey, or poítin to wash them down. It was also a time for storytelling and cardplaying, music and dance, contests of strength and "funeral games" such as The Bull and the Cow, Kick the Cobbler, The Fox in the Hole, and The Minister's Cat.

2½	cups chopped dates
1	pound raisins
3	cups sugar
3	cups water
½	cup butter
5	cups flour
2	teaspoons salt
2	teaspoons soda
3	teaspoons cinnamon
2	teaspoons cloves
1½	cups assorted nuts
1	pound candied fruit

This produces a dark fruit cake. Combine dates, raisins, sugar, water, and butter in a medium saucepan. Simmer for 20 minutes. Allow to cool. Sift together dry ingredients and pour into three well-greased bread tins. Bake 1 hour and 45 minutes at 325 degrees.

Associated Holidays: Funerals, Wakes, Samhain

The Black Book of Carmarthan

I am the wind that breathes upon the sea,

I am the wave upon the ocean,

I am the murmur of leaves rustling,

I am the rays of the sun,

I am the beam of the moon and stars,

I am the power of trees growing,

I am the bud breaking into blossom,

I am the movement of the salmon swimming,

I am the courage of the wild boar fighting,

I am the speed of the stag running,

I am the strength of the ox pulling the plough,

I am the size of the mighty oak tree.

◆

The fort beside the oakwood grove,

It was Bruidgi's, it was Cathail's,

It was Aedh's, it was Aillil's,

It was Conaing's, it was Cuilín's,

It was Mael Dúin's.

The fort remains after each in turn,

and the kings sleep in the ground.

ANONYMOUS

◆

Faerie Cakes

In Ireland, faerie cakes are served on Nollaig na mBan, *Women's Christmas, which is celebrated on December 12. Like hot cross buns, these faerie cakes have magical properties. Besides enabling you to see faeries, they work as a fertility charm and will heal the sick—but only if baked on that day.*

1	stick butter
⅔	cup sugar
2	eggs, beaten
½	teaspoon vanilla extract
	Grated rind of one orange
¾	teaspoon baking powder
1¼	cups flour
1	tablespoon milk
⅓	cup sultanas

Sugar Icing:

2	cups powdered sugar
2	tablespoon water, boiling

Cream the butter and sugar together until light and fluffy. Beat in eggs, vanilla, and orange rind. Sieve the baking powder and flour together and add to the butter mixture. Add a little milk to create a batter of dropping consistency. Fold in the sultanas and spoon the mixture into well-greased muffin cups. Bake at 375 degrees for 25 minutes. Drizzle on sugar icing and serve.

For sugar icing, combine powdered sugar with boiling water.

ASSOCIATED HOLIDAYS: NOLLAIG NA MBAN, YULE, ESBAT DINNERS, NAME DAYS/BIRTHDAYS

Yellow butter sells best.

SCOTTISH PROVERB

Mincemeat Parcels with Irish Whiskey Cream

A cherry year, a merry year (Scottish proverb).

½ pound currants
¼ pound raisins
¼ pound white raisins
¼ pound chopped candied peel
¼ cup chopped glacé cherries
2 cooking apples, peeled and chopped
Juice and grated rind of 1 lemon
¼ pound dark brown sugar
¼ teaspoon allspice
¼ teaspoon ground nutmeg
¼ teaspoon ground cinnamon
Pinch of cloves
½ cup butter, melted
⅓ cup Irish Whiskey
1 pound phyllo pastry

Irish Whiskey Cream:
1 cup whipped cream
1 teaspoon powdered sugar
3 tablespoons whiskey, or to taste

Mix the fruits, lemon juice and rind, sugar, and spices together; pour in the melted butter and Irish Whiskey. Mix thoroughly. Pour into clean, sterilized glass jars, seal, and store for at least 2 weeks before using.

To prepare the parcels, cut the sheets of phyllo pastry into 3-inch squares and layer three or four squares, brushing with melted butter between each layer. Put a tablespoonful of the mincemeat in the center and shape the pastry like a drawstring purse, tying the top loosely with string. Bake for 15 to 20 minutes at 400 degrees. Serve with ice cream or Irish Whiskey Cream. To make cream, fold the sugar and whiskey into the whipped cream. Serve a dollop on each parcel.

ASSOCIATED HOLIDAYS: YULE, NEW YEAR'S EVE, ESBAT SUPPERS

Figgy Pudding

In many parts of Europe, it is still considered an insult to "fig" someone: to stick your thumb through the fingers of a closed fist. Yet this gesture, with its obvious lingam/yoni connotations, was also thought to protect one from the Evil Eye. I have a wooden charm from my grandmother of a hand carved into the shape of a fig. The head of a woman is carved into the other end. She said it was powerful magic and would keep me from harm. I was too young at the time to ask her how she came to possess it, or what it really meant. But I still keep it in my spirit pouch as a memory to her.

¼	cup dried apricots
½	cup prunes
¼	cup dried apples
½	cup raisins and sultanas
¼	cup dates
½	cup lard
1	cup flour
1	cup milk
1½	cups dried figs
1	tablespoon honey
1	wineglass brandy
¼	teaspoon ginger
¼	teaspoon cinnamon

The day before starting the figgy pudding, place the apricots, prunes, and apples in a dish and cover with water. Soak overnight. In another bowl, put the raisins and sultanas to soak overnight in the brandy.

The next day, fill a large saucepan one-third full of water. Remove the stones from the dates and prunes and discard. Butter a large pudding basin. Mix the lard and flour; gradually add the milk to make a stiff dough. Roll the dough out ¼ inch thick and line the pudding basin, leaving enough dough to sufficiently seal the top. In a small saucepan melt the honey; stir in the ginger, cinnamon, and brandy mixture. Pack the fruit into the basin and pour the honey-brandy mixture over it. Seal the basin with the suet-crust lid. Cover with foil and tie it down tightly, leaving a long end of string to make it easier to lift out of the saucepan later. Bring the water in the large saucepan to a boil and place the pudding basin in the pan; continue to let the water boil and cook the pudding for two hours. Add more water when necessary. Turn out onto a dish and serve.

ASSOCIATED HOLIDAYS: YULE, NEW YEAR'S EVE

Oh bring us some figgy pudding,

oh bring us some figgy pudding,

oh bring us some figgy pudding,

and bring it right here!

BRITISH FOLKSONG

Tansy Pudding

Tansy has been used in spells of immortality and invisibility, and if hung above the front door will prevent evil from entering the house. If hung above the bed, it can aid in conception. It also makes a great spring tonic.

2	cups milk
1	tablespoon butter
½	cup fresh breadcrumbs
¼	cup sugar or honey
2	tablespoons tansy leaves, chopped fine
2	eggs, beaten
	Honey and cream, to serve

Boil the milk and butter together and pour over the breadcrumbs. Set aside for 30 minutes. Beat together the sugar and the tansy leaves with the eggs, and fold into the breadcrumb mixture. Pour into a pudding bowl or Pyrex dish and bake at 350 degrees until set. Serve cold with cream and honey.

ASSOCIATED HOLIDAYS: OSTARA, BELTAINE, MIDSUMMER

Rum Balls

The vanilla plant has a long association with love magic. Its purple flowers are used in amulets, sachets, and love potions.

    1   cup vanilla wafer crumbs
    1   cup pecans, chopped fine
    1   cup powdered sugar
    2   tablespoons cocoa
    ¼   cup rum
        More powdered sugar and nuts for rolling

Combine all ingredients together. Form in small bowls and roll in powdered sugar and nuts. Store in airtight containers.

ASSOCIATED HOLIDAY: YULE

MAKES 6 DOZEN

Steamed Orange Pudding

It was once a tradition for young brides to carry orange blossoms in their bridal bouquet or to wear them in their hair. Because flowers and fruit could both appear on the same tree, the orange became a symbol of the Goddess in her Virgin and Mother aspects. To wear orange blossoms would serve as a fertility charm and as a testament to the bride's virginity.

    1   tablespoon corn syrup
        Grated rind and juice of 2 oranges
    1   stick butter
    ½   cup sugar
    2   eggs, beaten
    ½   cup flour
    ¼   cup fine white breadcrumbs

Heat the syrup and add the orange rind and juice; pour into a well-greased pudding bowl. Beat the butter and sugar until light and fluffy and gradually add the beaten eggs. Add the flour and breadcrumbs. Pour this mixture into the basin with the orange sauce; do not stir. Cover with a double layer of foil. Tie tightly with string and lower the basin into a large saucepan of boiling water. Put the lid on the saucepan tightly and boil for 1½ hours. Check periodically to make sure water does not boil away. Turn pudding out onto a large dish.

ASSOCIATED HOLIDAYS: BELTAINE, MIDSUMMER,
LUGHNASADH, SUN FESTIVALS

Cornish Saffron Cakes

The saffron plant is an important magical herb. It is used in healing rituals and love spells, and is used as an aid in raising storms. Ingesting the herb or drinking a potion can boost clairvoyant powers.

½	teaspoon saffron
1	cup boiling water
½	cup butter
1½	cups sugar
¼	tablespoon lemon juice
2	eggs
2¾	cups flour
1	cup currants
1	cup candied fruit
1	cup raisins
	Sugar for sprinkling

Pour boiling water over saffron and let set until cool. Combine all the ingredients and bake in a 9 by 13-inch pan at 350 degrees for 50 minutes. Sprinkle with sugar before serving.

ASSOCIATED HOLIDAY: MIDSUMMER

Lughnasadh Pie

Blueberries, also known as fraughans, herts, *or* bilberries, *are connected with the ancient festival of Lughnasadh. In later years this Sabbat came to be known as Garland Sunday, a time when the whole village would gather for a day of singing, dancing, feasting, courting—and picking wild blueberries.*

1	cup sugar
¼	cup flour
	Grated zest of ½ lemon
	Salt to taste
5	cups fresh blueberries
	Pastry for a 9-inch, 2 crust pie
	Juice of 1 lemon
1	tablespoon butter

Combine sugar, flour, lemon zest, and salt to taste. Add blueberries, tossing to thoroughly coat fruit. Pour mixture into a pie crust, drizzle with lemon juice and dab with butter. Place top crust over pie; seal and flute edges. Cover edge of pie with foil. Bake for 20 minutes at 375 degrees. Remove foil and bake for another 25 minutes. Cool on a wire rack.

ASSOCIATED HOLIDAY: LUGHNASADH

Many a lad met his wife
on Blueberry Sunday.

IRISH SAYING

◆

Apple and Rowanberry Tart

Rowan trees are native to Celtic lands, but they were not usually cultivated for their fruit. People often planted them beside their cottage to ward off the evil eye, and their wood was used for wands and other magical purposes. Burning a bit of the wood enhances visions and strengthens spells.

Rowan trees growing near stone circles produce the most potent of woods—carve the wood into a walking stick or magic wand, or fashion it into a divining rod. Rowan is the most magical of all trees, as shown in its other names: witchwood and witchbane.

As a general spell of protection, an equilateral cross can be made by tying together two pieces of rowan wood. Wrap a black thread, a white thread, and a red thread around the middle. In Scotland these were sewn into clothes and in Cornwall they were kept in pockets. Equilateral crosses were a symbol of the Goddess.

If living in North America, it is best to purchase rowanberries from an online source as some species of American rowanberries may be toxic.

     Pastry for a 9-inch, 2-crust pie
4   **cooking apples, cored and sliced**
1   **cup rowanberries**
1   **cup sugar**
3   **cloves**
1   **egg, beaten**
     Superfine sugar
     Whipped cream and brown sugar to serve

Combine apples, rowanberries, and sugar. Pour mixture into a 9-inch pie crust, add cloves, and sprinkle with additional sugar. Place top crust over pie; seal and flute edges. Cut a small slash in the center to allow steam to escape and brush with beaten egg. Cover edge of pie with foil. Bake for 20 minutes at 475 degrees. Remove foil and bake for another 45 minutes at 350 degrees. Serve hot with whipped cream and soft brown sugar.

ASSOCIATED HOLIDAYS: LUGHNASADH, MABON, SAMHAIN

I will eat good apples in the glen

and fragrant berries of the rowan tree.

TWELFTH CENTURY, IRELAND

Baked Apples

Nutmeg was prescribed by wise women for a number of inflictions, including back-aches, boils, and rheumatism.

6	large baking apples
¾	cup fruit and nut mixture (currants, nuts, lemon rind, et cetera)
½	cup dark brown sugar, packed
½	cup water
1	tablespoon butter
½	teaspoon cinnamon
½	teaspoon nutmeg
	Whipped cream

Core the apples and place in a baking dish large enough to accommodate the apples without them touching. Fill the apples with the fruit and nut mixture. In a small saucepan, combine the brown sugar, water, butter, and spices. Bring to a boil and pour sugar mixture around apples. Bake, uncovered, for 1 hour at 350 degrees. Baste occasionally with the sugar mixture; they will be done when they are fluffy and slightly burst. Serve with whipped cream.

ASSOCIATED HOLIDAYS: SAMHAIN, YULE, ESBAT DINNERS

SERVES 6

Apple tree, little apple tree,

violently everyone shakes you.

Rowan, little berried one,

lovely is your bloom.

EARLY CELTIC POEM

Bread Pudding

One cannot go far without bread, for bread is life (Manx proverb).

⅓	loaf of stale bread
8	eggs
1	cup sugar
	Grated lemon zest
4	cups milk
	Butter to dot on top
	Lemon juice, cherries, strawberries

Break bread into bite-sized pieces. Place bread pieces in a 9 by 9 by 2-inch pan. Beat eggs and sugar together, add zest and cold milk and pour over bread. Dot with butter and bake in a 375-degree oven till custard is set. Do not heat milk before mixing. Sprinkle with lemon juice, cherries, and strawberries.

Variation: Add raisins, nutmeg, and brown sugar for a sweeter version.

ASSOCIATED HOLIDAYS: EVERYDAY DESSERT, ESBAT DINNERS

Burnt Sugar Cake

Keep a pecan in your coat pocket to attract silver (British belief).

½   cup plus 1 cup sugar
½   cup boiling water
⅔   cup butter
1   teaspoon vanilla extract
2   eggs, separated
3   cups flour, sifted
3   teaspoons baking powder
1   teaspoon salt
1   cup milk
     Caramel frosting, pecan halves

Slowly heat ½ cup sugar in a small saucepan, stirring all the while. When sugar is melted and begins to smoke, slowly add water while continuing to stir. Cook until syrup measures ½ cup, stirring until sugar is dissolved. Cool. Cream butter; gradually add 1 cup sugar, beating until light and fluffy. Add vanilla, then yolks, beating thoroughly after each. Stir in syrup. Add dry ingredients alternately with milk; beat until smooth. Beat egg whites until stiff and fold into flour mixture. Pour into three 9-inch round greased and floured layer pans. Bake at 375 degrees about 20 minutes. Cool and frost with caramel frosting (below) and top with nuts.

Caramel frosting

2   tablespoons butter
⅓   cup cream
⅔   cup brown sugar, packed
⅛   teaspoon salt
2   drops vanilla
3   cups sifted powdered sugar

Combine butter, cream, sugar, and salt in a saucepan. Bring to a boil. Remove from heat and add vanilla. Gradually add powdered sugar and blend until it is of spreading consistency.

ASSOCIATED HOLIDAYS: NAME DAYS/BIRTHDAYS

Nut Cake

As most nuts are fertility charms, this makes an excellent wedding cake.

1	cup soft butter
1¾	cups sugar
1	teaspoon vanilla extract
3	whole eggs plus 1 egg yolk
3	cups sifted flour
2	teaspoons baking powder
¾	teaspoon salt
¾	cup milk
1	cup finely chopped nuts

Cream butter; gradually add sugar. Beat until light and fluffy. Add vanilla. Add eggs and yolk, one at a time, beating thoroughly after each addition. Add sifted dry ingredients alternately with milk, beating until smooth. Fold in nuts. Pour into greased 9-inch tube pan, lined on bottom with waxed paper. Bake in 375-degree oven for 1 hour, or until done. Cool in pan for 10 minutes, remove to rack.

ASSOCIATED HOLIDAYS: NAME DAYS/BIRTHDAYS, SAMHAIN, MABON, ESBAT DINNERS, WEDDINGS

Maura O'Byrne's Christmas Cake

I first met Fiach O'Byrne when he came to live with his brother Rory in the apartment downstairs from my own. They had grown up at Ballykealy Farm in Ballon, County Carlow, and they spoke often of their mother's fine country cooking. They were not able to return to Ireland that first winter, and I phoned their mother to get her recipe for Christmas Cake, a favorite with the O'Byrne boys. On Christmas Day we cheerfully argued over how to apply the marzipan topping and the white icing, and what to use for the snowmen and faerie decorations. Although Fiach is no longer with us, I make this cake each Yule time in memory of him.

2	cups golden raisins
2	cups currants
½	cup glacé cherries
½	cup candied peel
⅔	cup almonds, chopped
1	lemon rind
4–6	tablespoons brandy
2	sticks butter, softened
1½	cups sugar
7	eggs, beaten
2	cups flour
1	teaspoon salt
	Apricot preserves

Place fruit, nuts, and rind in a baking dish. Cover with foil and heat at 275 degrees until heated through, about 15 minutes. This will make the fruit sticky and prevent it from sinking during baking.

Let the fruit cool completely, then combine with the brandy and set aside. Cream the butter and sugar until light and fluffy. Add the eggs, one at a time, with a little flour to prevent curdling. Sift the flour with the salt and fold into the egg mixture. Fold fruit and nuts into batter. Put the mixture into a deep, 10-inch greased cake pan that has been lined with waxed paper. Bake for 3 hours at 350 degrees. Bake an additional two hours at 300 degrees. Let the cake grow cold and spread with a thin layer of apricot preserves. The cake should then be topped with an almond paste.

Almond Paste

⅔ cup sugar

⅔ cup powdered sugar

2 cups ground almonds

2 eggs

2 tablespoons brandy or whiskey

 Almond extract

Sift together the sugars and the ground almonds. In a separate bowl, whisk the eggs with the whiskey, and add a drop of the almond extract. Fold into the sugar mixture. Blend to form a stiff paste. Sprinkle the work surface with powdered sugar, turn out the almond paste, and knead until smooth. Roll out ⅛ inch thick and place over cake, covering top and sides completely. Frost with white icing and decorate with any sort of winter figurines you may have.

White Icing

2 egg whites

4 cups powdered sugar

2 teaspoons lemon juice

 Glycerine

Whisk the egg whites until they begin to froth; add the powdered sugar a tablespoon at a time, beating well with each addition. Add the lemon juice and a few drops of glycerine. Beat until the icing forms stiff peaks. Cover with a damp cloth for about an hour until ready to use. This cake is best when aged a week or two.

Teatime Spice Loaf with Raisins

In Celtic nations, "tea" usually means just tea, rich with fresh cream and sugar. To "make tea" usually implies that some food, most often bread and butter but perhaps biscuits or cake, will accompany the hot beverage. I was served this delicious spice loaf during a visit to a friend's farm in Carlow.

1	cup brown sugar, packed
1	cup raisins
1¼	cups water
½	cup shortening
1	teaspoon cinnamon
½	teaspoon nutmeg
½	teaspoon allspice
2	cups flour
1	teaspoon soda
1	teaspoon baking powder
½	teaspoon salt

Boil brown sugar, raisins, water, shortening, cinnamon, nutmeg, and allspice together for five minutes. Let cool completely. Sift remaining dry ingredients; stir into first mixture. Pour into well-greased 9 by 5 by 3-inch loaf pan. Bake at 350 degrees for one hour. Turn out onto wire rack and cool. Serve plain or frost as desired.

ASSOCIATED HOLIDAYS: ESBAT DINNERS

Triple Citrus Curd

Use as a filling for tart shells, cakes, jelly rolls, cream puffs, or spread it on scones or toast.

½	cup butter
1	cup sugar
2	tablespoons lemon juice
2	tablespoons lime juice
2	tablespoons fresh orange juice
2	teaspoons lemon zest
2	teaspoons lime zest
2	teaspoons orange zest
5	eggs, beaten

Melt butter over medium heat. Remove from heat and stir in sugar, juices, zests, and eggs. Return to heat and cook, stirring constantly, until mixture begins to bubble—do not boil. Cool quickly by setting pan in a bowl of ice and stir for several minutes. Cover and refrigerate overnight.

ASSOCIATED HOLIDAYS: MIDSUMMER,
LUGHNASADH, SUN FESTIVALS

"*I never eat a meal,*" said Cormac,

"*without fifty in my company.*"

THE ADVENTURES OF CORMAC MAC ART

The Vision of Mac Conglinne

The Vision of Mac Conglinne is perhaps the only piece of early Celtic narrative that was composed expressly to make people laugh. It was written down in the Twelfth Century but is believed to be much older. It is a satire of contemporary religious writings as well as a burlesque on royal gluttony.

A vision that appeared to me,

An apparition wonderful I tell to all:

A lardy coracle all of lard

Within a port of New Milk Loch,

Up on the World's smooth sea.

We went into the man-of-war,

'Twas warrior-like to take the road

O'er ocean's heaving waves.

Our oar-strokes then we pulled

Across the level sea,

Throwing the sea's harvest up,

Like honey, the sea-soil.

The fort we reached was beautiful,

With outworks of custards thick,

Beyond the loch.

New butter was the bridge in front,

The rubble dyke was wheaten white,

Bacon the palisade.

Stately, pleasantly it sat,

A compact house and strong.

Then I went in:

The door of it was dry meat,

The threshold was bare bread,

Cheese-curds the sides.

Smooth pillars of old cheese,

And sappy bacon props
Alternate ranged;
Fine beams of mellow cream,
White rafters—real curds,
Kept up the house.
Behind was a wine well,
Beer and bragget in streams,
Each full pool to the taste.
Malt in a smooth wavy sea,
Over a lard-spring's brink
Flowed through the floor.
A loch of pottage fat
Under a cream of oozy lard
Lay 'tween it and the sea.
Hedges of butter fenced it round,
Under a blossom of white-mantling lard,
Around the wall outside.
A row of fragrant apple trees,
An orchard in its pink-tipped bloom,
Between it and the hill.
A forest of real leeks,
Of onions and of carrots stood
Behind the house.
Within, a household generous,
A welcome of red, firm-fed men,
Around the fire.
Seven bead strings and necklets seven,
Of cheeses and of bits of tripe,
Hung from each neck.
The Chief in mantle of beefy fat

Beside his noble wife and fair
I then beheld.
Below the lofty cauldron's spit
Then the Dispenser I behold,
His fleshfork on his back.
The good Cathal mac Finguine,
He is a good man to enjoy
Tales tall and fine.
That is a business for an hour,
And full of delight 'tis to tell
The rowing of the man-of-war
O'er the Loch Milk's sea.

◆

Honey

In very early mythology it was thought that the bees carried the soul back to the country where there is no room for death and where the souls fly free, ranging the heavens to join the stars, imperishable in number (Virgil).

Centuries before sugar became widely available, the sweetness of honey was used to enhance the flavor and palatability of a variety of foods. Prehistoric cave paintings in Western Europe depict early man gathering wild honey in much the same manner as today.

Honey was one of the few preservatives known to the ancients. In addition to its use as a food additive, it was also considered a powerful source of resurrection magic, and many are the myths showing how the Goddess restored her followers to life with her sacred bee balm. Along the Mediterranean the dead were once placed in the fetal position and embalmed in a jar of honey to await rebirth in the next world. Worshippers of the Goddess as Demeter referred to her as Mother Bee, and wild bees were looked on as her representatives on earth. They were believed to be the souls of priestesses who had once been in her service, so you should never attempt to harm a bee or move the hive. Nor should you argue in the presence of bees.

To the Greeks, bees were called *hymenoptera*, a word meaning "veil-winged," which referred to the veil that covered the inner chambers of the Goddess' temple. The Goddess was patroness of marriage, the wedding night, and honeymoon, and to deflower a maiden was to symbolically penetrate the veil of the Goddess. Christian mythology says that bees have their origin in the tears Christ shed during the crucifixion.

Traditionally, the honeymoon was the month of May, following the hand-fasting ceremonies of Beltaine. The honeymoon would include a menstrual cycle, the blood of which was called Moon Honey. Menstrual blood was held sacred, for the very magic of creation was thought to dwell in the blood women gave forth. Therefore, to copulate during this time would afford a man the opportunity to touch the very source of life. The Nordic tribes considered the elixir of life to be a combination of honey and the "wine blood" that came from the great cauldron of the Goddess' womb. The Celts believed that their kings could become gods by drinking this same "red mead" (mead being an alcoholic beverage made of honey).

Honey was so important in Celtic lands that the Irish Brehon laws devoted a whole section to bees and beekeeping. Tributes to chieftains could be paid in honey and mead, and a banquet was not considered complete unless there was plenty of mead to drink and honey for basting or dipping meat, fish, and poultry. Ireland has been described by many poets and bards as the "land of milk and honey."

There has always been a strong connection between bees and the bee-keeper's household. Beekeepers were careful to speak to their bees with the utmost respect, and to never shout or curse at them. It was believed that bees could not only understand human speech, but knew their keeper's voice and his particular smell.

It is still a common practice to "tell the bees" if a death occurred in the family. The beekeeper will go to the hive after sunset and pin a piece of black crepe on the hive, then lean over and whisper to the bees news of the sad occasion. If this was not done, the bees might swarm or else pine away and die without ever leaving their hives. In some areas it was common to turn beehives around to face the

opposite direction when a corpse was removed from the home. Even in late Celtic mythology, bees were identified with mortality. If bees left their hive, it was taken as a sign that the hive's owner would soon die.

Bees can keep secrets. The Scots say, "Ask the wild bee for what the druid knew." Hives were never sold for money, but always given away with the understanding that future payment would arrive in the form of fresh honey and honeycomb. They were so valuable that it became a capital offense in many regions to steal a beehive.

Bees were not to be found in North America when the Europeans first settled here, and so hives were carefully shipped overseas. Native tribes called them "white men's flies," and since that time bees have become a well-established feature of the landscape.

Today, honey is a welcome addition to any kitchen cupboard, where it is used to spread on toast, stir into stew, and pour over waffles and ice cream. Honeys vary in flavor—they can be full-bodied or smooth, depending on the flowers that the bees have gathered their nectar from. Honeys made from a single plant species, such as strawberries or lavender, tend to be more expensive than multifloral honeys, but it is simple enough to create a reasonable imitation in your kitchen.

Planting Your Own Bee Garden

If you wish to tend your own hive of bees, there are certain herbs and flowers you should plant that will attract bees to your garden and guarantee a steady supply of nectar for honey production. A bee garden should be planted in an area with an abundance of sunlight, and have individual herb species planted in groups of four or more. If your garden is not well sheltered, you may wish to erect some form of windbreak. A trellis looks beautiful when covered in roses, while a hedge of holly and ivy looks nice and provides flowers in spring and autumn. Select herbs that will provide pollen and nectar all season long, and remember to keep your hives out of the perimeter of the garden, as bees ignore plants within a 50-foot radius of the hive. The most important nectar-producing plants are fruit trees, clover, dandelion,

charlock, and mustard; you should include these in your yard if at all possible. You may also wish to consider the following plant species:

anise, basil, bee balm, borage, calendula, catmint, chamomile, chicory, coriander, crocus, fennel, flax, forget-met-not, goldenrod, horehound, hyssop, jacob's ladder, lavender, lemon balm, marjoram, meliot, mint, muskmellow, poppies, Queen Anne's Lace, rosemary, safflower, sage, savory, smallage, sunflower, thyme, valerian, verbena, viper's bugloss, woad, yarrow

Basic Herbed Honey

The most common flavored honeys include mint, lavender, thyme, cinnamon, and basil, but many other herbs can be used to flavor honey. Look on pages 66 and 67 for a list of herbal blends that work well together. There's plenty of room for experimentation here!

  2 **cups honey**
  ¼ **cup of the fresh herb of your choice**

Heat the honey gently over a low flame. Place the herbs in a clean jar and pour the warm honey over them. Seal and allow to age for at least a month before using.

Variation: Heat the honey gently over a low flame. Add herbs. Remove from heat and let cool. Strain and pour into sterilized jars.

He who would harvest honey
must endure the sting of the bees.

BRETON PROVERB

Honey of Roses

The following recipe comes from A Treatise of Cleanness in Meates, *1692:*

"Cut the white heels from red roses, take half a pound of them and put them into a stone jar, and pour on them three pints of boiling water. Stir well and let stand twelve hours. Then press off the liquor, and when it has settled add to it five pounds of honey. Boil it well, and when it is of the consistence of a thick syrup it is ready to put away."

Caramel Honey Apples

Try this honeyed variation of an autumnal favorite.

- 1 cup dark brown sugar
- ½ cup unsalted butter
- ½ cup clover honey
- ¼ cup cream
- ¼ teaspoon cinnamon
- ¼ teaspoon nutmeg
- ¼ cup chopped peanuts
- ¼ cup chopped almonds
- 4 large apples
- 4 sticks or apple sturdy apple twigs

Combine sugar, butter, honey, cream, and spices over medium heat. Cook until it reaches 265 degrees on a candy thermometer. Insert a stick in each apple and dip into caramel mixture. Roll the apples into the nuts and place on waxed paper to cool.

Honey Butter

Where the scythe cuts, and the plow rives, no more faeries or bee hives (Cornish proverb).

½ cup butter, cut in small pieces
¼ cup honey
½ teaspoon lemon zest

Soften butter to room temperature. Stir in honey and lemon zest. Serve with soda bread and hearty glasses of milk.

Honey Almond Candy

Carry an almond in your pocket during the waxing moon to make your money increase and to have general success in all your business ventures.

2 cups sugar
1 cup clover honey
½ cup peanuts
¾ cup almonds
½ stick butter
2 teaspoons vanilla
1 teaspoon baking soda
Pinch of salt

Combine sugar and honey in a large saucepan. Simmer over medium heat until sugar dissolves. Add peanuts, almonds, butter, and vanilla; combine thoroughly. Remove from heat and stir in soda and salt. Stir until light and creamy and spread onto a greased cookie sheet. Let cool. Break into pieces and store in an airtight container.

ASSOCIATED HOLIDAYS:
IMBOLG, BELTAINE,
SAMHAIN

The three most difficult things to understand:

the mind of another,

the labor of bees,

and the ebb and flow of the tide.

WELSH TRIAD

Bibliography and Recommended Readings

Adler, Margot. *Drawing Down the Moon*. Boston, 1986.

Angus, S. *The Mystery Religions*. New York, 1975.

Apocrypha (authorized version). New York, 1962.

Asala, Joanne. *Irish Saints and Sinners*. New York, 1995.

———. *Whistling Jigs to the Moon: Tales of Irish and Scottish Pipers*. Iowa City, 1993.

Ashe, Geoffrey. *The Virgin*. London, 1976.

Attwater, Donald. *The Penguin Dictionary of Saints*. Baltimore, 1965

Bacon, Edward. *Vanished Civilizations of the Ancient World*. London, 1963.

Baring-Gould, Sabine. *Curious Myths of the Middle Ages*. New York, 1967.

Barth, Edna. *Shamrocks, Harps, and Shillelaghs: The Story of the St. Patrick's Day Symbols*. New York, 1977.

———. *Lilies, Rabbits, and Painted Eggs: The Story of the Easter Symbols*. New York, 1970.

———. *Witches, Pumpkins, and Grinning Ghosts: The Story of Halloween Symbols*. New York, 1972.

———. *Holly, Reindeer, and Colored Lights: The Story of the Christmas Symbols*. New York, 1971.

Bates, Katharine Lee. *Ballad Book*. Boston, 1890.

Best, R. I. and Osborn Bergin, eds. *Book of the Dun Cow*. Dublin, 1929.

Best, R. I., Osborn Bergin, and M. A. O'Brien. *The Book of Leinster*. Dublin, 1954-67.

Bergin, Osborn and R. I. Best, eds. *The Wooing of Étain*. Dublin, 1937.

Binder, Pearl. *Magic Symbols of the World*. London, 1972.

Brandon, S. G. F. *Religion in Ancient History*. New York, 1969.

Branston, Brian. *Gods of the North*. London, 1955.

Bremness, Lesley. *The Complete Book of Herbs*. New York, 1988.

Brewster, H. Pomeroy. *Saints and Festivals of the Christian Church*. New York, 1904.

Bromwich, R. *The Welsh Triads*. Cardiff, 1961.

Brooks, J. A. *Ghosts and Legends of Wales*. Norwich, England, 1987.

Budge, Sir. E. A. Wallis. *Egyptian Magic*. New York, 1969.

Butler, Sharon and Constance B. Hieatt. *Pleyn Delit: Medieval Cookery for Modern Cooks*. Toronto, 1976.

Campbell, Joseph. *The Masks of God: Primitive Mythology*. New York, 1959.

———. *The Masks of God: Oriental Mythology*. New York, 1962.

———. *The Masks of God: Occidental Mythology*. New York, 1964.

———. *The Masks of God: Creative Mythology*. New York, 1970.

———. *The Power of Myth*. New York, 1988.

———. *The Flight of the Wild Gander*. Chicago, 1969.

Campbell, Joseph F. *Popular Tales of the Western Highlands*. Edinburgh, 1860.

Carmichael, A. *Carmina Gadelica* (2 volumes). Edinburgh, 1928.

Cavendish, Richard, ed. *Man, Myth, and Magic* (Volumes 1-30). New York, 1970.

———. *Mythology: An Illustrated Encyclopedia*. London, 1992.

Chadwick, Nora. *The Celts*. Harmondsworth, 1970.

Chaucer. *The Canterbury Tales*. Harmondsworth, England, 1951.

Clough, S. D. P. *A Gaelic Anthology.* Dublin, 1987.

Cole, William. *Folk Songs of England, Ireland, Scotland, and Wales.* New York, 1969.

Collins, Joseph B. *Christian Mysticism in the Elizabethan Age.* New York, 1991.

Colum, Padraic. *An Anthology of Irish Verse.* New York, 1948.

Conway, D. J. *Celtic Magick.* St. Paul, Minnesota, 1990.

Crawley, Ernest. *The Mystic Rose.* New York, 1960.

Croker, Thomas Crofton. *Fairy Legends and Traditions of the South of Ireland.* London, 1828.

Cross, Tom. P. and Clark Harris Slover. *Ancient Irish Tales.* Dublin, 1936.

Cunningham, Scott. *Earth Power.* St. Paul, Minnesota, 1992.

Curtain, Jeremiah. *Myths and Folklore of Ireland.* New York, 1969.

Delehaye, Hippolyte. *The Legends of the Saints.* New York, 1962.

de Lys, Claudia. *The Giant Book of Superstitions.* Secaucus, New Jersey, 1979.

de Paor, M. and L. *Early Christian Ireland.* London, 1978.

Doane, T. W. *Bible Myths and their Parrallels in Other Religions.* New York, 1971.

Doble, G. H. *Lives of the Welsh Saints.* Cardiff, 1971.

Doel, Geoff and Fran Doel. *Mumming, Howling, and Hoodning: Midwinter Rituals in Sussex, Kent, and Surrey.* Ashford, England, 1992.

Dossey, Donald E. *Holiday Folklore, Phobias, and Fun.* Los Angeles, 1992.

Douglas, Sir George. *Scottish Fairy and Folk Tales.* New York, 1900.

Ebbutt, M. I. *The British.* New York, 1985. (Originally published in 1910.)

Elder, Isabel Hill. *Celt, Druid, and Culdee.* London, 1990.

Ellis, Albert. *The Folklore of Sex.* New York, 1951.

Ellis, Peter Berresford. *Dictionary of Celtic Mythology.* Oxford, 1992.

Evans-Wentz, W. Y. *The Fairy Faith in Celtic Countries.* New York, 1966.

Fielding, William J. *Strange Customs of Courtship and Marriage.* New York, 1942.

Frazier, Sir James George. *The Golden Bough.* London, 1922.

———. *Folklore in the Old Testament.* New York, 1927.

Funk, Wilfred. *Word Origins and their Romantic Stories.* New York, 1978.

Gantz, Jeffrey. *Early Irish Myths and Sagas.* New York, 1981.

———. *The Mabinogion.* Harmondsworth, 1976.

Garmey, Jane. *Great British Cooking.* New York, 1981.

Gascoigne, Russell. *The Haunting of Glamorgan and Gwent.* Gwynedd, Wales, 1993.

Gaster, Theodor. *Myth, Legend, and Custom in the Old Testament.* New York, 1969.

Geoffrey of Monmouth. *History of the Kings of Britain,* in various translations.

Giraldus Cambrensis. *The History and Topography of Ireland,* in various translations.

Glassie, Henry. *All Silver and No Brass.* Indiana, ca. 1975.

Gmelch, Sharon. *Irish Life and Traditions.* Dublin, 1986.

Graves, A. P. *A Celtic Psaltery.* London, 1917.

Graves, Robert. *The White Goddess.* New York, 1973.

Greene, D. and O'Connor, F. *A Golden Treasury of Irish Poetry* A.D. *600 to 1200.* London, 1967.

Gregory, Lady Isabella Augusta. *Cuchulain of Muirthemne: The Story of the Red Branch of Ulster.* New York, 1924.

———. *Gods and Fighting Men.* New York, 1904.

Guerber, H. A. *Legends of the Middle Ages*. New York, 1924.

Guest, Lady Charlotte. *The Mabinogion*. London, 1904.

Guignebert, Charles. *Ancient, Medieval and Modern Christianity*. New York, 1961.

Hamilton, Edith. *Mythology*. Boston, 1940.

Hazlitt, W. Carew. *Faiths and Folklore of the British Isles*. New York, 1965.

Henderson, George. *Bricriu's Feast*, in *Fled Bricrend*. Dublin, 1899.

Higginson, Thomas Wentworth. *Tales of the Enchanted Islands of the Atlantic*. New York, 1898.

Hitching, Francis. *Earth Magic*. New York, 1978.

Hole, Christina. *English Custom and Usage*. London, 1941.

Hull, E. *The Poem Book of the Gael*. London, 1912.

Hyde, Douglas. *The Religious Songs of Connacht*. Dublin, 1906.

————. *Legends of Saints and Sinners*. Dublin, 1915.

Jackson, K. H. *A Celtic Miscellany*. London, 1971.

Jacobs, J. *English Fairy Tales*. London, ca. 1890.

————. *Celtic Fairy Tales*. London, ca. 1890.

————. *More Celtic Fairy Tales*. London, ca. 1890.

Jeffery, P. H. *Ghosts, Legends, and Lore of Wales*. Cambridge, date unknown.

John, Brian. *Pembrokeshire Folk Tales*. Newport, Wales, 1992.

Johnson, Walter. *Folk Memory*. New York, 1980.

Jones, Kathy. *The Ancient British Goddess*. Glastonbury, England, 1991.

Jones, Sally. *Legends of Somerset*. London, Cornwall, 1984.

Jones, Thomas and Gwyn Jones. *Mabinogion*. London, 1970.

Keightley, Thomas. *The World Guide to Gnomes, Fairies, Elves, and Other Little People*. New York, 1978.

Kee, Robert. *Ireland: A History*. London, 1980.

Kinsella, Thomas. *The Taín*. Oxford, 1986.

Larmine, William. *West Irish Folk Tales and Romances*. London, 1893.

Larousse Encyclopedia of Mythology. London, 1968.

Leamy, Edmund. *Irish Fairy Tales*. Dublin, 1978.

Lee, F. H. *Folk Tales of All Nations*. New York, 1930.

Luzel, J. *Folk Tales of Brittany*. Paris, 1890.

MacCana, Proinsias. *Celtic Mythology*. London, 1970.

Malory, Sir Thomas. *Le Morte d'Arthur*. London, 1961.

Mason, J. H. N. *West Country Walks and Legends*. London, 1980.

Matthews, Caitlín. *Mabon and the Mysteries of Britain*. New York, 1987.

————. *Arthur and the Sovereignty of Britain*. New York, 1989.

Matthews, John. *Taliesin: Shamanism and the Bardic Mysteries in Britain and Ireland*. New York, 1991.

McCoy, Edain. *Witta: An Irish Pagan Tradition*. St Paul, Minnesota, 1993.

McLean, G. R. D. *Poems of the Western Highlanders*. London, 1961.

McManus, Seamus. *The Story of the Irish Race*. New York, 1921.

McAnally, D. R. *Irish Wonders*. London, 1888.

Meyer, K. *Selections from Ancient Irish Poetry*. London, 1911.

Miles, Clement A. *Christmas in Ritual and Tradition*. London, 1912.

Munford, G. F. *Ghosts and Legends of South Somerset*. London, 1922.

Neuman, Erich. *The Great Mother: An Analysis of the Archetype*. Princeton, New Jersey, 1963.

Northall, G. F. *English Folk-Rhymes*. London, 1892.

Norton-Taylor, Duncan. *The Celts*. Alexandria, Virginia, 1974.

Ody, Penelople. *The Herb Society's Complete Medicinal Herbal*. London, 1993.

Oliver, Edith and Margaret K. S. Edwards. *Moonrakings: A Little Book of Wiltshire Stories*. London (facsimile edition reprinted 1979, original date unknown).

O'Neill, Captain Francis. *Irish Minstrels and Musicians*. Chicago, 1913.

O'Sheridan, Mary Grant. *Gaelic Folk Tales*. Chicago, 1910.

Pepper, Elizabeth and John Wilcock. *Magical and Mystical Sites*. New York, 1977.

Piggot, Stuart. *The Druids*. New York, 1968.

Powell, T. G. E. *The Celts*. London, 1958.

Rank, Otto. *The Myth of the Birth of the Hero*. New York, 1959.

Rees, Alwyn and Brinley. *Celtic Heritage*. New York, 1961.

Rhys, Sir John. *Celtic Folklore*. London, 1911.

Robertson, J. M. *Pagan Christs*. New York, 1967.

Rolleston, T. W. *Myths and Legends of the Celtic Race*. London, 1917.

Ross, Ann. *Everyday Life of the Pagan Celts*. London, 1970.

———. *Pagan Celtic Britain*. London, 1967.

Sargent, H. C. *English and Scottish Popular Ballads*. Boston, 1932.

Sharp, E. *Lyra Celtica*. Edinburgh, 1896.

Sikes, Wirt. *British Goblins*. London, 1880.

Spence, Lewis. *The History and the Origin of Druidism*. New York, 1971.

Squire, Charles. *Celtic Myth and Legend*. New York, 1979.

Stewart, R. J. *Celtic Gods, Celtic Goddesses*. London, 1990.

———. *Celtic Myths and Legends*. London, 1996.

Stone, Merlin. *When God Was a Woman*. New York, 1976.

Thurneysen, Rudolf. *The Tale of Macc Da Thó's Pig*, in *Scéla mucce Meic Dathó*. Dublin, 1935.

Trevelyan, Marie. *Folklore and Folk Stories of Wales*. London, 1909.

Tuleja, Tad. *Curious Customs*. New York, 1987.

Turville-Petre, E. O. G. *Myth and Religion of the North*. New York, 1964.

van Hamel, A. G. *The Birth of Cú Chulain, Compert Con Culainn*. Dublin, 1933.

Walker, Barbara. *The Women's Encyclopedia of Myths and Secrets*. San Francisco, 1983.

Walker, Peter N. *Folk Tales from York and the Wolds*. London, 1992.

Wilson, Barbara Ker. *Scottish Folktales and Legends*. Oxford, 1954.

Wiltshire, Kathleen. *Ghosts and Legends of the Wiltshire Countryside*. Salisbury, England, 1973.

Wimberley, Lowry Charles. *Folklore in the English and Scottish Ballads*. New York, 1959.

Yeats, W. B. *Fairy and Folk Tales of the Irish Peasantry*. London, 1910.

Glossary

Baste. To moisten food during cooking with pan drippings.

Bean sidhe. Woman faerie; the shrieking spirit who visits houses where a death is imminent.

Beat. To make a mixture smooth by adding air with a whipping or stirring motion, usually with a spoon.

Beltaine. One of the four major Celtic festivals, falling on May Eve or May 1.

Blanch. To precook in boiling water, usually to loosen the skin.

Blend. To thoroughly combine two or more ingredients to make a smooth mixture.

Boil. To cook in liquid to boiling temperature.

Book of the Dun Cow. Eleventh-century book in which the Tain Bo Cuailgne appears.

Bridgit. A triune Celtic goddess who often appears as a goddess of healing, of smiths, and of fertility and poetry. Often identified with the maiden aspect of the Goddess, she is usually honored in springtime.

Cailleach. "Old woman" or "hag;" usually in reference to the Goddess as crone.

Carrageen moss. A type of moss used to thicken anything from soups to puddings.

Celt/Celtic. In modern terms the Celts are divided into two groups, the Goidelic Celts who are Irish, Manx, and Scots, and the Brythonic Celts who are Welsh, Cornish, and Breton. Today, there are only about sixteen million people who live in a Celtic country, with less than three million who still speak a Celtic language.

Celtic Feast of the Dead. *See* Samhain.

Celtic Tree Calendar. Druidic system of determining the thirteen lunar cycles, each assigned a sacred tree that represents the month.

Ceridwen. Mistress of the Cauldron, an aspect of the Goddess as crone. She possesses the cauldron of regeneration, where the dead can be cast into and return to life.

Cernunnos. "Horned one," also known as lord of the animals. An early aspect of the God.

Changeling. A faerie left in exchange of a human child.

Chop. To cut into pieces about the size of peas.

Cool. To remove from heat and let stand at room temperature.

Cream. To beat a mixture until it becomes soft and smooth.

Crone. The Goddess as old woman.

Dagda. In Irish tradition, he is the father of all the gods. He possessed a magic harp and a cauldron that never was emptied.

Danu. Mother Goddess from which the Tuatha de Danaan take their name.

Deosil. The act of moving clockwise.

Dollop. Adding a small amount of a semiliquid food—such as sour cream—to garnish another.

Elementals. Archetypal spirit associated with each of the four elements of earth, air, fire, and water.

Equinox. Days of balance between light and dark, until the arrival of the Norse, these days were noticed but not observed by the early Celts as a Sabbat.

Esbat. The time of the full moon that is celebrated monthly.

Faerie ring. Also called a sidhe ring, it is either a circle of grass that appears darker than the surrounding grass or a ring of mushrooms. Often leads to a faerie mound, where the race of faeries live. Once believed that to be caught in such a ring would mean the faeries could imprison you if they so chose.

Fold. To gently add ingredients to a mixture. The best method is to use a spatula to cut down through the mixture, across the bottom of the bowl, and then back up and over the surface.

Fry. To cook in hot fat. *See also* pan-fry.

Glaze. To brush a mixture on food to give it a glossy appearance.

Grate. To rub food across a rough surface that breaks it down into small pieces.

Grain Mother. A name of the Goddess in her role as provider.

Green Man. Early form of male deity, his figure is still found on early Christian churches.

Guinness. A type of dark Irish beer.

Gwyn ap Nudd. A king of the otherworld who appears as a warrior and hunter in many sagas.

Hallowe'en. *See* Samhain.

Harvest suppers. Feasts to celebrate the harvest season.

Holly King. In Ireland, the Holly King is the king of the waning year, from Midsummer to Yule. Holly is a sacred plant and has long been used in protective spells.

Horned God. The earliest form of male deity.

Imbolg. Celtic celebration of Bridgit celebrated on February 1 or 2.

Knead. To work dough with the heel of your hand in a pressing or folding motion.

Lammas. *See* Lughnasadh.

Lugh. An important Irish god, he is a solar deity and god of arts and crafts. When the old gods were driven underground and reduced in status to faeries, Lugh became a faerie craftsman known as Lugh-chromain. This was later Anglicized as leprechaun.

Lughnasadh. A sabbat, observed on August 1, which celebrates the first harvest and honors the god Lugh. The name survives in modern Irish as Lunasa (August), in Manx as Luanistyn (August), and in Scottish Gaelic as Lunasad, for the Lammas festival.

Mabon. Sabbat observed at the Autumn Equinox, named for Welsh God. Originally of little importance to the Celts, it was latter added as a second harvest festival. In modern society it is associated with Thanksgiving.

Maiden. Youngest aspect of the Goddess.

Michaelmas. Fomhar na nGeanna, on September 29, celebrates the Feast of St. Michael the Archangel.

Midsummer. Sabbat observed at the summer solstice.

Midwinter. Winter solstice, when the sun has reached its lowest point in the sky.

Mince. To chop food into very small, irregular pieces.

Mull. To heat beverages, such as wine or mead, with sugar and spices.

Mother Goddess. Second aspect of the triune female deity, she is associated with fertility and the harvest.

Mumming. Ancient custom where groups of people dressed in outlandish costumes would travel from house to house to perform ritual plays.

Name Day. In some cultures, name days are celebrated rather than birthdays, if a person shares the same name as a particular saint; may also refer to the day you were initiated into a pagan group and took a new name.

Oak King. God as King of the Waxing Year, from Yule to Midsummer.

Ostara. Sabbat observed at the vernal equinox, it was not an important Celtic festival until Nordic Pagan influence brought it to prominence in the nineteenth century.

Pagan. Generic term for anyone who practices an earth religion.

Pan-fry. To cook in a small amount of fat.

Peel. To remove the outer skin from a fruit or vegetable.

Picts. British Celts; the name was given to them by the Roman soldiers garrisoned at Hadrian's Wall to describe their painted appearance. *Pictii* is the past participle of the Latin *pingere*, to paint.

Pinch. To use your fingers to pinch one ingredient into another, such as butter into flour.

Poach. To cook food in hot liquid, being careful that the food holds its shape.

Poitín. Home-brewed whiskey, also known as mountain dew.

Purée. To convert food into a heavy paste or liquid, usually in a blender or food processor.

Sabbat. Festival or observance of the pagan year.

Samhain. Sabbat that marked the beginning of the Celtic year, now associated with Halloween.

Sauté. To cook or brown food in a small amount of fat.

Sift. To put one or more dry ingredients through a sieve or sifter to add air and break up lumps.

Saxon. Germanic tribes who conquered the British Isles, bringing with them many new holidays and traditions that would later influence Celtic culture.

Shielings. Temporary dwellings.

Simmer. To cook food in liquid over low heat where bubbles form at a slow rate.

Slainte agus saol agat. *Health and long life to you!* A traditional toast.

Solstice. Points in the solar year where the sun reaches its highest and lowest points in the sky.

Summer Solstice. Also known as midsummer, it is when the sun is at its zenith.

Tain bo Cuailgne. A *tain* is a cattle raid, the most famous of which is the Tain bo Cuailgne. In Irish mythology, this saga is the equivalent of the *Iliad*, and describes how the Queen of Connacht, Medb, sets out to capture the famous Brown Bull of Ulster.

The Fionn Cycle. Stories of the exploits of Fionn Mac Cumhail, a famous Irish hero.

Tir-na-nOg. Land of the ever young, the Celtic version of heaven. Tir-na-nOg is presided over by the the Goddess as crone and her cauldron of regeneration, to which all life returns to await rebirth.

Treacle. A type of sweetener that can be replaced with molasses.

Triple Goddess. The one Goddess in her three aspects as maiden, mother, and crone. The theory of a triple female deity is found throughout every culture in the world, and predates all patriarchal religions.

Tuatha de Dannann. The people of the goddess Danu. According to myth, they were driven underground when the Milesians conquered Ireland, and later became the faeries of popular folklore.

Usquabath. Gaelic word for whiskey.

Waning moon. Phase of the moon where it decreases in size.

Waxing moon. Phase of the moon where it increases in size.

Wheel of the Year. The Celtic festival calendar, often depicted as a wheel.

Widdershins. To go backwards, the act of moving counterclockwise.

Yule. Sabbat celebrated at the winter solstice. Most of the traditions come from the Pagan Roman holiday of Saturnalia.

Index

Note: Recipe page numbers are in bold type

Llewellyn publishes hundreds of books on your favorite subjects.

LOOK FOR THE CRESCENT MOON

to find the one you've been searching for!

To find the book you've been searching for, just call or write for a FREE copy of our full-color catalog, *New Worlds of Mind & Spirit*. *New Worlds* is brimming with books and other resources to help you develop your magical and spiritual potential to the fullest! Explore over 80 exciting pages that include:

- **Exclusive interviews, articles and "how-tos" by Llewellyn's expert authors**

- **Features on classic Llewellyn books**

- **Tasty previews of Llewellyn's latest books on astrology, Tarot, Wicca, shamanism, magick, the paranormal, spirituality, mythology, alternative health and healing, and more**

- **Monthly horoscopes by Gloria Star**

- **Plus special offers available only to *New Worlds* readers**

To get your free *New Worlds* catalog, call 1-800-THE MOON

or send your name and address to

Llewellyn
P.O. Box 64383, K044-2
St. Paul, MN 55164–0383

Many bookstores carry *New Worlds*— ask for it! Visit our web site at www.llewellyn.com.